Sam Choy's Polynesian Kitchen

Sam Choy's

Polynesian Kitchen

More Than 150 Authentic

Dishes from One of the

World's Most Delicious and

Overlooked Cuisines

Written by **Sam Choy** with U'i and Steven Goldsberry
Food photographs by Douglas Peebles
Location photographs by Douglas Peebles and Houserstock
Food styling by Faith Ogawa

HYPERION

NEW YORK

Book design by Richard Oriolo

My travels through the South Pacific have confirmed for me one thing: the people of these exotic places are as beautiful as their islands. My father used to say that a good person was someone beautiful on the inside. The people of Polynesia are beautiful inside and out.

I dedicate this book to those wonderful Polynesians who love their culture enough to share it with the world.

Contents

The Marquesas

New Zealand

Tonga   249

Introduction

IF I EVER TOOK THINGS for granted, my father would say, "You wait. Someday you'll see the value." As always, he was right. IN THE RURAL COMMUNITY OF La'ie on the north shore of O'ahu, our family owned a little mom-and-pop grocery store. It was a wood-frame building with a sliding barn-style door that opened onto a narrow residential street. The floor was just painted cement, polished to a glossy shine by the steady stream of customers, some in bare feet, some wearing rubber slippers. A 2-inch drop from the cement floor led to a 3-foot-wide sidewalk, then another little 2-inch drop to the road. Only four houses lined each side of this short side street. It seemed like the smallest part of our very small town. AT THE FRONT OF THE store under the checkout counter was a glass case where we kept all the candy. My dad got a kick out of watching the neighborhood children kneel in front of the Baby Ruths, Jawbreakers, and Mounds bars. They studied the bright wrappers, then looked up at him and pointed, and their tiny fingers always smudged the glass—something that drove my mom crazy. MY JOB WAS TO STOCK the shelves. Alongside the regular grocery store fare, we sold fresh coconut milk, green cooking bananas, ripe breadfruit, mountain apples, star fruit, sweet papaya, dried cuttlefish, imported Samoan cocoa, raw and cooked taro, and 1-pound bags of ground kava root used to make kava, the ceremonial drink of the South Pacific.

Once a week, women from the community would bring homemade Tahitian coconut bread, Tongan lupulu, and Samoan panipopo to sell. People lined up outside the store, waiting for these delicious treats. I loved delivery days.

The panipopo was my favorite, yeast buns floating in a sweet coconut pudding. When the women arrived, carrying trays of ti leaf bundles and pans filled with domes of the lightly browned rolls, the store filled with the rich aroma of coconut and bread. People bought them up by the dozen. My dad would scoop the rolls, one at a time, onto dishes and plates the customers brought from home. The panipopo came in at 8 A.M., and were all gone by 10.

Lupulu was delivered on Thursdays around noon. The tightly wrapped ti leaf bundles, the size of fists, had been plucked right out of the imu (earth oven) and brought to the store steaming. Inside each packet were chunks of corned beef, chopped onions, and coconut milk all snugly encased in succulent taro leaves. Just thinking about the smell of that heavenly steam rising from the hot lupulu makes my stomach growl.

Every day after school, my friends and I would head to the beach to fish or surf. By dinnertime, we were starving. The streets in the old part of La'ie had one lane, just wide enough for a car. If two met coming from opposite directions, one car had to pull onto the grassy side to let the other pass. Large mango, breadfruit, and avocado trees shaded the small wooden houses that lined the streets. We always walked home along the same route, down the meandering roads coated with only a thin layer of asphalt. There was one spot where the salt air from the beach mixed with the aroma that whisked out of the neighborhood kitchens, the evening meals of sautéed corned beef, spicy curries, steaming coconut milk, garlic, ginger, grilled fish, and simmering chicken. It was heaven.

I knew that my friends at school were from different countries. Many of their parents and grandparents had arrived as labor missionaries from Samoa, Tonga, Fiji, New Zealand, Tahiti, and the Marquesas to help build the Mormon Temple and the Church College of Hawaii. Then, when the college opened in 1955, students from the South Pacific were invited to enroll. Many of the men and women who came to school stayed on and raised families. They brought with them the traditional dances, culture, and foods from their home islands.

We had community parties, where children danced to the music of Samoa, Tahiti, Tonga, and Fiji. Everybody wanted to learn how to swing the poi balls of New Zealand. I was introduced to classic South Pacific cuisine at these gatherings. When it was time to build new church houses, we all got together and put on a public lu'au on the beach at Hukilau. Tourists came from all over to watch the community children dance, and to sample Polynesian cooking—an array of mouthwatering dishes from all over the Pacific. The event turned into a weekly affair, and became so popular that Elvis Presley re-created a Hukilau scene—shot on our beach—for his film *Blue Hawaii*. The Hukilau organizers then decided to expand the show at a site a few blocks south, and they created the Polynesian Cultural Center, which has since become the most visited tourist attraction in the Islands.

I never realized it as a kid, but I grew up in a hotbed of pan-Polynesian culture, a small Hawai'i town where you could find native islanders from all seven of the Pacific Island nations living in one place. La'ie represented (and still does today) a microcosm of Polynesia. It wasn't until I became a successful chef and traveled around to the homelands of my old friends that I understood how lucky I was, especially in terms of ethnic cooking, to have experienced what I did growing up. My father was right, I see the value.

For years now, I've been experimenting with dishes that combine the traditional tastes I took for granted in old La'ie with new techniques I've learned as a chef and restaurateur. I've always been what you might call a "food tourist," even if I'm just attending a dinner party in the neighborhood. But recently my travels have taken me to where those tastes from my childhood originated. I discovered on these far-flung Pacific Islands new dishes and variations of the old, and I decided in a fit of both nostalgia and adventure to bring my expanding collection of "Choy-style" Polynesian recipes together into one book.

I guarantee that in these pages you'll find some of the most unusual and delectable dishes you've ever tried. To truly appreciate this wonderful cuisine, however, you should know a little about where it all comes from.

The islands of Polynesia form a triangle: Hawai'i, at the northern tip; New Zealand at the south; and the Marquesas to the east. Fiji is along the western side, and Samoa, Tonga, and Tahiti are located in the middle. Connected by the warm waters of the Pacific, all of the island countries have a similar climate. They share the fish and shellfish of the ocean, and their basic agriculture is made up of bananas, coconuts, breadfruit, taro, and papayas.

Anthropologists theorize that Polynesian culture began in Fiji around 1500 B.C. From there, people moved to Tonga around 100 B.C., then to Samoa. The Marquesas were settled around A.D. 500. The Hawaiian migrations were going strong at around A.D. 500. And New Zealand was settled last.

In the 1800s, colonists from many of the world's maritime countries traveled into the South Pacific in search of whales, and to work the copra and sugarcane plantations. They brought with them their dances, their conservative style of dress, and their foods. Each immigrating group of people influenced the cooking and flavors of Polynesia, creating an exotic culinary environment with their new spices and new ingredients. The flavors of each of the colonizing cultures had enormous impact on the cuisines of each specific island country.

In Fiji, Chinese workers brought their love of rice, parsley, cabbages, turnips, ginger, and garlic. East Indians introduced peppers, chutneys, and delectable curries. The English brought their livestock, and added densely rich beef and lamb stews to the amalgamation that is known as Fijian cuisine.

Traditional Tongan cooking is refined, with subtle flavorings. This style of cooking easily incorporated the techniques and flavors introduced by the English colonists. The family land divisions worked well in the raising of livestock, and the Tongan people readily adapted to the flavors of British-style lamb, beef, and chicken.

German and Chinese settlers arrived soon after the English "discovered" Samoa. The dense, hard-crust Samoan bread comes from the German method of leavening, and the soft yeast biscuits baked atop a pool of coconut pudding called panipopo is reminiscent of a European cobbler. Chinese influence is seen in the cultivation of herbs and greens used in down-home favorites like stir-fried corned beef and cabbage.

Tahiti and the Marquesas are part of French Polynesia. French is still the national language of both these countries. Everyone knows about Tahitian dancing, the fast-moving skirts and the strong rhythm pounded out on wooden drums. But Tahiti also exports the world's most delicate vanilla, and the tart, sweet Tahitian lime. Tahitian and Marquesan cooking have strong French tones in their sauces, soups, and stews. A Tahitian chef once told me that "Tahitian food is rough French cuisine. The flavors are bolder, the sauces are stronger, and the dishes are very basic. But there is a tropical elegance in everything we make."

I didn't fully understand the beautiful subtleties of all these island countries until I toured them. While traveling through the South Pacific, I recognized the heavy influences of the colonizing cultures on each of the islands. Many of the local dishes are hybrids using German, English, French, Chinese, and East Indian flavors, combined with ingredients found in the islands. I saw how their unique cooking styles and flavors were a part of me, and felt it was high time the rest of the world experienced the relaxed harmony and savory balance of Polynesian cooking. It's nice to know that in the midst of our daily rushing around, we can enjoy the slower pace of the South Pacific by connecting with these island cultures through their food.

So, if you love adventure and good food, take notice of this fascinating region of the world. Kick off your shoes, put on your aloha shirt, whip up a Fijian Passion drink, and enjoy the sunset. From New Zealand, haere mai; from Tahiti, maeva; from Hawai'i, e komo mai, and from me, welcome to the exotic and tantalizing cuisine of the seven island groups of the South Pacific.

How to Use
This Book

I'M NOT A CULINARY ANTHROPOLOGIST, I just have a love for really good food. Many of the recipes in *Sam Choy's Polynesian Kitchen* are my adaptations, my take on some of the traditional dishes from the islands of Fiji, Samoa, Tonga, Tahiti, New Zealand, the Marquesas, and my home, Hawai'i. Other recipes are creations, inspired by the flavors, textures, and unique ingredients that make each island cuisine distinct. I'VE ALWAYS FELT THAT THE simpler the recipe, the better. So, I've applied my "easy-to-follow" cooking techniques to each dish, and have provided ingredient substitutions that retain the essence of the islands' cooking. All substitutions can be found in most major grocery stores and Asian markets. The recipes are simple, with few ingredients. LISTED BELOW ARE INGREDIENTS THAT are staples in South Pacific cooking but may be difficult to find in American markets. I've included a description of each item, the availability in U.S. markets, viable substitutions, and storage recommendations. When substituting, it's important to remember that the flavor and/or texture will change as a result of the substitution.

Banana Leaves

Description: Every part of the banana tree was important to the people of the South Pacific. They ate the fruit, used the moisture-rich trunks as cooking buffers in underground ovens, and wrapped their food in the wide, green leaves for steaming. These leaves add a tantalizing, woodsy flavor to the traditional dishes of the Islands.

Use: If you are using fresh leaves, cut away the center vein of each leaf, and discard. If the leaves are too stiff to mold around the food bundles, hold them briefly over a gas flame or pour boiling water over the leaves in a colander to make them pliable. I recommend using an outer wrapping of foil around the leaf bundles while cooking to prevent leaking. The steamed food should be served in the leaf, but the leaf is not eaten.

If you are using frozen leaves, they should be thawed, then rinsed and patted dry. Glide the flat surface of the leaves across a gas flame or electric element on the highest heat setting. In just a few seconds, the leaves will become shiny and pliable, and give off a pleasant aroma. Set aside until ready to use (up to several hours). Leaves can be stored frozen for several months.

Availability: In U.S. markets, you can find banana leaves in Asian or Latin food shops. They come fresh, dried, or frozen in 1-pound packages.

Storage: Fresh leaves should be wrapped tightly in foil and stored in the crisper of the refrigerator. They can last for 3 months. Frozen leaves will keep in your freezer for virtually as long as you want.

Substitution: Ti leaves are the best substitute for banana leaves. Oiled parchment paper or foil can also be used, but these do not have the natural appearance and flavor of the banana or ti leaves.

Breadfruit

Description: Breadfruit is native to the South Pacific. The large and imposing green fruit is covered in short, knobby spines, can weigh up to 9 pounds, and grows to a diameter of 8 to 10 inches. It's usually picked and eaten before it ripens and becomes too sweet. The flesh is bland tasting with a cream-colored, breadlike center. Breadfruit can be baked, grilled, fried, or boiled.

The breadfruit tree is one of the most handsome of the tropical flora, with thick, lobed dark-green leaves and a sturdy trunk. Trees start bearing after five or six years, and with good soil conditions and correct climate, can produce fruit for 50 years. Male and female flowers are grouped separately in catkins on the same tree. Depending on the variety of tree, the fruit can be oval, spherical, or pear-shaped and can be found at all stages of its development on the same tree. There are usually two ripening seasons a year.

Use: Breadfruit must be cooked to be edible. One fresh breadfruit weighing about 2 pounds, or one packed in a 26-ounce can, serves 6. For a vegetable side dish, peel fresh breadfruit and cut out the core, or drain canned breadfruit. Cook with desired seasonings in water to cover for about 15 minutes until tender; drain, and mash with butter to the consistency of mashed potatoes. Breadfruits have a starchy taste that makes them an excellent substitute for potatoes or rice.

Traditionally, the Pacific Islanders preserve the fruit by fermentation. But when fresh or canned, the breadfruit may simply be sliced and dried out in the sun or in an oven, or it may be cooked and pounded to a paste.

Availability: In the United States, you can find breadfruit fresh or in 26-ounce cans in some Latin and specialty produce markets.

Storage: Whole breadfruit will keep for weeks in a cool place.

Substitution: Irish or baking potatoes are the nearest practical substitution for breadfruit. The recipes in this book will work well using these potatoes.

Chutney

Description: Chutneys are very spicy Indian relishes that are served either cooked or raw. The immigrants from India that arrived in Fiji to work on the copra and sugarcane plantations brought chutneys with them. Today, chutney is a staple in Fijian cooking.

Use: Chutneys are made fresh with fruits, vegetables, spices, sugar, and vinegar. They are served as a side dish with curried dishes.

Availability: Chutneys are available in Asian markets, specialty food stores, and well-stocked supermarkets. Those found in U.S. markets are usually a golden-colored mango variety. Indian markets carry a well-rounded variety of bottled or canned chutneys, and occasionally carry their own fresh versions.

Storage: Prepared chutneys are usually sold in jars and look like fruit preserves. These are stamped with shelf-life dates and can be stored in your pantry or cupboard for months. Once opened, they should be kept in the refrigerator. Fresh chutneys should be stored in the refrigerator, and will usually last 1–2 weeks.

Substitution: Chutneys are very easy to make. They are basically a combination of tomato, fresh mint, pineapple, coconut, onion, garlic, or any other ingredient that is refreshing to the palate. Please feel free to experiment with the recipes I've included in this book.

Coconut Crab

Description: Coconut crabs, also known as robber crabs, are found on the islands of the South Pacific and Indian Oceans. These large land crabs are related to the hermit crab and have a symmetrical abdomen covered with horny plates. They grow up to 16 inches long and may weigh as much as 9 pounds.

The coconut crab derives its name from its habit of climbing palms to get coconuts for food. The crab cracks the coconuts with its powerful pincers and eats the sweet meat inside the nut. The back of the coconut crab's body is red and striped like a yellow jacket, and this is where it stores all the nutrients it gathers from eating coconuts.

Use: Because coconut crabs consume so much rich coconut, their flesh is juicy with a buttery, oily texture. These huge crabs are considered a delicacy in the South Pacific.

Cooked with onions, peppers, and garlic, coconut crabs have the best flavor in the world. I always eat the back first. It's the most succulent part, where you find most of the juicy, nutrient-rich meat.

Availability: Coconut crabs are generally not available in the United States, except in Hawai'i and major West Coast cities, but they can be ordered frozen through Internet markets and specialty food supply houses.

Storage: If you can get fresh or frozen coconut crabmeat, purchase and requirements are the same as for any other fresh crab. When acquiring live crab, buy it—on the day you are going to cook it—from a reliable fish market, and take care that it is alive and kicking. If it has been kept on crushed ice, its reactions will be slow. Live crab should be purchased on the day of use and refrigerated until just before cooking. Raw crabmeat should be cooked within 24 hours.

Any cooked crabmeat purchased in a fish market should smell sweet and fresh. If it smells strong, don't buy it. Cooked crabmeat can be refrigerated for use within 3 days. Remember that freezing crabmeat damages its flavor and texture, and should be done only if it is not to be used quickly. Use frozen crabmeat within 3 months.

Substitution: Any large crab (spider, king, or Dungeness crabs) can be substituted for coconut crabs. Canned crab, precooked and sold in 6- to 8-ounce cans, can be found in every supermarket. Canned crabmeat varies greatly in price, depending on the type. It tends to be stronger in flavor than fresh or frozen. Crabs can also be found fresh or frozen in fish markets or in the fish section of large supermarkets.

Coconut Milk

Description: Traditionally, the people of the South Pacific drench their food in coconut milk, the sweet liquid from the staple fruit of the Islands. In legend, the coconut was named by Spanish and Portuguese traders that visited the South Pacific and Asia. They thought the coconut shell's three "eyes" resembled the face of a clown; loosely translated, the Spanish word *coco* means "grinning face."

The coconut tree is a tall, slender tropical palm that can grow as high as 60 feet. The fruits or nuts are a single seed with an outer fibrous husk that allows the fruit to float in seawater for weeks without coming to any harm. A tree in full production can bear up to 120 fruits a year.

Native to the tropics, the coconut is used in hundreds of different ways. The liquid you hear sloshing around inside the fresh coconut is called coconut water, and is drunk fresh. It's important not to confuse this splashing liquid with coconut milk, a creamy solution made by grating and squeezing the flesh of a ripe coconut.

Fresh, fully ripened coconuts make the most flavorful coconut milk. To check for freshness, shake the coconut. If you can hear the coconut water splashing around inside, the coconut is fresh. Another way to check for freshness is to husk the outer shell. All three eyes should be closed and sealed.

Use: Coconut milk is used throughout the South Pacific and Asia to season the local traditional dishes. The creamy milk imparts a gentle, pleasing flavor that provides a unique identity to these island foods.

Availability: Prepared coconut milk is available canned or frozen in most Asian markets and in some well-stocked supermarkets. Many brands are imported from Hawai'i, Thailand, and the Philippines. Check the label to make sure that the coconut milk you buy is unsweetened. Most brands of canned coconut milk are as thick as homemade (hand-squeezed) coconut milk, and are just as good.

Storage: Purchased canned or frozen, coconut milk will keep indefinitely. Fresh-squeezed coconut milk must be used immediately.

Substitution: You can make a convenient (though not authentic) substitute for fresh or canned coconut milk by mixing whipping cream with coconut extract. Use ½ teaspoon each of sugar and coconut extract and 1 cup whipping cream for every cup of coconut milk.

NOTE: Coconut milk, adored by all Asians and Pacific Islanders, may not hold as much appeal for certain Western palates. A key ingredient in Thai and East Indian cooking, coconut milk has become widely available in the United States, and is much more accepted as a flavoring to meat and fish dishes.

I do love coconut milk, but if you find it's not to your taste, simply use heavy cream as a substitute, or try experimenting with smaller portions than those I recommend.

Coriander

Description: Coriander, also known as Chinese parsley or cilantro, is a very pungent and aromatic herb. It resembles the flat-leaf Italian parsley.

Use: All parts of the plant are used in Asian cooking: the seeds are used in curries, the fresh green leaves as an herb, and the roots in some Thai dishes.

Availability: Sold by the bunch, fresh coriander is available year-round in most Asian markets and in many supermarkets in the United States. If possible, buy the coriander with its roots attached.

Storage: Coriander should be stored in a plastic bag in the refrigerator. It will stay fresh for about 1–2 days.

Substitution: There is no true flavor substitution for fresh coriander, but it is possible to use fresh curly parsley (found in most supermarkets) for texture and color. Coriander is often sold as "cilantro"; they are the same plant. Because of the distinct flavor difference between coriander and parsley, you may opt to leave out the parsley altogether.

Curry

Description: Curry powder is not a natural spice. It is a combination of anywhere from 7 to 20 separate ingredients.

Use: In India, cooks combine their fresh spices daily to complement the curry they are preparing. Curry powders are as different as the cooks. It's very common for a cook to prepare a different curry powder for each different recipe.

Availability: Bottled curry powders and pastes are available on supermarket shelves and in Asian markets throughout the country. These are premixed convenience items, combined spices. As a rule, the brands of curry powder from India are the best.

Storage: Bottled or premixed curry powder can be stored, tightly sealed, on your pantry or cupboard shelf for up to a year. If you prepare your own spices, it is best to use the mixture immediately.

Substitution: For convenience, use store-bought, premixed curry powder. For the best flavor you should blend your own. This takes trial-and-error practice, but the process can be a flavor blast.

Daikon

Description: Daikon, a variety of white radish from the turnip family, is in season most of the year. It has a sharp, sweet flavor. There are many types of daikon; all are slightly different, but are interchangeable in recipes. The most common come from Japan and China. The Japanese variety is long and slender. It can grow to 14 inches in length and weigh as much as 4 to 5 pounds. Chinese daikon is slightly shorter and wider.

Use: Japanese cooks serve daikon in soup, preserved and pickled, or shredded raw as a garnish for sushi or sashimi.

Availability: Fresh daikon is usually available year-round in Asian markets, specialty food stores, and in the produce section of supermarkets. When selecting daikon, make sure the root is firm and white with healthy-looking dark green leaves attached to the top. Smaller roots are moister and more delicate.

Shredded and dried daikon, called kiri-boshi daikon, can be found in Japanese markets.

Storage: Fresh daikon will keep in the crisper drawer of your refrigerator 2–3 days. It's important to use any of your fresh ingredients as soon as possible. They lose their flavor the longer they are kept in storage.

Substitution: In the recipes in this book, any variety of raw turnip is a suitable substitute for fresh daikon.

French Beans

Description: French beans are a narrow, completely edible variety of string bean.

French explorers introduced many types of European produce in the lands they visited. French green beans grew well in the South Pacific volcanic soil and became very popular in French Polynesia.

Use: French beans are interchangeable with other string beans in any of the recipes in this book.

Availability: French beans are available in specialty produce markets or in national supermarkets.

Storage: Fresh French beans will keep well in the crisper drawer of your refrigerator 2–3 days. It is important to use all fresh ingredients as soon as possible. Flavor dissipates during prolonged refrigeration.

Substitution: String beans work best as a replacement for French beans.

Green Papaya

Description: The unripe papaya is used like a vegetable in the new cuisine of the South Pacific. It tastes like a squash and can be served stuffed or baked with butter, added to salads, or pickled.

Use: Green papaya is much like winter squash and can be prepared in the same way.

Green papaya can also be stuffed, fried, added to fricassees or ratatouille, marinated, or served with dressing. To prepare a green papaya, it is sometimes necessary to drain its white, acidic sap.

Availability: Papayas are picked green and shipped, and are available year-round in most Asian markets and in the produce sections of most large supermarkets.

Storage: I always recommend that produce be used on the day it is purchased to ensure freshness. Green papaya may be stored in the refrigerator for up to 2 days, depending on the ripeness of the fruit.

Substitution: In salads, substitute cucumbers for green papaya. This substitution will change the flavor of the recipe, but the texture, consistency, and refreshing tenor of the dish will remain the same. In soups, substitute winter melon.

Guava Juice

Description: Guava trees can grow up to 30 feet tall and have aromatic flowers. There are more than 150 species that bear fruit in a variety of shapes, sizes, colors, and tastes. Pink- or yellow-fleshed, this sweet fruit can be as small as a walnut or as large as an apple. The average guava has a diameter of 2–3 inches, with a thin edible skin that ranges in color from white to bright red. It contains small, hard, edible seeds.

Use: Guava can be pureed or baked, or eaten fresh with sugar and cream, and it goes well with fruit such as pineapple or banana. Guavas make a delicious jelly, and a sauce of pureed guavas can be served with meat or duck.

Availability: Guava grows wild in tropical and subtropical countries like Africa, Australia, India, the southern United States, Brazil, Taiwan, throughout the South Pacific, and Hawai'i. The fresh fruits are usually available only in regions where they grow. Guavas make excellent jams, preserves, and sauces. You should have little trouble finding canned whole guavas, as well as juice, jams, jellies, preserves, and sauce. Guava juice is available in most supermarkets in the freezer section.

Storage: Store ripe guavas in the vegetable drawer of the refrigerator for up to 4 days. Ripen green guavas at room temperature.

Substitution: Substitute orange juice if you can't find frozen or fresh guava juice.

Heart of Palm

Description: Heart of palm is a delicious and quite expensive vegetable. Every palm has a "heart," the ivory-colored interior at the top of the trunk where the new leaves form. But the most commonly used source of this delicacy is the cabbage palmetto, the official state tree of Florida. These are such expensive items because small trees must be chopped down to harvest the heart. Maybe the greatest characteristic of heart of palm is its texture, like a cross between stringless celery and nutmeat—incredible!

Use: Heart of palm is firm and smooth and the flavor is reminiscent of an artichoke. Once out of the package, the hearts should be transferred to a nonmetal container with an airtight cover. They can be refrigerated in their own liquid for up to a week. Heart of palm can be used in salads and in main dishes, or deep-fried.

Availability: In the United States, hearts are available fresh only in Florida, but can be found, packed in water, in 10- or 30-ounce cans in fancy-food stores across America.

Storage: Fresh heart of palm can be kept in the refrigerator to up to 2 days, but should be used as soon as possible after harvest or purchase. Canned varieties may be kept in your pantry or cupboard for up to a year.

Substitution: Canned heart of palm is relatively easy to get. But celery hearts, asparagus tops, or artichoke meat may be substituted.

Japanese/English Cucumber

Description: Cucumbers are believed to have originated in either India or Thailand, and have been cultivated throughout the world for thousands of years. A part of the squash and melon family, this long, cylindrical, green-skinned fruit has edible seeds surrounded by a mild, crisp flesh.

Cucumbers grow on a climbing plant 3 to 10 feet long. The plant's tendrils allow it to cling to other plants or objects. The fruit emerges after the plant's long yellow flowers have blossomed. There are over 40 varieties of cucumber. The English or Japanese varieties, also known as hothouse cucumbers, are the longest, with fewer seeds and a very thin skin. They are often sold in a tight plastic jacket to keep them fresh.

Use: Cucumbers are best when young and tender. They are used in cold soups and in delicately flavored, refreshing salads.

Availability: English or Japanese cucumbers are available in major supermarkets and Asian markets year-round, with the peak season between the months of May and August.

Choose firm fruit with smooth, brightly colored skins; avoid those with shriveled or soft spots.

Storage: Japanese or English cucumbers can be stored in the refrigerator for a week at most. Store whole cucumbers, unwashed, in a plastic bag in the refrigerator up to 10 days. Wash thoroughly just before using.

Substitution: Japanese or English cucumbers are available throughout the United States and Canada year-round. But if not available in your area, the shorter, fatter American variety is an acceptable substitute.

Lemongrass

Description: Named for its subtle lemony flavor, this tall, gray-green grass has an aromatic, scallionlike base and grows to a height of about 2 feet. For centuries, lemongrass has been used by Asian cooks. It adds a light, spicy flavor to many Thai and Indonesian dishes.

A tropical and subtropical plant, lemongrass grows best in a frost-free place like any other herb.

Lemongrass is also called citronella and *sereh*.

Use: Lemongrass stalks are tough on the outside and contain layers of tender inner leaves. Used to flavor soups, curries, pork, seafood, and chicken dishes, the stalks are usually cut into rounds—much like chefs use green onions or scallions—or shredded.

Peel the fresh stems first, removing all but the lower 2½ inches. This outer layer and the upper portion of the stems are too stringy to eat, but are great in flavoring stocks, sauces, soups, stews, fish, and poultry dishes, and herbal teas. Use the portion of the white base up to the place where the leaves begin to branch. This is the tender part. Discard the gray-green leaves. Bruise the fresh stalks to release the lemony flavor.

To use dried lemongrass, soak it in warm water for 2 hours and then finely chop before adding to recipes.

If you are using the powdered type, add it directly to recipes, substituting 1 teaspoon for each fresh stalk.

Availability: Today, lemongrass is cultivated in Africa, the United States, South America, the Caribbean, and Australia, and is available in the produce sections of most Latin and Asian markets. In Latin markets lemongrass can be found under the label *nativeto*, and in Asian markets it is known as *sereh*.

Dried lemongrass is also available, labeled *daun sereh*. This dried variety must be soaked or ground to a powder. In international supermarkets and in herbal tea shops, lemongrass is commonly found in a powdered form.

Storage: Lemongrass is best used fresh, and can be kept for up to 2 months in the crisper of your refrigerator. I like to keep a bunch of lemongrass, wrapped in plastic, in the refrigerator. It can be frozen without blanching. Just be sure to freeze the lower and upper stems separately.

If you are using the dried variety, store it as you would any herb, but make a point of using it as soon as possible.

Substitution: It's best to use fresh lemongrass, but when this isn't available, substitute equal quantities of dried or powdered. If fresh, dried, or powdered are not available, 2 strips of lemon peel (or 1 teaspoon of finely grated lemon rind) per stalk provides an acceptable substitute.

Liliko'i Juice—Passion Fruit

Description: Passion fruit, a climbing vine native to Brazil, is known throughout South America by its Spanish name, *granadilla*. People often mistake the name for passion fruit as having something to do with lust. But it was the Catholic missionaries in South America who gave it its name, after observing that parts of the plant's flowers resembled the symbolic nails, hammer, and crown of thorns of the Passion and Crucifixion of Christ.

Many different varieties of this sweet, aromatic fruit are grown in Australia, California, Florida, Hawai'i, the West Indies, and New Zealand. In Hawai'i, it is called *liliko'i*, and in the West Indies it's called *calabesh*. Worldwide, there are approximately 400 different varieties of passion fruit. Only about 30 are sold commercially.

Skin hue and the color of the jellylike flesh vary, depending on the variety of passion fruit. In commercially sold fruits, the skin is yellow, orange, or purple. The most common variety sold in the United States is oval-shaped and about the size of an egg.

The passion fruit is entirely edible, from its thick, smooth skin (which is very tough, and rarely eaten) to the sweet, juicy pulp and crisp, black seeds. As the fruit ripens, the skin becomes thin and crinkled. The pulp has a very fragrant, slightly tart, gelatinous texture. The small black seeds are inseparable from the sweet-sour pulp.

Unripe passion fruit pulp is very tart. To test for ripeness, press the skin gently. When it is ripe, the skin will yield to the gentle pressure.

Use: In the wild, passion fruit is just cut in half, sprinkled with lemon or lime juice, and eaten out of your hand, seeds and all. Or, the fruit can be halved and drizzled with sherry or cream for a delicious dessert. The pulp and seeds are also mixed into fruit salads, and make a delicious flavoring for mousses, sorbets, ice cream, or sauces.

The seeds and pulp are virtually inseparable, but it's possible to sieve the pulp in an attempt to remove the seeds. It's much easier to buy commercially bottled or canned juice. On its own, passion fruit flavor can be very strong and is often mixed with other fruits or fruit juices.

Availability: Fresh passion fruit is available from March through September and can be found in Latin American markets and some supermarkets. Choose fruits that are wrinkled, unbruised, and heavy. Smooth skin is a sign that the fruit is unripe. Commercial passion fruit nectar is available in cans or bottles in many supermarkets and health food stores. This nectar is usually sweetened with sugar.

Storage: Ripe passion fruit can be stored in the refrigerator. With the skin, the fruit will stay fresh for up to 5 days. Without the skin, wrapped in a plastic bag, it will keep for a week. The pulp can be frozen in an ice-cube tray, and will keep for several months if well wrapped.

Substitution: Passion fruit contains vitamins A and C, and is high in citric acid. It is possible to substitute orange juice for this delicious juice, but much of the unique, sweet-sour flavor of the passion fruit will be lost.

Lu'au Leaves—Taro Leaves—*Callaloo*

Description: The taro plant's leaves are broad, green, and shaped like elephant ears. Each South Pacific Island culture has its own name for taro leaves. In Hawai'i, they are called *lu'au*. In Fiji, they are known as *rourou*. In Tahiti, taro leaves are called *fafa*. And in Tonga and Samoa, they are called *lu*.

Taro leaves are also used in the Caribbean and in some areas of South America. There they are called *callaloo*. The name callaloo refers to two different plants that are used interchangeably. One plant, the *malanga*, has large green leaves shaped like elephant ears, and the other plant is the *amaranth* or "Chinese spinach," which has small green leaves.

Use: Used throughout the South Pacific as a wrap and to flavor the food placed in earth ovens, these large, moisture-rich leaves provide enough dampness to allow adequate steaming of meats and vegetables. Once cooked, the dark-green "taro tops" have the consistency and nutritional value of spinach (and have a similar flavor), and are used as a vegetable.

Availability: You can find fresh taro leaves or lu'au year-round in most Asian and Latin American markets. In Caribbean markets, it is sold in cans labeled callaloo or "chopped spinach in brine."

Storage: When purchased fresh, lu'au greens can be stored in a paper bag inside a plastic bag in the refrigerator for up to a week. Once opened, the canned greens should be stored in a nonmetal container in the refrigerator (and will last for up to 4 days).

Substitution: Spinach, Swiss chard, or mustard or turnip greens can be substituted for lu'au.

Mango

Description: Mango, known originally as *tamil*, is sacred in its native India. This extraordinarily beautiful tree has been cultivated in Asia for over 6,000 years. Portuguese explorers introduced the fruit they called mango to Brazil in the eighteenth century. It gradually spread throughout the world.

A relative of the pistachio and cashew, mango trees grow in tropical, temperate climates. Today, Thailand, India, Pakistan, and Mexico are the world's largest producers, with California and Florida providing seasonal supplies in the United States.

Mango trees grow to an average height of 50 feet, and can sometimes reach as high as 100 feet. Each tree produces an annual yield of about 100 fruits. There are over 1,000 different types of mango that grow in a wide variety of shapes: oblong, kidney, oval, tear-shaped, or round. Certain varieties, especially wild mangoes, have very little flesh. Some are as large as melons or as small as apples. The average size of cultivated fruit ranges from 6 ounces to 4 pounds, with an average length of about 4 inches. Before the fruit ripens, the skin is green, with a smooth, thin surface. When ripe, the skin should be yellow with red mottling, have a strong fragrance, and give with a slightly gentle pressure.

The flesh of green mangoes is green and hard, while ripe mango flesh is fragrant and ranges in color from golden yellow to the rosy red hues of a peach. The best ripe mangoes are very juicy and without fiber, and possess a spicy-sweet and tart flavor, often compared to peaches, apricots, and pineapples. The only negative to this beautiful fruit is the oversized, flat seed. The flesh clings tenaciously to the seed, and must be carefully carved free with a sharp knife. The larger the mango, the higher the fruit-to-seed ratio.

Use: While occupying India, the British developed a liking for the taste of mango chutney, which can be found under the label of Major Grey's mango chutney in almost any American supermarket.

Mangoes should be eaten peeled: the skin may irritate the mouth. Ingenious ways have been developed to separate the large mango seed from the sweet flesh. The best way to cut a mango is called "hedgehog." The mango is cut into three pieces by slicing down on both sides of the large pit or seed. The circle of fruit left around the pit may be cut away, and the pit discarded. Place the two remaining bowl-shaped halves meat-side up. Without piercing the skin, the meat or flesh is scored from top to bottom diagonally at ½-inch intervals in both directions. When each section is pushed inside out, little squares of the mango spread out over the inverted skin, making it easy to eat with a spoon, or slice over ice cream, sorbet, or salad. Chilled mangoes are sometimes served halved in their skin, sprinkled with lemon juice, sugar, rum, or ginger.

One medium mango will serve 1 or 2 and will yield approximately 1 cup of pulp. It is also important to remember that mango juice will stain clothing.

In India, green mango, the unripe fruit, is widely used in chutneys, relishes, condiments, beverages, and pickles. One of the most popular uses for dried green mango is in *amchoor*, an Indian seasoning used to flavor many dishes. In Malaysia, green mangoes are a main ingredient in lentil dishes, and like papaya, green mango is a wonderful tenderizer for meat. In the Caribbean, the seed is roasted and the inner kernel is eaten.

Availability: Fresh mangoes are in season from May through September, with imported fruit available in the stores sporadically throughout the remainder of the year. When buying fresh mangoes, look for fruit with an unblemished, yellow skin blushed with red. The outer skin should be soft, with a sweet, light fragrance and a few black spots that indicate that the fruit is very ripe. Mangoes that are picked too early have shriveled skin and a very fibrous flesh with an unpleasant acidic taste. Choose mangoes that are not too hard, and not too soft. Because they can vary so much in flavor, and because they are so expensive, buy one first and taste it before purchasing a quantity of them.

Canned mangoes are sold in many supermarkets and Latin American grocery stores. Packaged dried mango comes in chunks and strips and is available in health food stores and many gourmet markets. It must be rehydrated in warm water for about 4 hours before being used in baked goods or preserves. Green mango may be purchased in various forms in Asian and Indian markets.

Storage: Mangoes taste best when eaten at peak ripeness. Ripe mangoes will keep for up to 5 days in a plastic bag in the refrigerator. Unripe fruit should be left to ripen at room temperature for about a week. To speed things up, place fruit in a paper bag.

Once opened, canned mangoes can be stored in a nonmetal container in their own syrup in the refrigerator for up to four days.

Mangoes can be frozen, cooked in syrup, or pureed. Sugar and lime or lemon juice may be added as desired.

Substitution: Fresh mangoes are available year-round in supermarkets and Latin American markets. If you are having difficulty finding mangoes, then fresh peaches or apricots may be used instead.

New Zealand Oysters

Description: New Zealand oysters, also known as rock oysters outside of the United States, are a type of Pacific oyster similar in shape and size to the Nelson Bay or Fanny Bay varieties. Originally from Japan, this type of oyster thrives in the shallow waters off the New Zealand coast. The shells can reach up to one foot in length.

The New Zealand oyster, like most other Pacific varieties, has a creamy, ocean taste.

Use: Known for their delicate flavor and juicy meat, the New Zealand oysters are best eaten raw with cayenne pepper, a little lemon juice, red wine vinegar, or chili peppers. New Zealand oysters may also be eaten smoked or canned, but are best raw. It is important to remember that because raw foods, including oysters, may carry bacteria, persons with chronic liver disease, impaired immune systems, or cancer should avoid eating raw oysters.

Oysters in the shell can be served raw, baked, steamed, or grilled. All oysters have a tendency to become rubbery or pasty if even slightly overcooked, but when prepared correctly, cooked oysters are delicious hot or cold. Oysters are often used in soups, pâtés, and sauces, or cooked au gratin.

Shucked oysters can be eaten raw if they are very fresh, but they are often less fla-vorful than just-shucked oysters, and are more suitable for use in cooked dishes. Although canned smoked oysters are sold "ready to eat," they should be rinsed and marinated.

Availability: Oysters are at their best when the sea is coldest. In New Zealand, which lies in the Southern Hemisphere, oysters are harvested from the end of May through late August.

New Zealand oysters are an import item in America, and are sold by the pound, freshly shucked, or frozen. They are also available canned in water or their own liquor, or smoked. Shucked fresh oysters should be firm, fleshy, and shiny, and the liquid they are stored in should be clear, not milky. Shucked oysters are more expensive than unshucked.

Fresh, unshucked oysters are usually sold by the dozen or the crate. The general rules for buying oysters are (1) always purchase your shellfish from a reputable fishmong-er, and (2) do not buy fresh unshucked oysters unless they are still alive and full of water. Live oysters are usually closed, and if they are slightly open, will close when tapped. Oys-ters that are filled with water are quite heavy.

Storage: Unshucked oysters can be kept for up to 6 weeks in a container covered with a damp cloth. Never store them in a bag or a tightly sealed container. They will not be able to breathe. Never freeze unshucked oysters.

Fresh, shucked oysters should be stored in their own liquid, and will keep for up to 2 days in the refrigerator, or for about 3 months in the freezer, depending on how fresh they were when purchased.

To ensure the best flavor, both shucked and unshucked oysters should be eaten as soon as possible.

Substitution: New Zealand oysters are difficult to get in the United States, but there are many varieties of Pacific oysters that will substitute nicely.

Ota Seisei—Fiddleheads

Description: There are thousands of varieties of fern throughout the world, but only a few produce edible shoots. Fiddleheads, appreciated by North American Indians, the Japanese, and the aboriginal people of Australia and New Zealand—long before the arrival of Europeans to these countries—are the tightly curled new sprouts (heads) of the ostrich, buckhorn, or cinnamon ferns. These young shoots, named fiddleheads because of their resemblance to the spiral end of a violin, stay coiled for only about 2 weeks. They must be gathered during the spring when they are bright green, firm, and still tightly curled. When they open and mature into feathery green fern leaves, they become poisonous.

Fiddleheads grow wild along the eastern seaboard of the United States, ranging from as far south as Virginia to as far north as Canada. Fiddleheads can be gathered for about 15 days between mid-April and early July, depending on the region. They grow to about 2 inches long and 1½ inches in diameter.

The flavor of this vegetable delicacy has been described as a mixture of artichokes, asparagus, green beans, and mushrooms. And the texture of the rich green shoots is pleasant and chewy.

Use: Fiddleheads have a fragrant, woodsy flavor. They are sometimes cooked as a first course or side dish, or marinated and served raw in salads. They are wonderful sautéed in butter with lemon juice and black pepper; or cooked for 3 to 4 minutes in lightly salted water until tender, and served with melted butter or hollandaise sauce; or cooked with salt pork and garlic, and creamed to serve on toast. Fiddleheads are also sometimes deep-fried and served as an appetizer, or served in a delicate cream sauce and tossed with pasta.

When buying fiddleheads, always choose small, firm, brightly colored ones that have been gathered no more than 2 days prior to your buying them, and still have their brown scales. The stems should be short.

Pull off any brown sheaths. To rid the heads of scales, rub them between your hands or place them in a bag and shake it. Wash and drain well. Trim all ends just before cooking, steaming, simmering, or sautéing. For best results, add a little salt to the water. Baking soda will affect their bright green color. Do not worry if the water turns a little brownish, this is normal. Be sure not to overcook.

Frozen fiddleheads should not be thawed before cooking.

Availability: Depending on the region, fiddleheads are sold fresh, frozen, or canned. Fresh fiddleheads are available in the spring, from early May to the middle of July, and are occasionally sold in specialty produce shops that carry gourmet delicacies. A warning: they are quite expensive.

Canned fiddleheads don't taste much like fresh.

Storage: Fresh fiddleheads are highly perishable and should be refrigerated as soon as possible. To store fresh fiddleheads, wrap them in dampened paper towels and place them in a plastic bag in the refrigerator. Be sure to use them within 2 days.

To freeze the shoots, blanch for 1 or 2 minutes, then plunge into an ice bath immediately. Dry them thoroughly, then lay them out on a cookie sheet in the freezer. Once they are frozen, move them to an airtight container. Remember not to thaw them before cooking.

Substitution: There really is no flavor substitute for fiddleheads, but none of the recipes in this book that call for this vegetable delicacy depend on its unique flavor. If you are unable to find fiddleheads, omit them from the recipe. The dish will still turn out fine.

Panko

Description: Panko is a coarsely ground mixture of dried crumbs. It has been used in Japan for centuries to provide the deliciously crunchy crust to traditional Japanese fried foods. The panko sold in the United States is usually ground to a finer texture than panko sold in Japan.

Use: In Japan, panko is used to coat deep-fried dishes from *tongatsu* (deep-fried pork cutlet) to shrimp. In the United States, we've found use for it as a topping for all kinds of casseroles and au gratin dishes.

Availability: Panko is packaged in cellophane bags, and can be found on the shelves of most Asian markets.

Storage: Unopened, panko will keep indefinitely, but, as with any bread crumbs, will stale quickly once the package is opened.

Substitute: Use panko as you would any coarse bread crumbs—to coat foods for deep-frying, or to create a crispy Japanese-style breading.

Rice Vinegar

Description: In the United States, you can find a number of different types of rice vinegar—there's a relatively mild seasoned vinegar from Japan that contains sugar and salt, and there are also three types of vinegar from China. All are made from fermented rice, contain monosodium glutamate, and are sweeter and slightly milder than vinegar sold in the West.

The Japanese rice vinegar is almost colorless with a sweet, delicate flavor. It is used in a variety of Japanese dishes from sushi rice to *sunomono* (vinegar salads). Maruken is the most widely known brand. Home-style Japanese cooks usually prefer to create their own vinegar by combining rice wine and sugar to taste.

The three types of Chinese seasoned rice vinegars in the market all have a stronger flavor than the Japanese variety, and each has its own distinct purpose and function. The "white" rice vinegar has a pale amber tint, a mild flavor, and is used mainly in sweet-and-sour dishes. The "red" rice vinegar has a pale, pink hue. It is slightly tart and is used as an accompaniment for boiled or steamed crab. The Chinese "black" rice vinegar has a complex, rich, smoky flavor. Usually made from grains, this dark, thick, and very aromatic mixture is used as a table condiment.

Use: In Japan, rice vinegar is served at every meal. It is added to water (about 2 teaspoons per quart) to soak vegetables that discolor when exposed to the air. In the U.S., we have developed a taste for this mild flavoring, and use it liberally in salad dishes as a simple low-calorie dressing, or sprinkled over shredded cucumbers topped with toasted sesame seeds.

Availability: Today, both the Japanese and Chinese varieties of rice vinegar are available in most U.S. supermarkets and Asian specialty markets.

Storage: Opened or unopened, rice vinegar will keep indefinitely on the pantry shelf.

Substitution: Substitute white wine vinegar for Japanese rice vinegar or Chinese white vinegar if the color is important to the recipe. Otherwise, red vinegar can also be used as a substitute. Black vinegar is generally too strong for most recipes, but is wonderful as a dipping or drizzling condiment with Chinese meals.

If you choose to make your own rice vinegar, combine about 2 teaspoons of sugar and salt to every ¼ cup of unseasoned vinegar. Adjust the flavor to taste.

Roti

Description: Roti, an unleavened bread made from finely ground whole wheat flour, was introduced to Fiji by immigrants from India who came to work the plantations. Similar to India's traditional pancakelike chapati, the dough is rolled into thin rounds and is cooked over an open flame for 10 to 15 minutes until it fills with steam and puffs up like a balloon.

Use: Eaten hot like chapati, roti is torn into pieces and used to scoop up the delicious curries, chutneys, and sauces used in many East Indian dishes.

Availability: Frozen roti is available in some Asian and specialty food markets. A recipe for homemade roti can be found on page 56.

Storage: Fresh roti, stored tightly wrapped in a plastic bag, will stay fresh for 2 days, but it's best to use it as soon as it comes off the griddle.

Substitution: Pita bread, popular with the health-conscious consumer and available in most health food stores, can be used as a substitute. The flavor is quite different, but the texture is comparable.

Samoan Crab

Description: Samoan crab, a member of the mud crab family, likes the flat, muddy low-lying coastlines of the Samoan islands. These large, black crustaceans are scavengers, and will eat almost anything.

Samoan crab meat is tender and flaky, but not as rich as a Dungeness or snow crab.

Use: Growing to a weight of nearly 6 pounds, these large crabs are prized for their delicate texture, and are usually marinated in coconut milk then steamed, or steamed in brine.

Availability: Samoan crabs are rarely available in the United States, so a substitute should be used.

As I recommend for all fresh seafood, be sure to purchase your crab from a reputable fishmonger. Fresh, frozen, and canned crabmeat are available in supermarkets across the country.

Storage: Fresh crab should be used on the day of purchase and stored in the refrigerator until it is time to be cooked.

Cooked crabmeat should be refrigerated, then used within 3 days. If you have selected the canned variety, use the meat as soon as you open the can.

Freezing damages the juicy flavor and delicate texture of the meat. If at all possible, avoid frozen crabmeat. When frozen is your only option, be sure to use the meat within 3 months, or immediately after thawing.

Substitution: Substitute with meat from any other large crab (Dungeness, snow, or Alaskan King).

Sarso (Mustard Seeds)

Description: There are two major types of mustard seeds currently on the international markets: white (or yellow) and brown (or Asian). A third variety, the black mustard seed, has been replaced for most purposes by the brown or Asian species because black seeds are expensive and very difficult to find. White mustard seeds are larger, but a lot less pungent than the brown variety.

Sarso or sarson is a large brown mustard seed, a favorite seasoning among East Indian cooks.

Use: Sarso is used in making a variety of East Indian spice mixtures from curry to masalas, sauces to marinades. Sarso is sold whole or ground into powder. Whole seeds can be eaten raw or roasted. In India, cooks brown them in very hot oil until they burst open like popcorn.

Storage: Fresh sarso should be stored in an airtight container until use. Once the seeds have been roasted or cooked, they tend to release their flavor.

Availability: Whole and raw sarso mustard seeds are available in Asian markets and specialty food stores. They are also available over the Internet from on-line vendors.

Substitution: If black mustard seeds are not available in your area, substitute with whole brown mustard seeds. White mustard seeds are not a recommended substitute because of their tendency to overpower the spice mixture.

Sweet Potato

Description: Sweet potatoes are a staple in the South Pacific. Thought to have originated in the Americas, the popular variety grown throughout the South Pacific is very similar to plants that grow wild in the West Indies and Central America. Even the Polynesian names for sweet potato resemble those used by the indigenous peoples of Peru, Colombia, and Ecuador. In Tahiti, they call sweet potato *umara*, in the Marquesas it's known as *uara*, the Samoans call it *umala*, Hawaiians *'uala*, and in New Zealand the Maori people called it *kumara*. In both Fiji and Tonga, it is known by the name *kumala*.

Everywhere it grows, this nutritionally rich plant is considered a high food value crop. It is easily propagated in the light, well-drained soils on the volcanic islands of the

South Pacific. Stem cuttings are simply shoved into loose mounds of earth that allow the tubers to mature quickly.

Use: Throughout the South Pacific, the sweet potato tubers are simply baked or steamed in an earth oven or *imu*. When cooked, the thick skin is peeled away, exposing the sweet, starchy meat. Sweet potatoes are rarely peeled and boiled like regular potatoes, although in Tahiti they are sometimes boiled, then mashed with coconut milk.

Availability: Sweet potatoes are uniformly available year-round throughout the United States in most major supermarkets. Specialty varieties can be found in Latin American markets by the Mexican name *camotl*.

Storage: Store fresh sweet potatoes as you would any potato, in a dark, cool, and airy place.

Substitution: For any recipe in this book, it's possible to substitute one sweet potato variety with any of the others recommended. Yams may also be used.

Tahitian Vanilla

Description: For centuries, the Aztecs of Mexico and Central America cultivated the yellow pods of a certain orchid plant and processed them into an aphrodisiac and a flavoring for their cocoa drink called *xocolatl*—chocolate. Even then, the process of curing the orchid pods was so intense and laborious that the flavoring was reserved for royalty.

Near the end of the sixteenth century, as Spanish conquistadors pushed through Central America, they developed a taste for this cocoa drink flavored with the dried pods of an Aztec orchid. The Spaniards named the flavoring *vainilla*, because when dried, the curved orchid pod looked like a small sheath (*vaina*) or sword. The conquerors were so impressed with the rich, sensuous vanilla-flavored cocoa drink, they introduced it to Europe.

Today, there are over 20,000 varieties of orchids in the world, but only 50 produce vanilla. The vanilla planifolia orchid, a native of the rain forests of Mexico, the West Indies, and Central America, is the only one that gives us what we call "real" vanilla.

The complicated, labor-intensive regimen required for pollinating, growing, harvesting, and drying the vanilla, along with the fermentation processes for extracting it, makes pure vanilla one of the most expensive flavorings in the world.

In the wild, the long orchid tendrils attach themselves to trees, and climb high into the forest canopy, up to 200 feet above the ground. Picked while still unripe and odorless, the thin 8-inch-long pods—featuring aromatic pulp and a number of small seeds—resemble green beans.

The difficulty of extracting the delicate vanilla flavor begins with pollination. The vanilla orchid opens for only a few hours, one day a year, and is naturally pollinated by the Melipona bee. In today's farming environment, this type of pollination isn't possible. Each blossom has to be artificially pollinated, one at a time. The pods take 6 weeks to reach their optimum size of 6 to 10 inches, and up to 9 months to mature. Then they are handpicked while still green, placed into a vat of water, and boiled for 10 seconds. The hot pods are removed, wrapped in blankets, and allowed to "sweat" in the sun for 3 to 6 months. The pods shrink about 400 percent in size, and are dried until they become soft and turn dark brown. These are the vanilla "beans." During this curing process the aged vanilla develops its distinctive aroma and sweet flavor. The grade quality of a bean is determined by the amount of "vanillin" or "givre" that coats it. The vanillin spreads itself over the bean skin like a kind of sticky mist, a thin, white powder that has the effect of deepening the vanilla flavor.

There are three common types of vanilla beans grown in the world today: Bourbon-Madagascar, Mexican, and Tahitian. Each is prized for its unique flavor. Ninety percent of the world's vanilla is generated in Madagascar, where it's produced in mass. Mexico, the land of the original vanilla orchid, produces stronger, smoother, more flavorful beans, while Tahiti's volcanic soil and endless sunshine provide the thickest, darkest, and most aromatic vanilla.

Use: Vanilla brings its clean flavor to many types of desserts. An old-time favorite way of using the beans is to keep them in a jar of sugar. The sugar is then used to sweeten comfort foods like whipped cream, rice pudding, and baked custard. A popular application for vanilla is to flavor milk or cream by splitting a bean and soaking it in the liquid. The bean is then removed, washed and dried, and stored for use at another time. It's also used as the predominant flavoring for ice cream and crème brûlée.

Availability: Vanilla is available in whole bean, powder, liquid, and sugar form, and is sold in glass tubes, jars, or pouches. Pure vanilla has a finer, smoother taste and is much more expensive than synthetic vanilla. Read the label on liquid and powdered vanilla to be sure there are no artificial ingredients or chemicals added. The terms "pure vanilla extract" or "fine vanilla" should appear on the label.

Quality whole beans are sold in glass tubes, and can be found in gourmet specialty markets and bakers' supply houses. When shopping, look for beans that are soft, ribbed, and pointed at one end. Beans should be coated in "givre."

Storage: Whole beans should stay hard and dry. When storing, wrap them tightly, or seal them in a jar and place them in the freezer or refrigerator. Extracts should be kept in a cool, dry place.

Substitution: The only substitute for vanilla that will ensure genuine flavor is pure vanilla extract. Imitation vanilla is synthetic and has a bitter aftertaste.

Tamarind Paste

Description: The word *tamarind* is short for the Arabic *tamar hindi*, which means "date of India." Indigenous to India, and closely related to carob, the tamarind tree grows to a height of 80 feet. The tropical and subtropical climates of Africa, Southeast Asia, the West Indies, and parts of the South Pacific are perfect for the cultivation of this legume plant.

The tamarind fruit grows into large, cylindrically shaped brown pods that measure 4 to 6 inches in length. Each pod contains a sweet-sour pulp that surrounds 1 to 12 hard, shiny, dark, cinnamon-colored seeds. When the fruit dries, it becomes very sour and highly acidic.

Use: A popular seasoning for chutneys, curries, and pickled fish in East India and the Middle East, tamarind pulp concentrate is used much like lemon juice is used in Western cultures. It is also widely used to make a sweet syrup flavoring for soft drinks. Worcestershire sauce, the time-honored Western beef condiment, gets its rich, spicy flavor from tamarind.

If you can obtain fresh tamarind pods, it's possible to make the sour tamarind liquid to flavor sauces. First, soak the pulp for about 15 minutes, or until it softens. Then run it through a sieve to remove excess fiber or seeds, and you've got it: purified tamarind.

Availability: A sweetened tamarind syrup called *asem toelen*, used as a primary-ingredient syrup and to make soft drinks, is sold in Dutch, Indonesian, and East Indian markets. This mixture should not be mistaken for tamarind pulp. It is not a suitable substitute.

Tamarind is sold as instant paste (merely add a bit of water) or compact cubes, and is available in many specialty food stores.

Asian markets provide tamarind in various forms: whole pods, powder, bricks (make sure to choose the softest), and jars of prepared pulp. There is also an "instant" powder available.

Storage: Tamarind, whether in pod, powder, or jar form, can be kept indefinitely on your pantry shelf at room temperature. Once the packages are opened, tamarind will keep in the refrigerator for a few weeks, or in the freezer for several months.

Prepared pulp will last up to 1 week in the refrigerator. It also freezes well.

Substitution: Lemon juice is often substituted for tamarind, at a ratio of 2 parts lemon juice for 1 part tamarind pulp. Although this is a reasonable substitute, there is a big difference in flavor.

Tapioca-Cassava

Description: Tapioca, from the family Euphorbiaceae, originated in tropical America, and was grown as a food plant from Mexico to Peru before the arrival of Europeans. Portuguese explorers transported the plant to Africa in the sixteenth century, and from there it spread to Madagascar, Java, Asia, and the islands of the South Pacific, becoming a staple in these regions. It is also known as cassava, manioc, and yuca.

Originally, tapioca grew in tropical and subtropical climates, but today it is found throughout the world's tropic zones. The main producers of tapioca are Nigeria, Brazil, Thailand, Zaire, and Indonesia. Propagated by cutting, a cassava plant will grow in a wide range of soils as long as there is adequate drainage. In the South Pacific, where the soil is often sandy, a rotation system is used to prevent continuous cropping that exhausts the soil.

Several cuttings are often planted in the same mound of earth, and when harvested the tubers can be gathered as needed without actually pulling up the entire plant.

A tapioca shrub generally measures 6 to 9 feet in height, and can be harvested between 6 months to 1 year from planting.

There are two species of tapioca: the bitter cassava and the sweet. The flavor distinction is determined by the quantity of a substance called cyanogentic glucoside on the outer layers of the tuber. The bitter variety, poisonous unless cooked, is a hardy shrub with very dark, reddish leaves and stems. Sweet cassava, the more widely used variety, is a more fragile plant with light green leaves and stems.

Cassava root, which is the part of the plant that is eaten, is conical or cylindrical in shape with a dark brown skin. When it is small, the tubers resemble a sweet potato, and can grow to as much as 10 to 20 pounds. Its flesh ranges in color from whitish to red, and is thick, fleshy, and starchy.

Use: Tapioca is very bland and tends to absorb the other flavors present in a dish. The tubers are usually eaten peeled and boiled in water, broiled, or baked in the earth oven.

Pearl-like tapioca balls are often used as a thickening agent in soups, sauces, stews, pies, fruits, and puddings, and are used to make into delicious desserts that are flavored with cream and wine. These tapioca pearls must be soaked for 45 to 75 minutes before cooking. The pulp and paper industry uses tapioca in the production of embossed paper, and it is also used to make the glue on the back of postage stamps.

Tapioca root can't be preserved fresh. So, in the South Pacific, the flesh is sliced and dried in the sun within hours of picking to extract the starch. The pulp can also be transformed into flour, although this is not used in the Pacific territories. Early Tahitians used to dry the pulp that was left after the starch was extracted. They considered this a delicacy. The juice collected during the extraction process was boiled and used to preserve meat.

Storage: Packaged tapioca pearls and flour will keep indefinitely on the pantry shelf.

Availability: Fresh tapioca is difficult to get in the United States, unless you have a tapioca plant in your backyard. Packaged tapioca flour and pearls can be found in Asian markets, health food stores, and major supermarkets year-round.

Substitution: As a thickening agent, arrowroot or cornstarch will work well as a tapioca flour substitute. Pearls may be purchased in most major supermarkets. There is no viable substitute for the tapioca's delicate flavoring.

Ti Leaves

Description: The ti tree, a tropical, palmlike bush, grows to a height of 2 to 4 feet. Its shiny, oblong leaves are used in Polynesia for everything from wrapping foods to being steamed to performing a spiritual anointing.

In South Pacific cooking, ti leaves are used in much the same way we use aluminum foil to seal in the flavor of steaming foods. The leaves range in size from 2 to 6 inches in width and up to 2 feet in length, and are perfect for wrapping small bundles of meats and vegetables to be put into the earth ovens.

Use: Ti leaves are used in Hawai'i to wrap chicken for a steamed dish called "laulau," and are wrapped around fish in a Tahitian dish that is then cooked in coconut milk. Once the food is cooked, the leaves are removed and discarded. They are not eaten.

Storage: If you can get fresh green ti leaves, don't dampen them before wrapping the food to be steamed. They will provide their own moisture. But if you are using dried leaves, it is important to soak them until they are pliable.

If allowed to breathe in a paper bag or perforated plastic bag, fresh ti leaves can be refrigerated for up to 2 months.

Availability: Ti leaves are readily available or can be special-ordered through most florists in the United States.

Substitution: If dried or fresh ti leaves are not available, lotus or bamboo leaves can be substituted; or simply use foil or parchment paper.

Wasabi

Description: Wasabi, the hot, green condiment of Japan, is made from the root of the wasabi plant. It is commonly known as "Japanese horseradish" because of its pungent flavor, although there is no similarity, either botanical or by its appearance.

Used fresh in Japan, but sold grated or powdered in foreign countries, wasabi gives a fiery, eye-watering punch to sushi, sashimi, kamakoko, and raw fish dishes.

Wasabi is very popular in the United States and throughout the world where the Japanese influence is felt.

Use: In Japan, fresh wasabi is peeled, and the eyes are cut out of the root. It is then grated on a fine grater, and converted to a powder. This powder is mixed into a smooth paste, and covered for 10 minutes to allow the flavor to blend.

Wasabi is used as a spicy seasoning in sushi, as a flavoring for the Japanese soy sauce that accompanies sashimi or kamaboko, and as a dipping sauce for cold soba noodles.

Storage: Fresh wasabi should be refrigerated and used as soon as possible. The powdered form can be stored for years at room temperature, but after it's mixed with water, the paste should be stored in the refrigerator. Ready-to-use pastes keep well in the refrigerator for several weeks.

Availability: Fresh wasabi root is not available in the United States, but a fresh-grated wasabi can be found in some specialty produce markets. Both paste and powdered wasabi are always available in specialty and Asian markets. The powdered wasabi, sold in cans, is mixed with water to make a stiff wasabi paste. Ready-to-use wasabi paste is sold in tubes.

Substitution: Regular horseradish is not a substitute for wasabi. Powdered wasabi or paste is available in most Asian markets.

BUYING AND STORING SEAFOOD

Here are some quick guidelines to help you make informed decisions when you're buying and storing fresh fish, frozen fish, and shellfish. First and foremost, I recommend that you: (1) stay away from roadside stands; (2) always buy your fresh fish and seafood from a reputable fishmonger whom you know and trust; and (3) use your senses of sight, smell, and touch to guide you.

Buying Fresh Fish

There are four basic questions that should be asked before you begin to select your fish.

1. Where was the fish caught? This will determine how long the fish has been out of the water.

2. When did the fish come into the market?

3. Was the fish previously frozen?

4. How long will it keep at home?

After you've had these questions answered to your satisfaction, it's time to make some judgments on your own. The general appearance and smell of the whole fish and fillet is very important. Look for the following:

1. The eyes should have black pupils that have translucent cornea.

2. The skin should have a bright, luminous sheen.

3. The gills should be a bright pastel rose color.

4. The flesh should be translucent and firm with an elastic texture.

If these requirements are met, you have a fish or fillet that was caught within the last 24 hours.

Storing Fresh Fish

Once you have made your selection and have the fish at home, it's important to keep it in good condition until you are ready to cook it. After you have washed the fish and removed the scales and foreign matter, place a layer of ice on the base of a storage container. Cover the ice with a sheet of plastic, then lay the fish or fillet on top. Place another piece of plastic over the fish, and cover it with ice. The object is to keep the fish and the ice separated. The iced fish container should be stored on the bottom shelf of your refrigerator. Be sure to replace the ice when it melts, and drain the runoff, to keep the water from making the fish soggy.

It is always best to use fresh fish on the day it is purchased. Remember, for every hour a fish sits at room temperature, it loses a day of shelf life.

Frozen Fish

When buying frozen fish, check to see if it has been correctly packaged and stored. Frozen fish should be kept frozen solid until it is needed. At home, a frozen fish should be stored for no longer than 2 months, but after 1 month it starts to lose its flavor.

Cooking Frozen Fish

Ideally, frozen fish should be cooked while it is still solid and icy. To adapt the recipes, cook the frozen fish for a longer time (approximately 10 extra minutes for each inch of thickness) at a slightly lower temperature.

Thawing Frozen Fish

If you have to thaw fish, it is best to place fish or fillets on the bottom of the refrigerator for several hours or overnight. DO NOT leave the fish out at room temperature on the countertop to defrost. The fish quality will deteriorate rapidly.

Shellfish

Shellfish die if they are stored at temperatures that are too high or too low. If they are covered with fresh water for a long period, they will drown. To test if mussels, cockles, or pipis are alive before cooking, leave them at room temperature for 20 minutes then tap them lightly or hold under fresh water until they close. If the shell remains open about 1 centimeter, the shellfish is dead and should not be eaten.

Live mussels and other bivalves should be stored between $+ 2°C$ and $+ 4°C$ under a cover of melting ice. It is important that the ice does not make direct contact with the shellfish.

Place the shellfish in a container (preferably one with drainage holes), cover them with a towel or sacking, then cover them with ice. The container should be kept in a cool place but not in the refrigerator.

FISH SUBSTITUTIONS

Listed below are fish used in the book's recipes, followed by some basic fish substitutions:

'ahi—any fatty, firm-textured fish, like swordfish, sturgeon, marlin, halibut, salmon, or mackerel.

mahimahi—any lean, firm-textured fish, like monkfish (not as sweet), shark (not as sweet), swordfish, tuna, catfish (fattier), or tilefish (flakier texture, not as sweet).

marlin—any lean, firm-textured fish, like Pacific blue marlin, kajiki, or swordfish.

onaga (red snapper)—any fish with a lean, flaky texture, like sea bass, rockfish, grouper, halibut, pompano, lemonfish, sole (more delicate), flounder (more delicate), cod (more delicate), orange roughy (more delicate), or catfish.

'opakapaka (pink snapper)—any lean, flaky fish, like sea bass, rockfish, grouper, halibut, pompano, lemonfish, sole, flounder, cod, orange roughy, or catfish.

ono (mackerel)—any fatty, flaky fish, like Spanish mackerel, shad, bluefish, herring, or small trout.

swordfish—any lean, flaky fish, like marlin, shark (not as sweet or flaky), tuna (not as sweet), sturgeon, halibut, or mahimahi.

uku (gray snapper)—any lean, flaky fish, like sea bass, rockfish, grouper, halibut, pompano, lemonfish, sole, flounder, cod, orange roughy, or catfish.

Fiji

MY FAVORITE WAY TO TRAVEL through the South Pacific

is by cruise ship. The pace is slow, and it allows for time to enjoy the spectacu-

lar beauty. One of my favorite things to do is to stand on the bow of the massive

ship as we enter the turquoise waters of Fiji. We usually arrive in the morning

when the air is cool and the sun glints off the water, making thousands of shim-

mering diamondlike sparkles. **OVER 800 ISLANDS MAKE**

UP the tiny country of Fiji; and I was very excited the first time I visited

this legendary place. I'd heard about the colors of the water, the reefs teeming

with fish too numerous to count, and the

rugged mountain peaks that towered

above the sandy shores like Poseidon ris-

ing from the depths of his ocean. I made

sure on that first arrival that I had a

place on the deck so I could take it all in.

I REMEMBER, FROM

MY VANTAGE point it looked like the boat was headed straight for the

main island of Vita Levu (also called Big Fiji). I could see the vaulting green

towers of Mount Tomanivi, the tallest mountain in the country, riding the waves

in the distance. The captain said we'd land in Suva, the capital, so I planned a day trip into the city to visit the public markets. They are famous for the cornucopia of fresh seafood and produce offered by the street vendors in their canopied shops.

I stood at the railing and watched Vita Levu rise higher in the water. I'd worked myself into a frenzy of anticipation, going over my mental lists of foods to sample, places to see, and restaurants to visit. We would be in Fiji for only two days, and there was so much I wanted to do.

I couldn't believe it when the ship veered right, and headed straight toward the eastern horizon. We were steering away from Suva, away from everything I wanted to do and see. One of the stewards walked past and I asked him why we were moving away from Vita Levu. He pointed toward the water in the distance. "Between the boat and the land are hundreds of coral heads and shoals," he said. "When we come around, you'll be able to see the change in the color of the water. The dark blue is the deep channel, the light turquoise is the shallow sandy bottom, and the greenish blue marks the coral heads. When the tide goes out, the surface between the boat and the island gets all choppy as the waves push around the exposed reefs."

I knew this, of course, but the light on the water hid all of the subtle shadings. It was two more hours before the tugboats guided us into port, but the views were worth every minute. Everything I'd heard about Fiji was true. I've always said that my islands of Hawai'i were the most beautiful in the world, but Fiji rivals everything I've ever seen. It was magnificent.

"Bula vinaka!" My driver called out the Fijian greeting as I walked toward his jeep. His name was Rashi, a Fijian of East Indian descent. The taxi from the harbor, a rickety open-air trolley, rattled over every bump in the road as we wove through the noon traffic to the center of Suva. People on bicycles with large baskets swerved in and out of the cars and trucks.

I had to yell at the driver to be heard above the din of horns honking and engines roaring without mufflers. "I want to see the markets!" I shouted.

"Food or tourist?" he yelled back.

"Food!" I shouted. "Food!"

"It's no problem!" Rashi took a hard right, veering into the other lane and cutting off a delivery truck. We turned the next corner and crept down a side street. In the distance, on a crossing street, I noticed a cluster of bright canopies and outdoor stands. I tapped the driver on the shoulder and pointed. He nodded and sped up. As we came to the corner, the scene unfolded before us, all the displays that gave this farmers' market its reputation. Lining the full length of the street, tables stood piled with arrangements of breadfruit, dalo (taro), bags of rourou (taro leaves), boxes of tovioka (cassava), bunches of bananas, rows of yams, sacks of rice, bottles of lolo (coconut milk), bushels of ferns, and dangling on strings above each stand were thousands of bright hot chilies. At the far end, fishmongers peddled their fresh catch—chests heaped with glistening ice and topped with assortments of pink, gray, and red snapper, groupers, mahimahi, slabs of marlin fillets wrapped in plastic, moon fish, mussels, clams, lobsters, and an array of different kinds of crabs.

A little Chinese woman yelled and waved me over. Her booth, decorated with a red-and-white canvas awning, offered red, pink, brown, yellow, and white sea salts. "You have!" she said, lifting a small bag of crystals. "I make special." She pointed to the black and yellow specks that floated between the coarse grains. "Special today," she said. "Seasoned just for you. Hot. Hot salt. You like."

She was so cute. She reminded me of the little ladies in the lei shops in downtown Honolulu. They said things like "Special today," "I make special fo' you." I bought three bags of different colored salts and left the Chinese lady smiling.

Down the road a ways, through the crowd of shoppers dressed in colorful patterns of ethnic clothing, there was a family that sold meats. Large slabs of pork, beef, and plucked chickens lay in glass-topped, portable refrigerator chests. And next to that was a kava booth. Kava, made from the root of a pepper plant, is the ceremonial drink of the South Pacific. There were bags of kava in different stages of processing—whole roots, chopped, or ground.

Back in the taxi, the driver told me the market was open all day, every day, even Sundays. People came from all over the city to shop. "It's the best," he said.

And I had to agree.

"All kinds of people live in Fiji—Indian, like me, Chinese, Fijian, everything. They all cook different. You like see?" he asked.

We drove through a string of side streets, and turned up an avenue lined with restaurants. "All kinds of food here!" the driver yelled. "All kinds."

He was right. There was a deli, then a place called Curry Café, then a Chinese take-out, a burger place, a small, French-style sidewalk café with baguettes and croissants in the window, a Chinese diner, a seafood place. You name it, you could get anything you wanted. There was even a pizzeria.

"You cook, yes?" the driver asked. "You like the good stuff."

Before I could answer, we were off again.

"I take you to the hotels. That's the place. Good food. Expensive."

"Let's try the restaurants in town first," I told him.

The influx of foreign cultures to Fiji is most evident in the cuisine. There are really four basic types of food in Fiji—the "local" or traditional Fijian, the Chinese, the European, and the Indian.

Traditional Fijian cooking is much like the cuisine of the rest of the South Pacific, using lots of coconut milk, fish, and salt. I'd sampled many of these dishes while growing up in La'ie.

The Chinese introduced Cantonese and Szechuan cooking in the early 1900s, and opened restaurants featuring dishes made with fresh local fish and produce. My style of cooking is heavily influenced by my Chinese heritage, so of course I had to try the Fijian/Chinese food. I chose a Szechuan restaurant, a little hole in the wall next to a number of other more upscale places, and ordered a mixed plate of local vegetables, rice, and a dish of sautéed red snapper with a side of deep-fried breadfruit. The flavors were typically Chinese, spicy in the Szechuan tradition, but the deep-fried breadfruit was unique and wonderful.

Many of the other restaurants in the area were a mix of European eateries, everything from French to Italian, German to British. I checked the menus, and found the standard fare.

It was in the Indian restaurants that I found the true flavor of modern-day Fiji. Between 1879 and 1916, East Indian laborers were imported to work the sugar plantations. They brought their cuisine and cooking styles with them. Today, the special dishes found only here are called Indo-Fijian, a hybrid where everything from coconut milk to seafood is cooked in spicy curries. There are Indian restaurants everywhere in Fiji, and each offers a different style, a unique flavor. I decided I'd wait for dinner to try a place.

Rashi drove out to the countryside where the roads changed from asphalt to ruggedly pitted dirt. I felt like we were traveling back in time. Men on bicycles rode by, smiling and waving as we jostled along. Dust plumed into the cab and I had it everywhere. The humidity and heat helped secure every speck of dust to my skin. I looked like a coated sugar cookie by the time Rashi decided to stop driving.

"Where are we?" I asked.

"Home," Rashi said. He jumped out of the taxi. "I have to get something. You want to come in? See my family?"

How could I refuse? I climbed out of the car and walked to the small wood-frame house. Rashi had disappeared inside, and as I got to the door, he came back out. "You want something to drink?" he asked. "We have tea." Rashi's wife, a rather large woman with deep brown eyes that looked almost black, stood behind him. She whispered something in his ear. Rashi smiled.

"My wife has some dinner almost ready," he said. "You stay and eat."

I shook my head. "I don't want to impose," I said.

Rashi laughed. "You stay. I take you back to the boat later. If you stay, I stay. See?" His smile got bigger.

It's not every day that you visit a country and get to sample a genuine local, home-cooked meal. I accepted.

Rashi's wife was named Mata. She hurried back into the house.

"I show you my garden," Rashi said. I followed him out into what looked like a jungle. "This is tovioka," he said, pointing to the cluster of bushes with spindly branches and big leaves. "You call cassava. Looks good. Tastes good. My wife is cooking some now."

"Yeah," I said. "We also call it tapioca."

"Yes," Rashi said. "Same. Over there." He pointed off into the distance. "That is the coconut trees, and over there is the breadfruit tree." He pointed back to his home. "The chilies are next to the house." All around the perimeter of the cottage were small bushes that looked like filigree against the yellow paint.

"We have chickens and pigs. But no cows," Rashi added. "I know you like food," he said smiling down at my stomach. Again he was right.

We walked back to the house. The sun was setting, and the spicy aroma from Mata's kitchen was so inviting I could taste the food in the air. "What is she fixing?" I asked. "It smells incredible."

"Beef stew with roti," Rashi said as he picked up his daughter. "It's full of tovioka. It's our favorite. The best."

Dinner was ready in no time. We all sat around the dinner table in the middle of a large central room. Mata placed an enormous stewing pot on the table. Rashi sat at the head with Mata to his right, then all of his five children took their places. His oldest son, Shringa, about 12 years old, sat at the other end. "Shringa, you move. Let Mr. Choy sit there," Rashi ordered.

When Mata opened the pot, the entire room filled with the aroma of tomatoes and beef. She passed around a plate of warmed roti. It looked like pita bread, flat and speckled brown. I watched as the children dished the thick stew onto their plates, then scooped helpings into the middle of their roti. They folded it together and ate it like a burrito. I followed their lead.

I took a bite. "Take more roti," Rashi advised.

The flavors were subtle and blended perfectly. It was the best stew I'd ever tasted. "It's like a Fijian burrito," I said. "This is wonderful, Mata."

She simply smiled.

"We eat roti with everything," Rashi added. "It's the best."

After dinner, I said my good-byes. Mata and all the children stood at the front door and bowed to us.

"You can eat at the fancy restaurants tomorrow," Rashi said as we drove away.

I said, "I doubt anything will be as good as Mata's cooking. What a fabulous introduction to Indo-Fijian cuisine."

The next day, I went with some people from the boat to sample as many Indo-Fijian dishes as possible. We tried curried chicken, beef, fish, and prawns with small helpings of dhal (soup), roti, and rice. My favorite traditional Fijian dish was a marinated raw fish called kokoda.

After it was all over and we were sailing away from Vita Levu, I realized that I'd already set my standard of Fijian excellence, and nothing compared to Mata's beef stew. I've included the recipe in this book. I wanted to add some curry to the mixture, but I thought you'd like to experience Mata's delicate blend yourself.

Moce. Au sa tatau meu sa lako.
(Good-bye. With your permission, I'll take my leave.)

Lovo Pork in Roti

IN FIJI, ROASTED pork is called *vuaka vavi* when it's prepared in a lovo, or earth oven. The meat is wrapped in banana leaves, placed over hot stones, then covered with more leaves, cloth, and dirt. This style of cooking is common throughout Polynesia. In Hawai'i, the name for this type of cooked pork is kalua pig. Vuaka vavi is easy to prepare at home.   SERVES 4

4 tablespoons vegetable oil

1½ cups Kalua Pig, or pua'a (see page 87)

¾ cup diced onion

1 clove garlic, minced

1½ teaspoons curry powder

2½ cups shredded cabbage

¼ cup chopped cilantro

Salt and pepper to taste

6 roti (see page 56), or four 6-inch tortillas

In a hot skillet, add the oil and sauté the pua'a, onion, garlic, and the curry powder for 4 minutes. Add shredded cabbage and salt and pepper to taste, and cook for 3 more minutes. Remove from the heat, and mix in chopped cilantro.

Wrap roti or flour tortillas in aluminum foil, and heat in 350°F oven for 5 minutes, or until warm and pliable. Divide pork filling into 6 equal parts and spread in 2-inch mounds down the center of each roti, one end to the other. Roll the roti burrito-style, and serve immediately with pineapple or tomato chutney.

Curried Citrus Chicken Papaya

CURRIED DISHES ARE an intricate part of Fijian-style cooking, and set it apart from the rest of the South Pacific fare. This dish can be served as a main dish or appetizer. Guests break off pieces of roti (the Fijian flat bread) and use it to scoop the curried filling, much like chips and dip.   SERVES 4

Curry Mixture
1 cup flour

2 teaspoons curry powder

1 teaspoon paprika

1 teaspoon seasoned salt

1 teaspoon white pepper

3 pounds chicken thighs, boned, skinless

Papaya Sauce
1½ cups orange juice

2 teaspoons curry powder

1 tablespoon cornstarch

⅓ cup brown sugar

2 cups sliced papaya

Spices
2 teaspoons minced ginger

2 teaspoons minced garlic

2 teaspoons chopped cilantro

Garnish
Sliced papaya, sliced citrus fruit, cilantro, and flowers

6 Roti (see page 56), or four 6-inch flour tortillas

Combine curry mixture ingredients in a large bowl. Dust chicken in curry mixture, and pan-fry in a wok at high heat. Mix papaya sauce ingredients together and set aside. Combine ginger, garlic, and cilantro in a bowl. Place pan-fried chicken in a baking pan, and pour papaya sauce over the top. Sprinkle with ginger-garlic-cilantro mixture. Bake at 350°F for 45 minutes. Pour chicken curry on top of a bed of rice and garnish with papaya, citrus fruit, cilantro, and edible flowers.

Serve with warm roti. Wrap roti or flour tortillas in aluminum foil, and heat in 350°F oven for 5 minutes, or until warm and pliable.

Potato and Pea Samosa

P O T A T O   A N D   P E A Samosa, a popular Indo-Fijian appetizer, is easy to prepare and very tasty. Samosas are fried, triangular pastries that are filled with vegetables or meat. This recipe has an interesting combination of Indian flavors and Chinese presentation when prepared with wonton wrappers and spicy curry powder, and served with the piquant flavor of fruit chutney.

YIELDS 3 DOZEN

3 tablespoons salad oil

1½ teaspoons sarso (black mustard seeds)

½ teaspoon jerra (cumin seeds)

1 small chili pepper, minced

1 medium onion, finely diced

1 tablespoon minced garlic

2 teaspoons curry powder

½ teaspoon turmeric

½ cup water

1½ cups diced potatoes

1 box frozen green peas (10 ounces)

Salt to taste

2 tablespoons minced coriander leaves

36 wonton wrappers (4-inch squares)

Egg wash

Oil for deep-frying

Tamarind Chutney (see page 64 for recipe)

Heat oil in a pan, add the sarso, jerra, and minced chili pepper, and sauté for about 2 minutes. Add the onion, and cook until onion is translucent. Add the garlic, curry powder, and turmeric; sauté for 1 minute. Add the water, potatoes, and the green peas; sauté until the potatoes are cooked and the water has evaporated. Season with salt and add the coriander leaves. Set aside until cooled.

In the meantime, separate the wonton wrappers. Arrange wrappers on a clean surface and place about a tablespoon of the pea and potato filling in the center of each wrapper. Brush the edges of the wrapper with the egg wash, and fold in half to make triangular-shaped packets. Heat deep-frying oil, and cook samosas until golden brown. Drain well on paper towels, and serve hot with Tamarind Chutney.

Dhal Soup

DHAL IS A term traditionally used to describe a spicy dish made with lentils or other legumes. This dhal soup is delicious, nutritious, and totally vegetarian. Serve a multigrain or Basmati rice on the side and some homemade yogurt for a filling lunch or winter afternoon snack.   SERVES 8

2 cups dried yellow split peas

12 cups water

4 tablespoons ghee (clarified butter) or unsalted butter

1 to 2 chili peppers, minced

1 teaspoon cumin seeds

1½ medium onions, diced

8 cloves garlic, thinly sliced

1½ teaspoons turmeric

Salt to taste

Chopped cilantro leaves for garnish

Rinse the split peas, and place in a pot with the water. Bring to a boil, and simmer for 30 minutes; skim occasionally.

Heat the ghee in a frying pan, brown the chili and cumin seeds, then add onions and garlic. Sauté until onions are golden brown on the edges; add turmeric. Add spicy butter mixture to split peas, and simmer for about 1 hour. Season with salt to taste.

If the soup appears to be too thick, add more water for a medium-thick consistency. Fold in the cilantro leaves before serving. Serve hot.

Kai Soup

BLACK RIVER CLAMS are sold in open air markets throughout Fiji. Kai means clams in Fijian. Any fresh clams make wonderful substitutes. If you are using Black River clams, make sure to simmer for about 30 minutes, or until they are tender.

SERVES 4 TO 6

2 pounds river kai (Fijian river clams) or fresh clams

6 cups water

4 tablespoons butter

1 medium onion, finely diced

1 clove garlic, minced

¼ cup flour

1 cup coconut milk

Salt and pepper to taste

Lemon juice to taste

Chopped green onion for garnish

Clean clams, and rinse. Place clams in a pot with the water. Simmer until clams open. Remove from heat. Strain the clam stock, and set aside.

In a separate pot, heat the butter, and add the diced onion and garlic. Cook until the onion is translucent. Stir in the flour, and cook for 1 minute. Do not brown. Slowly stir in the clam stock. Simmer for 10 minutes, add the coconut milk, and cook for 5 more minutes. Season with salt and pepper and lemon juice to taste. Divide soup among bowls. Just before serving, add the clams, and garnish with the chopped green onion.

Deep-fried Calamari Salad

I LOVE THIS layered salad. The paprika-spiced calamari rings have a wonderful, crunchy texture. Spanish onions have a mild, spicy flavor. Bermuda or Maui onions are great substitutes.   SERVES 4 TO 6

Oil for deep-frying

2 cups flour

2 tablespoons paprika

2 pounds calamari, cleaned and cut into rings

Salt and pepper to taste

1 pound salad greens

½ red bell pepper, julienned

½ yellow pepper, julienned

½ medium Spanish onion, julienned

1 medium cucumber, peeled, seeded, and sliced

2 medium tomatoes, cut into wedges

Chopped cilantro for garnish

Cilantro Vinaigrette (see page 59)

Heat the oil to 350°F. Combine the flour and paprika. Moderately season the calamari with salt and pepper. Add calamari to the flour mixture. Remove, and dust off the excess flour. Deep-fry the calamari until golden brown or until done. Arrange the salad greens, peppers, onion, cucumber, and tomatoes on a platter. Place the calamari on the top, and garnish with fresh cilantro. Serve the dressing on the side.

Ota Seisei (Fijian Fern Shoot Salad)

OTA ARE WILD ferns that grow near streams. In Fiji, young leaves are
stripped off the mature stems and boiled in salted water or coconut milk. Ota seisei is the young, unfurled fern top. Substitute with fiddleheads.   SERVES 6

1½ pounds fresh ota seisei or fiddleheads
1 can coconut milk (14 ounces)
½ medium onion, diced
1 large tomato, diced
½ red pepper, diced
1 chili pepper, minced
Salt to taste

Clean the tender part of the fern shoot, and cut into ½-inch slices. Add salt to a pot of
boiling water. Blanch the fern shoots, then cool in ice water to keep the ferns green.
Drain, place in a bowl, and add coconut milk, onion, tomato, red pepper, and chili
pepper. Season with salt to taste. Chill until ready to serve.

Fiji Bitter Beer Batter-Fried Fish

YOU CAN USE any white fish fillet for this recipe. It works well with 'ahi, marlin, or any of the snappers. Fiji Bitter is the premier beer of Fiji. It tastes so good on a warm, humid day. If you can't get Fiji Bitter beer, substitute with your favorite lager. I do.   SERVES 6

2 pounds white fish fillet

2 teaspoons lemon juice

¼ teaspoon five-spice powder

2 teaspoons salt

2 teaspoons paprika

1 cup flour

6 ounces Fiji Bitter beer

2 tablespoons water

Oil for deep-frying

Cut fillets into 2½-ounce portions, and sprinkle with lemon juice, five-spice powder, and ½ teaspoon salt. In a bowl, mix remaining salt, paprika, and flour. Gradually stir in beer and water. Beat until batter is smooth. Dip fish into batter, drain slightly, then fry in hot oil at 350°F for about 5 to 7 minutes or until fish is brown and will flake easily. Drain on paper towels and serve hot with tartar sauce and lemon wedges.

Fiji Beef Parcel

ROUROU LEAVES ARE leaves from the taro plant. In Hawai'i, these leaves are called lu'au leaves. Fresh, whole spinach leaves can be used as a substitute. If you are using fresh spinach, place the beef, onions, sweet potatoes, tomatoes, and coconut milk directly onto the aluminum foil, and cook without leaves. Spinach must be steamed and served separately to avoid overcooking. SERVES 6

1½ pounds beef or beef chuck, stew cut

2 teaspoons minced garlic

2 tablespoons Hawaiian or rock salt

2 pounds fresh rourou (taro) leaves

2 medium onions, julienned

2 cups peeled and stew-cut sweet potatoes

2 large tomatoes, stew-cut

1 can coconut milk (14 ounces)

Coconut Chutney (see page 59)

Cut beef into cubes and rub with garlic and salt.

To make the parcel, place two large sheets of foil in a baking pan. Place one-half of the fresh rourou leaves in a thick layer in the middle of the foil. Place the beef, onions, sweet potatoes, tomatoes, and coconut milk on the leaves. Top with the rest of the rourou, and carefully seal the parcel by creasing the foil wrap. Carefully lift the parcel from the baking pan and place in a large steamer. Cook for 2½ to 3 hours. Meat should be tender. Serve hot with Coconut Chutney.

Mata's Beef Stew

MATA IS THE wife of a taxi driver I met on my first trip to Fiji. I had dinner at their home, and was so impressed with the simple, light stew Mata made, I decided to let you try it. It's so simple and down-to-earth and can be made in a crockpot. Fresh tapioca has a delicate and wonderful flavor. This stew is best the next day, after all the flavors have had a chance to blend.

SERVES 8 TO 10

3 pounds beef chuck roast, stew-cut

Salt and pepper

⅔ cup flour

¼ cup salad oil

3 cloves garlic, minced

2 medium onions, stew-cut

2 stalks celery, stew-cut

3 medium carrots, peeled and stew-cut

8 cups beef stock

2 cups chicken stock

1 can whole peeled tomatoes (28 ounces), cut in halves

4 pounds fresh tapioca, peeled and cut into 2½-inch dice; or substitute 4 pounds potatoes, peeled and stew-cut

6 Roti (see page 56), or four 6-inch tortillas

Sprinkle beef with salt and pepper, then dust with flour. Heat a heavy pot and add the salad oil. Brown meat with garlic and onions until golden brown. Add the celery and carrots, cook for 3 minutes. Add the stocks and tomatoes; simmer for 1¼ hours. Skim off the fat that rises to the top of the stew. Add the tapioca, and cook until meat and tapioca are tender. Season with salt and pepper. Serve with roti or tortillas on the side.

Pea and Potato Curry

I LIKE THIS mixture best when it's wrapped in warm roti, then dolloped with generous portions of yogurt and chutney. My favorite is Tamarind Chutney.

SERVES 4

8 ounces whole dried peas or whole soybeans
½ teaspoon cumin seeds
1 small chili, minced
¼ cup canola oil
1 medium onion, finely chopped
3 cloves garlic, minced
2 teaspoons curry powder
3 russet potatoes, peeled and cubed
1 cup water
Salt to taste
¼ cup finely chopped cilantro leaves

6 Roti (see page 56), or four 6-inch tortillas
¼ cup plain yogurt
¼ cup Tamarind Chutney (see page 64)

Soak the dried peas or whole soybeans overnight. Rinse peas, and cook until tender. Remove from heat, rinse under water, then drain.

Heat the cumin seeds and chili in the oil over medium-high heat. Add the onion, and cook until golden brown. Add garlic and curry powder. Fry for 1 minute, then add potatoes, cooked peas, and water. Cover and simmer for 25 minutes. Season with salt to taste. Stir in the chopped cilantro.

Serve with Roti, yogurt, and chutney.

Mr. Dean's Incredible Chicken Pilau

PILAU IS A rich and flavorful rice dish that originated in northern India and Pakistan. Indian Muslims brought this dish to Fiji. Mr. Dean, a second-generation Fijian citizen, was gracious enough to share this old family recipe with me. It is so good that I just had to share it with you. SERVES 8

1 whole chicken (3 to 4 pounds)
4 tablespoons canola oil
4 medium onions, diced
2 tablespoons chopped garlic
2 tablespoons chopped fresh gingerroot
2 tablespoons Pilau Masala (see page 63)
½ cup ghee or unsalted butter
1 teaspoon whole cloves
1 teaspoon whole cardamom
1 cinnamon stick, about 4 inches long, broken in half
3 cinnamon leaves (optional)
7 cups boiling water
4 cups long-grain rice
Tamarind Chutney (see page 64)

Preheat oven to 325°F. Wash chicken under cold water, dry the chicken, then chop into 1½-inch pieces.

In a heavy pot, heat the oil and fry half of the onions until edges are golden brown. Add 1 tablespoon each of the garlic and ginger. Sauté for 1 minute and add the chicken. Sauté until chicken is golden brown and liquid is almost evaporated. Add the Pilau Masala; cook for 2 minutes. Remove from heat and set aside.

In a similar-sized pot, heat the ghee or butter. Add the cloves, cardamom, cinnamon stick, cinnamon leaves, then the rest of the onions, garlic, and ginger. Sauté until the onions are golden brown, then add the 7 cups of boiling water. Simmer on medium heat for 4 minutes. Add the rice. Season with salt to taste. Stir, and simmer for about 8 minutes or until most of the liquid has evaporated. Add the prepared chicken, and mix.

Transfer to a baking dish, cover, and place in the oven. Cook for 20 minutes, until all moisture is dried off and the rice is cooked. Serve with Tamarind Chutney.

Spicy Suva Fried Fish

IN FIJI, THE cuisine is ripe with blends of coconut and East Indian spices. I developed this simple recipe for fried fish while in Suva. We went to a fish market and selected some great red snapper steaks. I wanted to make something different, something easy to fix, and something typically Fijian. Voilà! My Spicy Suva Fried Fish. SERVES 6

2 pounds white fish

1 can coconut milk (14 ounces)

1 cup flour

1 tablespoon curry powder

2 teaspoons garlic salt

½ cup oil for frying

Lemon wedges for garnish

Miti Sauce (see page 61)

Cut fish into about 12 pieces. Marinate the fish in the coconut milk for 1 hour. Combine the dry ingredients in a bowl. Heat oil in a frying pan. Drain the marinated fish and coat with the curried flour mixture. Carefully fry the fillet of fish on both sides until golden brown and cooked through. Serve with lemon wedges and Miti Sauce.

Prawn Curry

IN MY OPINION, coconut milk is needed to successfully blend the spicy curry and chili garlic paste in a dish like this. The rice serves as a refreshing equalizer for the palate. If this dish isn't hot enough for your tastes, add a little more chili garlic. It has the potential to make you sweat and clear your sinuses. This curry is wonderful when served over a mound of hot Basmati rice and crowned with a dollop of your favorite chutney.　　SERVES 4 TO 6

½ cup vegetable oil

½ teaspoon cumin seeds

1 teaspoon mustard seeds

1 large onion, diced

6 cloves garlic, crusted

1½ teaspoons ground coriander

1 teaspoon ground turmeric

1 tablespoon chili garlic paste

¼ cup tomato paste

3 pounds fresh whole prawns, with tail shells removed

1 can coconut milk (14 ounces)

Salt to taste

½ cup chopped fresh cilantro for garnish

Heat the oil, then add cumin seeds, mustard seeds, and onion. Cook until onion is golden brown. Add garlic, coriander, turmeric, chili garlic paste, and tomato paste. Sauté for about 3 minutes over medium heat. Add the prawns. Cook for another 2 minutes. Add the coconut milk, and simmer for a few more minutes. Season with salt to taste. Remove from heat, and stir in the chopped cilantro. Serve over hot Basmati rice with your favorite chutney.

Ginger-Scallion Fried Rice

THE NAME BASMATI is literally translated as "queen of fragrance." Grown in the foothills of the Himalayas, this long-grain rice has an aromatic, nutty flavor and a fine texture, and can be found in Indian and Middle-Eastern markets. YIELDS 5 CUPS

5 tablespoons peanut oil

½ teaspoon sesame oil

1 clove garlic, minced

2 tablespoons minced ginger

½ cup chopped scallions

¼ cup chopped cilantro

1 teaspoon sugar

2 teaspoons soy sauce

4 cups cooked Basmati rice

Salt and white pepper to taste

Cilantro for garnish

In a wok, heat the peanut oil and sesame oil. Add garlic, ginger, and scallions. Sauté for 1 minute, then add cilantro, sugar, and soy sauce. Cook for 1 minute. Add Basmati rice, and sauté until thoroughly warm and mixed well. Season with salt and pepper to taste. Garnish with cilantro, and serve immediately.

Roti

IN FIJI, ROTI is eaten for breakfast, as a snack, for lunch, and as a bread accompaniment at dinner. This versatile, easy-to-make, unleavened griddle-bread is filled with vegetable or meat mixtures, or broken up and used to sop up the savory juices of traditional Indo-Fijian dishes. Much like chapati, roti is a staple at Fijian tables. YIELDS 2 DOZEN 6-INCH ROTI

2 cups whole-wheat flour
1 cup all-purpose flour
½ teaspoon salt
1 tablespoon ghee (clarified butter) or canola oil
1 cup warm water (90°F to 100°F)

Cooked Tomato Chutney (see page 60)

Sift the dry ingredients together, and place in a food processor. Add ghee and mix for 10 seconds. Add half the warm water in a steady stream for 10 seconds. Turn off the machine, and scrape down the bowl. Drizzle the rest of the water into the bowl, and blend for another 10 seconds. Process dough until it looks smooth and shiny and feels soft and pliable to the touch. Carefully take the dough from the food processor container and place it in a bowl to rest. Cover with a moist towel and set in a warm place for 30 minutes. The dough can be made a day ahead of time, tightly covered, sealed, and refrigerated.

If kept in the refrigerator, remove and let stand for 30 minutes before you are ready to roll. Knead the dough for about 1 minute. Divide into 2 equal portions. Using your hands, roll each portion into a rope, then cut into 12 equal pieces. Roll them into 1-inch balls.

Dust the balls lightly with flour to prevent them from sticking to one another. Put them back into the bowl. Keep the bowl covered loosely with a damp towel at all times, to prevent the dough from drying out.

Heat a griddle over medium heat. Remove one ball from the bowl. Place on floured rolling surface. Start to roll out with a rolling pin in all directions to form a 6-inch circle.

Lightly grease a hot griddle with 1 teaspoon of oil. Fry for about 20 to 30 seconds, or until the side in contact with the griddle is cooked and several tiny brown spots appear. Flip the bread, and fry the other side the same way for about 10 seconds. Overfrying will cause the roti to be tough and hard. Place cooked roti in a dish to keep warm. Serve immediately.

Green Papaya Chanpuru

CHANPURU IS A traditional Indian dish, turned island-style by Fijian Indians using recipes like this. The result is healthful and surprisingly easy to make, and is satisfying as a side or lunch dish.   SERVES 4

¼ cup canola oil

4 ounces tofu, drained

⅛ teaspoon sea salt or rock salt

½ green papaya, peeled and coarsely grated

¼ cup thinly sliced carrots

¼ cup thinly sliced onion rounds

2 tablespoons canned tuna

½ cup chicken broth

½ teaspoon mirin (rice wine)

⅛ teaspoon shoyu

⅛ teaspoon sesame seed oil

Heat canola oil in pan. Add hand-broken tofu pieces, and sprinkle with ⅛ teaspoon salt. Brown tofu pieces thoroughly. Add coarsely grated green papaya, carrots, and onions. Add tuna and broth, and stir-fry, bringing broth to a rapid boil. Place mixture on a plate or in a shallow bowl, and season to taste with mirin, shoyu, and sesame seed oil. Do not overcook vegetables.

Kokoda

KOKODA, PRONOUNCED "KOH-CONE-DAH," is a very old, traditional Fijian dish. Much like poke (from Hawai'i), or Poisson Cru (from Tahiti), kokoda uses the citric acid in limes to "cook" the fish, before the crispy vegetables and coconut milk are added for flavor. **SERVES 6**

1 pound fresh 'ono (wahoo), cut in small cubes

1 cup fresh lime juice

1 can coconut milk (14 ounces)

½ cup finely diced onion

½ cup finely diced red pepper

½ cup peeled, seeded, and finely diced cucumber

1 cup diced tomato

4 stalks green onions, chopped, plus more for garnish

1 chili pepper (optional), minced

Salt to taste

Marinate the fish in the lime juice for 2 hours. In a large bowl, combine the coconut milk, onion, red pepper, cucumber, tomato, green onions, and the optional minced chili pepper. Strain the marinated fish and add to the coconut mixture. Salt to taste, then serve chilled, garnished with chopped green onions.

Cilantro Vinaigrette

YIELDS 2 CUPS

¼ cup cilantro leaves

1¼ cups orange juice

1 tablespoon rice wine vinegar

1 tablespoon lime juice

⅓ cup honey

1 clove garlic

2 teaspoons ginger

¼ cup canola oil

Salt and pepper to taste

Combine all the ingredients in a blender, and puree until smooth.

Coconut Chutney

YIELDS 1½ CUPS

1 cup unsweetened desiccated coconut, lightly packed

2 to 3 whole dried red chilies, broken into pieces and seeded

2 cloves garlic, minced

⅓ cup plain yogurt

3 tablespoons chopped cilantro

Salt to taste

In a food processor, combine coconut, red chilies, and garlic. Process until blended. Add the yogurt, cilantro, and salt to taste. Process for about 15 seconds or until chutney is well blended. Serve at room temperature. Keeps in the refrigerator up to 2 days.

Cooked Tomato Chutney

A FLAVORFUL CURRY condiment, this Cooked Tomato Chutney also works well when served with a good mozzarella or goat cheese wrapped in roti.

SERVES 6

½ cup salad oil

2 to 3 chili peppers, chopped

½ teaspoon cumin seeds

1 teaspoon sarso (black mustard seeds)

2 medium onions, julienned

5 cloves garlic, minced

2 teaspoons curry powder

12 medium tomatoes, cut into thin wedges

Salt to taste

Chopped cilantro leaves for garnish

Heat oil in a saucepan and add the chili peppers, cumin seeds, sarso, and onions. Fry until onions are golden brown. Add garlic and curry powder, sauté for 1 minute, then add tomatoes. Simmer until the chutney has a thick consistency. Season with salt to taste. Let cool to room temperature. Fold in chopped cilantro leaves, then serve at room temperature.

Fresh Tomato and Onion Chutney

CURRIES AND GRILLED or fried fish dishes zing when accompanied by this Fresh Tomato and Onion Chutney. Try it as a summer evening barbecue condiment, and bring the South Pacific home.

YIELDS 4 TO 5 CUPS

2 large, vine-ripened tomatoes, diced

2 medium sweet onions, finely chopped

¼ cup finely chopped cilantro leaves

1 small chili pepper, minced

Salt and pepper to taste

Combine all ingredients and chill.

Miti Sauce

MITI SAUCE, A traditional seasoning from India, is used in Fiji over grilled fish or other seafood dishes. It's a great seasoning anytime, for any type of fish.

YIELDS 2½ CUPS

2 cups coconut milk

Juice of ½ lemon

½ cup finely diced onion

½ cup finely diced green or red pepper

3 stalks green onion, chopped

Salt to taste

Combine ingredients in a bowl and store in the refrigerator until ready to use.

Pickled Watermelon

I'VE ALWAYS THOUGHT it unfortunate that we eat the meat of the watermelon and throw the rind away. The Fijians have found good use for it. Here's a refreshing recipe that can be served like a slaw or as a garnish or side for light salads.　　　　　　　　　　　　　　　YIELDS 4 CUPS

2 pounds watermelon rind

¾ cup salt

4 cups water

2 teaspoons whole allspice

1 cinnamon stick

2 teaspoons whole cloves

1 teaspoon black peppercorns

1 cup sugar

1 cup white vinegar

Remove dark skin and any pink flesh from rind. Cut the rind into ½ × 2-inch strips. Make brine from ¾ cup salt and 4 cups water; soak rind for 5 hours. Drain, rinse in cold water, and set aside.

In small saucepan, combine allspice, cinnamon stick, cloves, black peppercorns, sugar, and vinegar, and bring to a boil. Cook syrup and pour over melon.

Cover and seal. Let stand at room temperature until cooled. Refrigerate until ready to use.

Pilau Masala

MASALA MIX IS generally used for pilau, a traditional Fijian rice dish, curries, and seasoning meats such as lamb, mutton, goat, and game meats.

YIELDS 1 CUP

¼ cup cardamom

9 long cinnamon sticks (around 6 inches)

¼ cup coriander seeds

2 tablespoons cumin seeds

2 tablespoons whole cloves

1 tablespoon black peppercorns

3 whole nutmegs, grated

In a small saucepan, separately roast each of the spices: cardamom, cinnamon sticks, coriander seeds, cumin seeds, whole cloves, and black peppercorns. Turn or shake the pan back and forth so that the spices roast evenly. Each time the spice begins to smell fragrant, remove and place on a cool plate.

After roasting, peel the cardamom, discard pods, and use only the seeds. Put the roasted spices into a coffee or spice grinder, and grind to a fine powder. Finely grate the nutmeg and add to spice mixture. Store in an airtight container.

Tamarind Chutney

TAMARIND IS ALSO known as an Indian date. The pods are about 5 inches long. Tamarind can be found in Asian markets in pulp and seed and paste form. This is a chutney that is eaten with samosa, vegetable and meat curries, and pilau.

YIELDS 3 TO 4 CUPS

2 cups tamarind
4 cups warm water
4 tablespoons salad oil
2 chili peppers, minced
1 medium onion, finely diced
2 teaspoons curry powder
3 cloves garlic, crushed
1 tablespoon grated fresh gingerroot
1 cup sugar
Salt to taste

Soak tamarind in warm water for 2 hours or until soft. Break up and squeeze the tamarind by hand until the seeds are loosened from the sacs. Strain through a large-hole strainer. Discard seeds and fiber.

Heat oil in a heavy pot. Sauté the chili peppers and onion until golden brown. Add curry powder, garlic, and grated ginger, and sauté for 2 more minutes.

Pour the tamarind juice along with the sugar into the pot, and cook over medium heat for 45 minutes or until the chutney thickens; stir frequently. Add salt to taste. Cool and store in the refrigerator in a sealed container.

Almond Vermicelli

EVERYTHING ABOUT THE Indo-Fijian cuisine, including the desserts, is pleasantly spiced, and has an aromatic, very tropical flavor. The texture of this dish resembles that of a well-made tapioca pudding. Kana vakavinaka (eat heartily).

SERVES 6

1 cup vermicelli pasta, broken into ½-inch pieces
½ cup sugar
½ cup water
1 tablespoon butter or ghee (clarified butter)
1 teaspoon cloves
1 teaspoon cardamom seeds
3 cups milk
1 tablespoon raisins
¼ cup roasted almond slices

Preheat oven to 275°F.

Spread vermicelli onto a cookie sheet, and roast until slightly golden brown. Remove from the oven to cool. (Any unused vermicelli can be stored in an airtight container and used at a later date.)

Dissolve sugar in water, and set aside. Heat the butter in a pan. Add cloves and cardamom seeds, then the roasted vermicelli. Add the sugar water and milk, and slowly simmer, stirring occasionally. Turn off heat when the pasta is cooked. Add the raisins and almonds. Serve warm.

Fiji Rum Currant Scones

FIJIAN RUM IS a strong liquor. It adds a wonderful kick to the dessert scones. I enjoy these dense little cakes at breakfast. They are light, and bursting with flavor. Substitute Fijian rum with any dark rum found in your local liquor store.

YIELDS 12 SCONES

½ cup currants

3 tablespoons Fijian dark rum

2 cups all-purpose flour

1 tablespoon baking powder

½ teaspoon salt

¼ cup sugar

¼ cup butter, softened

2 eggs, beaten separately

½ cup buttermilk

Ground cinnamon

Confectioners' sugar

Soak currants until plump in Fijian dark rum.

Mix dry ingredients and sugar, then cut in the soft butter. Combine 1 beaten egg and buttermilk. Mix until dough holds together. Add the Fijian rum and currants. Wrap the dough in plastic wrap and chill well.

Preheat oven to 400°F. Divide the dough in half on a lightly floured board. Roll each half into a ¾-inch-thick circle, then score into 6 triangles. Place the two circles on a lightly greased cookie sheet and brush lightly with remaining beaten egg. A little cinnamon can be sprinkled on the scones before baking. Bake for 15 minutes.

As the scones cool, sprinkle with confectioners' sugar.

Fiji Ginger Tea

THIS SPICY FIJIAN tea is an excellent after-dinner soother, or a refreshing summertime iced beverage. Add a sprig of mint and an umbrella, and transport yourself into a tropical "Bula Vinaka" experience.   SERVES 4

6 cups water
1½ cups light brown sugar (or raw sugar)
2½-inch piece fresh gingerroot, peeled and sliced

Combine water, brown sugar, and ginger in a pan. Cook over low heat for 45 minutes, stirring occasionally. Strain and serve hot or chilled.

Fijian Passion

FIJIAN PASSION HAS got to be my favorite daquiri-like fruit drink. It brings back memories of tropical clouds glowing with that bright sunset orange. In Fiji they say that the sun blazes hot to intensify the colors of the land and sky. There are no truer words.   SERVES 4

6 ounces passion fruit juice
2 ounces pineapple juice
6 ounces dark Fijian rum
6 ounces Triple Sec
Fresh fruits for garnish

In a blender, combine juices, rum, and Triple Sec. Fill with crushed ice, and blend until slushy. Serve in margarita glasses, and garnish with fresh fruit.

Hawai'i

MAYBE IT'S BECAUSE of the ancient tradition of the lu'au,
maybe it's the beautiful weather, but however it came about, we love to celebrate in Hawai'i. THERE ARE THE REGULAR HOLI-
DAYS, like Valentine's Day, Mother's Day, Memorial Day, Easter, Fourth of
July, Father's Day, Summer Solstice, Labor Day, Halloween, Thanksgiving,
Christmas, New Year's, and family birthdays, weddings, and anniversaries. But
in addition to those, we commemorate Japanese Boy's Day and Girl's Day, when
families of Japanese ancestry fly carp kites for each of their sons and give their

daughters traditional Japanese dolls.
There are celebrations for Chinese New
Year, Passover, Boxing Day, Rosh
Hashanah, Bastille Day, and Samoan
Independence Day. And we join together
for Japanese Bon Dances, Chinese Ching
Ming ceremonies, and Lantern Festivals.

The intermingling of cultures that has developed over the past hundred years
has enriched our sense of ohana (family), and has carved the unique social landscape of these extraordinary islands. ONE OF THE MORE
INTERESTING festivities, a true celebration of Hawaiian life, is the

Baby Lu'au. Ancient Hawaiians lived for hundreds of years in isolation on this distant archipelago in the middle of the Pacific. Untouched by foreign influences, they developed no immunities to common illnesses like the cold or flu. In 1778, the year Captain James Cook and his men ventured into Hawaiian waters, there were estimates of 400,000 to 800,000 native Hawaiians living on the eight inhabitable islands. But after the introduction of foreign diseases, by 1900 there were only 29,799 natives still alive. Hawaiian families, devastated by the loss of their *ohaha* (family members), rejoiced with the birth of every child. The first year of life was the most dangerous; thousands of infants perished. So families celebrated with elaborate parties when a healthy baby reached its first birthday. People came and brought gifts of money, toys, and clothing. Today, it is a tradition to throw a huge party on the one-year anniversary of a child's birth. These lu'au range from small backyard barbecues to large fetes with guest lists of a hundred or more family and friends, local bands playing Hawaiian music, large inflatable castles for the children to play in, and flowers everywhere.

The menu at a Baby Lu'au has changed from the traditional raw fish and poi to a blending of the flavors and culturally rich dishes that have become the foundation of the culinary landscape of modern Hawai'i.

A few years ago, I went deep-sea fishing with my friend off the Kona coast on the Big Island of Hawai'i. We motored for about an hour before we spotted the telltale cluster of seabirds that marked the spot where a school of mahimahi were surface feeding. We anchored, dumped the chum into the water, and cast out. Alex went into the cabin and brought out a couple of cold drinks. "All we have to do is wait," he said.

We sat there, rocking with the waves and listening to the water lap against the hull. "Sam," Alex said at last. "Did you have a baby lu'au for your sons?"

"Yes," I said. "Of course."

"We are having one for our youngest this summer," he said, taking a sip of his iced tea. "My wife wants to have it catered. Do you know of anyone that could handle that?" Alex didn't look at me when he asked this question. He's a local man of Japanese ancestry. In our modern Island culture, it's considered rude to look a person in the eye when you are asking them for help. I think this point of etiquette comes from Japanese tradition, but it could be from the Chinese, too. I had the feeling that Alex was asking me to do more than recommend a caterer. "What's on the menu?" I asked.

"The usual," he said. "We were thinking of kalua pig, poi, lomi salmon, haupia. You know, the regular stuff."

"Why do you need a professional company to help you with that?" I asked. "You have family all over the island."

"That's the problem," he said, as he stood to check the fishing lines. "I got about a hundred people coming, and that's just my side."

"An intimate party," I said. We both laughed.

Hawai'i is a rather small place. Everyone is related in some way. It's understood that you need to treat people well because they may turn out to be a distant cousin or part of your extended ohana.

"Most of my wife's family still live in New Zealand," Alex added. "They think we're crazy for celebrating the baby's first birthday," he said. "In New Zealand, they wait until the child turns twenty-one, then they throw a big party."

"So?" I asked. "What are you planning to do?"

Alex came back and sat down. "What do you suggest?" he asked. "You the chef, man."

"I know a bunch of caterers," I offered. "I can have one of my restaurants do it for you if you want."

Alex smiled. The fish just weren't biting that day, so we sat on the coolers and talked about our favorite lu'au foods. Alex raved about his mom's chicken long rice and his uncle's kahl bi ribs. "How about lomilomi salmon?" I asked. "Who makes the best?"

"Oh," he replied, "Uncle Jesse. He makes huge vats of the stuff. It's great!"

"There you go. Have everybody make their favorite lu'au foods. You can even have several people bring the same thing so that you have enough for everybody. The stuff that your family doesn't make, you can order from the caterer. It's more fun that way."

He thought for a little while, then said, "So, do you want to come to the party, Sam?"

"I would love to," I said.

"What do you want to bring?" Alex's mouth turned up in a big "I got you" grin.

I was trapped. "Okay," I said. "Poke. I'll bring poke."

" 'Ahi?" Alex pressed.

"We'd better go out fishing before the party then, so I can catch one."

"It's a deal," Alex agreed.

Poke is one of my favorite foods. The Hawaiian word *poke,* pronounced "PO-kay," means "to slice into pieces." It is a raw fish dish, much like Fijian kokoda or Tahitian poisson cru, where the raw meat is cooked by adding citric acid in the form of lime or lemon juice.

We didn't catch any mahimahi that day, but Alex had sure reeled me in!

He and I fished for an entire week before we finally landed that 'ahi we needed, and on the morning of little Alex Junior's baby lu'au I was filleting 'ahi steaks, cutting them into one-inch squares, and mixing them together with my special seasonings to make gallons of poke. I used an entire refrigerator in my restaurant to store the stuff.

The party was fabulous. About an hour before the lu'au, my sons and I loaded the tubs of poke into the truck and drove toward Alex's house. We could see the big open-sided tent was set up in the large field next door. In the shade of the awning were rows of picnic tables covered with white butcher paper. Little kids were placing fern and ti leaves in the center of each table, then sprinkling plumeria and hibiscus blossoms over the top. Woven coconut fronds climbed each of the tent poles, and Hawaiian music, played on steel guitars and 'ukuleles, pounded through the five-foot speakers on either side of the small stage on the north end of the tent.

I drove the truck around to the back of the house where a group of women were setting out pineapple boats filled with chopped fruit. One of the women called out, "Kawehi!" and motioned to one of the girls, who came running. "You and Tasha put three of these on each table. Make sure you cover them." The girl ran off and brought four girls back with her. Each picked up two boats and walked back to the tent.

"Hi, Sam," the woman said. It was Moana, Alex's wife. "*E komo mai,*" she said, "thank you so much for coming." She smiled and gave me the traditional Hawaiian greeting, a kiss on the cheek. "Alex took Junior for a walk. They were both driving me crazy. What's in the truck?"

My sons had already started unloading the poke. "Oh my," Moana said, seeing what it was. "So much." She gave me another kiss. "Thanks, Sam. This will be the hit of the lu'au."

The feeling you get from friends is priceless. "No problem," I said, and I helped the boys carry the tubs. Three large, rented refrigerators lined one side of the garage. The poke took up all of the extra space.

We dropped everything off, said our good-byes, and left. When we came back, the lu'au was in full swing. Hawaiian music boomed from the PA while a long line of people filed past the buffet table. There were large trays and bowls of chicken long rice, kalua pig, lomilomi salmon, haupia, fruit salad, rice, poi, broiled ribs, chicken hekka, and poke. Every container that emptied was quickly replaced. I smiled and thought, That's the Hawaiian style. There's always more food than the crowd can eat.

Alex walked over to us. He was carrying little Alex, and they were both wearing matching aloha shirts. "Sam," Alex said. "The poke is a smash!" He smiled so big that his eyes almost squinted shut.

"It's a great lu'au," I said.

"You the man," Alex added. "When I asked everyone to bring something, they loved the idea. My grandmother said, 'That's how, you know. That's Hawaiian-style. Everybody helps, then everybody plays.' "

"The old folks really knew how to make people feel welcome," I said. I looked around. "I see you got Uncle Jesse to bring his pulehu ribs."

Uncle Jesse walked up. "Hey, Sam," he called. Uncle Jesse was a tiny little Japanese man, bent from years of hard work in the up-slope ranch lands of Kamuela.

"We're in for it now," Alex laughed.

"You know, Sam," Uncle Jesse said. "Alex told me that you wanted to taste my pulehu ribs. They are famous, yeah?"

I looked at Alex. He shrugged and smiled.

"Yes, Uncle," I said. "Can't wait."

"I thought that if you tasted them, you would guess my secret recipe. So, I wanted to tell you that if you want to put it in one of your books, you can."

"It won't be secret anymore," I said.

"Ugh!" Uncle said, with a wave in the air. "So what? If I die tomorrow nobody will taste the ribs again. You put it in the book." He smiled and gave me a pat on the arm. He couldn't reach my shoulder.

After the party, Alex and I went behind his house and sat on a couple of coolers.

"Good party, Alex," I said. My friend just smiled.

There was a long silence, then Alex said, "You know, the old folks used to make us work all the time, and I never realized the gift. I want to pass it on to Alex Junior."

"What gift?" I asked.

"The gift of work," Alex said. "Work to help the family. The kids had a great time today because they helped. They worked in the kitchen, they helped put up the tent, they helped decorate the tables, and they got to eat. Everybody was happy."

"It's the ohana," I said, thinking about my dad and mom, and how they taught us to work together. "My parents always said never to sit when someone is working. We always had to stand up and help. When the work was done, everyone relaxed."

We looked over at the tent. All of the women who had worked together in the kitchen were sitting at the picnic tables, listening to music, and talking. Little Alex was asleep in his mother's arms. "It's the ohana, man," Alex said. "What would we do without it?"

"*Kamau!*" I said, a toast. We raised our glasses. "*I ka ohana.*"

"To the family," Alex repeated.

Kamau I Ka Ohana to your family.

Aloha, a hui hou.
(Good-bye. Until we meet again.)

Baked Lu'au Oysters

IN THE HAWAIIAN language, lu'au has two meanings. The first is the tender, young taro leaves that are baked with coconut cream and chicken or beef. The second is a Hawaiian feast, named after these taro tops. So, in this recipe I combined young taro tops and oysters, and made a party. SERVES 4

3 eggs
1 tablespoon white wine
Salt and white pepper to taste
2 tablespoons steamed lu'au leaves
12 oysters, on the half shell
1 teaspoon minced gingerroot
1 teaspoon minced garlic
1 teaspoon finely chopped cilantro
1 tablespoon chopped green onion

Whip eggs and wine together. In a double boiler, cook egg mixture, stirring constantly. Add salt and white pepper to taste.

Stir in steamed lu'au leaves, and remove mixture from double boiler; set aside. NOTE: Be sure leaves are completely cooked; otherwise they will be scratchy on the palate.

Arrange raw oysters on a platter, and sprinkle with a little bit of ginger, garlic, cilantro, and green onion.

Scoop a spoonful of egg-lu'au sauce to cover each oyster. Pop oysters into the broiler for a couple of minutes, or until tops are brown. Ready to serve!

Auntie Sarah's Poke Cakes

AUNTIE SARAH IS a little lady who lives about three doors down the street from my home in Kona. She came over one day with a plate of poke cakes, and said, "Sam, my son Harry caught a big 'ahi this morning and I thought I'd make something good for your family." She wasn't kidding. These are fabulous! Enjoy. Thank you, Auntie. YIELDS 6 PATTIES

Patties

1 cup ⅜-inch cubes fresh 'ahi (yellowfin tuna)

½ cup minced onion

½ cup minced green onions

1 egg

3 tablespoons soy sauce

2 teaspoons sesame oil

Salt and pepper to taste

Panko (packaged Japanese-style fine bread crumbs)

4 tablespoons salad oil

1 medium tomato, diced, for garnish

2 tablespoons chopped green onion, for garnish

Sauce

¼ cup sliced mushrooms

4 tablespoons butter

2 teaspoons soy sauce

2 teaspoons oyster sauce

2 teaspoons chopped cilantro

Combine patty ingredients and form 6 patties. Press patties in panko to coat. In a frying pan, warm oil over medium-high heat. Gently place patties in pan and brown both sides, keeping the inside of the patties medium rare. Arrange on a platter, and garnish with tomato and green onion.

To make sauce, sauté mushrooms in butter for 2 minutes. Add remaining sauce ingredients, and cook for another minute. Pour sauce over patties, and serve.

'Ahi (Yellowfin Tuna) Poke

POKE (PRONOUNCED PO-KAY) is one of my all-time favorite dishes. The cubed raw fish in this traditional Hawaiian dish is seasoned and cooked by the juices of the tomatoes and soy sauce. It works well as an appetizer or as a main dish, seared and served over rice.   SERVES 4

1 pound 'ahi (yellowfin tuna), cubed

1 medium tomato, chopped

½ cup chopped onion

2 tablespoons soy sauce

1 teaspoon sesame oil

½ teaspoon granulated sugar

½ teaspoon crushed red pepper flakes, or 1 Hawaiian red pepper, minced

2 tablespoons chopped green onion for garnish

Combine all ingredients; mix well. Allow flavors to blend for 1 hour before serving. Serve chilled. Garnish with chopped green onion.

Kalua Pig Spring Rolls with
Pineapple Dipping Sauce

KALUA IS THE Hawaiian name for a style of underground cooking. Meat is put into an earth oven called an *imu* and roasted for hours. This recipe reflects the rainbow of cultures in Hawai'i—spring rolls from the East combined with kalua-style pork. **YIELDS 30 SPRING ROLLS**

1 pound Kalua Pig (see page 87)

2 tablespoons salad oil

¾ cup chopped onion

1 tablespoon minced garlic

1 can water chestnuts (8 ounces), coarsely chopped

6 cups shredded green cabbage

2 cups shredded red cabbage

¾ cup chopped green onions

¼ cup finely grated carrot

3 tablespoons oyster sauce

Salt and pepper to taste

1 package spring roll wrappers

1 egg, beaten, for egg wash

Oil for deep-frying

Pineapple Dipping Sauce (see page 96)

½ cup toasted macadamia nuts, chopped

Brown kalua pig in 2 tablespoons oil. Add onion and garlic, and cook for 2 minutes over medium-high heat. Add the water chestnuts, cabbage, green onions, carrot, oyster sauce, and salt and pepper to taste. Cook over high heat for about 2 to 3 minutes. Remove from the heat, drain excess liquid, and cool.

Separate the sheets of spring roll wrappers, and keep under a slightly damp towel. Place 2 tablespoons of kalua filling on a wrapper. Fold nearest edge of wrapper over filling; fold left and right corners toward the center. Roll tightly and seal with the egg wash.

Heat oil to 375°F. Fry spring rolls until golden brown. Place on paper towels to drain. Serve with the Pineapple Dipping Sauce and macadamia nuts.

Sam's Seafood Chowder

THE BEST WAY to describe this chowder is "dense." Whenever I add heavy cream to a dish, I feel like I need to add something that the thick cream can hold up, ingredients that will add flavor and texture to the smooth base. With all of my recipes, I encourage creativity. If you don't have some of the ingredients, substitute others. If you don't like some of the ingredients listed here, substitute with ingredients you prefer. Have fun with it. Once you get the base right, everything else is a cinch.   SERVES 8

Fish stock

3 pounds fish bones, rinsed

1 cup white wine

1 onion, chopped

1 stalk celery, chopped

1 carrot, chopped

1 slice of fresh gingerroot

2 bay leaves

1 teaspoon white peppercorns

2½ quarts water

8 strips bacon, diced

1 large onion, diced

2 stalks celery, diced

1 teaspoon minced garlic

4 branches fresh thyme

½ cup flour

2 quarts fish stock

2 cups clam juice

2 potatoes, peeled and ½-inch diced

1 medium sweet potato, peeled and diced

1½ cups fresh corn kernels

1½ cups creamed corn

1 pound firm white fish, cubed

¼ pound shrimp, cleaned and deveined

¼ pound scallops

1 cup clam meat, minced

1 cup heavy cream

Salt and pepper to taste

Chopped parsley as garnish

Place fish bones in a large pot. Add white wine, vegetables, ginger, bay leaves, white peppercorns, and water. Simmer for 45 minutes and strain.

In a heavy stockpot, fry bacon, onion, celery, garlic, and fresh thyme until onion is translucent. Add the flour, and stir for 2 minutes. Slowly add the fish stock and the clam juice; keep stirring to avoid any lumps forming. Simmer for 30 minutes, then add the potatoes, corn kernels, and creamed corn. Continue to simmer for 20 minutes, then add the fish, shrimp, scallops, and clam meat. Remove thyme branches. Stir in the heavy cream and heat thoroughly, but don't boil. Season with salt and pepper to taste. Garnish with chopped parsley and serve immediately.

Clam-Miso Soup

MISO IS ONE of the mainstays of Japanese cuisine. Immigrant plantation workers from Japan brought miso to Hawai'i and drank this comforting soup after a long day at work. Some Japanese plantation families even started their mornings with a bowl of miso soup and some rice. I prefer using Shinshu miso because of its golden color and mild flavor. You can find the miso paste, *dashi-no-moto* (powdered fish stock), and wakame (Japanese seaweed) in most Asian markets.   SERVES 4 TO 6

1 pound clams
6 cups water
2 slices fresh gingerroot
1 package dashi-no-moto (powdered fish stock)
½ cup miso
3 tablespoons wakame (Japanese seaweed)
Salt to taste
Green onions for garnish

Rinse clams, and place them in a heavy stockpot. Add 5 cups of water, ginger, and dashi-no-moto; bring to a rapid boil.

In the meantime, place miso paste in a bowl, and dilute with 1 cup water to avoid lumps in the soup. When soup comes to a boil, add the miso and wakame. Salt to taste. Simmer for 2 minutes, and serve hot. Garnish with chopped green onions.

Choy's Light Chinese Salad

I SOMETIMES DICE the lettuce into very small pieces, and serve this salad with chopsticks. It's a real challenge to eat, but it slows you down to appreciate the blending of the flavors. Try it. Your guests won't know what hit them.

SERVES 4 TO 6

2 medium heads of iceberg lettuce, torn into bite-size pieces

½ cup celery, thinly sliced diagonally

½ cup carrots, julienned

½ cup chopped green onions

Choy's Chinese Salad Dressing (see page 96)

½ cup chopped cilantro

4 tablespoons crushed macadamia nuts, chopped, or sliced toasted almonds

2 ounces rice noodles, deep-fried

In a large salad bowl, toss lettuce, celery, carrots, green onions, and dressing. Sprinkle with cilantro, macadamia nuts, and crispy rice noodles.

Upcountry Sweet Potato Salad

MY SONS AND I have made Sweet Potato Salad a staple at the local high school football tailgate parties. It's amazing how many friends you have when your grill is fired up and there's a big bowl of something so 'ono on the table.

YIELDS 6 CUPS

4 cups diced cooked sweet potatoes
3 hard-boiled eggs, chopped
¼ cup minced onion
½ cup minced celery
¼ cup grated carrot
1½ cups mayonnaise
Salt and pepper to taste

In a large mixing bowl, toss all ingredients lightly to combine. Adjust seasoning with salt and pepper.

Big Island Paniolo Tri-Tip Steak

I LOVE THE sweet smell of burning *kiawe* (mesquite) wood. In Hawai'i we call grilled meat *pulehu*. It is literally translated as "to broil." Tri-tip steaks are cut from the upper crescent of the sirloin, then sliced into ¼-inch thin sheets. Throw a few Maui onions on the grill, and serve this tri-tip with my sweet potato salad, and you'll get raves all the way around. SERVES 4

2 teaspoons rock salt

2 cloves garlic, minced

2 teaspoons minced fresh gingerroot

1 tablespoon soy sauce

1 tablespoon brown sugar

1 teaspoon sesame oil

Pepper to taste

1½ pounds tri-tip steak

In mixing bowl, combine rock salt, garlic, ginger, soy sauce, brown sugar, sesame oil, and pepper to taste. Add steak. Cover, and marinate for 1 hour. Place on a medium-flame grill with kiawe or mesquite wood. Cook to your preference, rare to well done.

Chinese-Style Steamed Snapper

THIS IS A simple but elegant way of eating a good-quality snapper. I prefer to use red snapper (onaga) or Uhu (parrot fish) for this particular dish, but any white fish will do.   SERVES 4

1 whole snapper, about 3 pounds
Salt and white pepper to taste
4 ounces fresh shiitake mushrooms, stems removed
¼ cup very thinly slivered fresh gingerroot
1 bunch green onions, slivered
1 bunch cilantro, coarsely chopped
¼ cup soy sauce
⅔ cup peanut oil
1 tablespoon sesame oil
Fresh cilantro for garnish

Clean and scale the fish. Rinse and pat dry. Rub salt and white pepper on fish meat. Place fish in a large fish steamer, and scatter with shiitake mushrooms. Steam for about 15 to 20 minutes on medium heat. Garnish with the ginger, green onions, and cilantro.

Pour the soy sauce over the fish. Heat peanut and sesame oils in a saucepan until they are smoking. Carefully drizzle the hot oil over the steamed fish, and garnish with the fresh cilantro. Serve immediately.

Kalua Pig

KALUA PIG IS a Polynesian feast favorite. Traditionally cooked in an underground oven, this roasted pig is called kalua pig in Hawai'i, *vuaka vavi* in Fiji, and *pua'a fauna'a* in Tahiti and the Marquesas. Here is a kitchen-friendly recipe that will give you the same flavor without having to go out in the backyard and dig an earth oven. SERVES 12

4 pounds pork butt

Hawaiian or rock salt

Liquid smoke

2 cloves garlic, minced

6 ti leaves, ribs removed (or aluminum foil)

1 tablespoon Hawaiian or rock salt

2 cups boiling water

Preheat oven to 350°F.

Score pork on all sides with ¼-inch-deep slits about 1 inch apart.

In a bowl, mix 2 tablespoons rock salt, 2 tablespoons liquid smoke, and garlic. Rub this mixture all around the pork butt. Line a 9 × 12-inch pan with foil. Place 3 ti leaves lengthwise in the foil-lined pan, then place the pork butt on top of the ti leaves. Place the other 3 ti leaves crosswise over the pork butt, and fold leaves to cover. Tie with string to hold them in place.

Cover pan very tightly with foil, and roast for 4 hours. Remove meat from roasting pan, and shred. In a large pot, dissolve 1 tablespoon rock salt and a few drops of liquid smoke in 2 cups boiling water. Add shredded pork. Simmer for 15 minutes before serving.

Ka'u Orange-Ginger Chicken

THE DISTRICT OF Ka'u on the Big Island of Hawai'i is famous for its incredibly ugly (on the outside) but remarkably juicy and sweet oranges. I like the combination of ginger and orange, and I use it a lot in my cooking. The spicy ginger flavor really gives the orange a kick of zest.   SERVES 4 TO 6

1 whole chicken, about 3 pounds
¾ cup fresh-squeezed orange juice
¼ cup dry sherry
2 tablespoons salad oil
1 tablespoon minced fresh gingerroot
1 clove garlic, minced
2 teaspoons Dijon mustard
1 tablespoon minced fresh basil
Salt and pepper to taste
Orange sections from 2 oranges, for garnish
Basil leaves, for garnish

Cut chicken into pieces. In a mixing bowl, combine orange juice, dry sherry, salad oil, ginger, garlic, mustard, basil, and salt and pepper. Add the chicken pieces to the bowl, and toss to coat. Cover, and refrigerate for 6 hours, turning occasionally.

Drain chicken, reserving the liquid. Place pieces in a large shallow baking pan, and bake in a 400°F oven for 25 minutes. Drain off fat, pour reserved liquid over the chicken, and continue to bake, basting occasionally, about 25 minutes until chicken is browned.

Place chicken on a serving platter, and drizzle pan juices over the chicken. Garnish with orange sections and basil leaves.

Kona Oyster Mushrooms with Tofu

THERE IS A produce company up the road from my family's restaurant in Kona that supplies us with the most beautiful oyster mushrooms. I've been all over the world, and these are the firmest, most flavorful mushrooms I've ever tasted. You can get fresh oyster mushrooms year-round in most Asian markets, but if you use the canned variety, make sure you rinse them first.

SERVES 4 TO 6

½ cup peanut oil

1-pound block firm tofu, cubed

½ sweet onion, diced

2 teaspoons minced gingerroot

½ red bell pepper, ½-inch diced

½ yellow bell pepper, ½-inch diced

8 ounces oyster mushrooms, stems removed, quartered

2 ounces fresh shiitake mushrooms, stems removed

2 tablespoons soy sauce

1½ tablespoons oyster sauce

Salt to taste

Chopped green scallions for garnish

Heat ¼ cup peanut oil in a wok, and stir-fry the tofu for 30 seconds. Set aside to drain on paper towel. Keep warm.

Heat wok with the remaining ¼ cup peanut oil, and stir-fry onion and ginger for 30 seconds on medium-high heat. Add peppers, oyster mushrooms, shiitake mushrooms, and stir-fry for another minute. Add soy sauce and oyster sauce; stir-fry for 1 minute more. Add the tofu, and season with salt to taste. Garnish with scallions.

Oven Laulau

LAULAU IS THE Hawaiian word for wrapped or wrapped package. A single *lau* means leaf, and since the packages of food were commonly wrapped in leaves, it makes sense that the old Hawaiians called wrapped packages of food laulau.

SERVES 12

2 pounds fresh lu'au (young taro tops) or large, fresh spinach leaves
½ pound salted butterfish or black cod
4 pounds pork butt, cubed
1½ tablespoons Hawaiian or rock salt

Wash spinach, and remove excess water. Soak butterfish in water for about 2 hours. Drain, and cut fish into ¼-inch slices.

In a 9 × 13-inch pan, layer in the following order: 1 pound spinach, pork cubes, sprinkle of Hawaiian salt, butterfish, and remaining spinach. Seal tightly with foil, and bake at 350°F for 1½ hours. Cut into 12 portions, and serve immediately with poi or hot rice.

Teriyaki Beef Roulade

THERE IS SOMETHING elegant about slicing into a roll of tender steak and finding your favorite vegetables cooked to perfection and seasoned with meat juices. It's really easy to get creative with this recipe. You need 4 cups of stir-fry vegetables. Substitute mushrooms or tomatoes, add more peppers or take them out. Mix and match your vegetables of choice. Just make sure they are cut small and not overcooked. Have fun with this one. It's really easy.

SERVES 4

1½ pounds beef rib eye steak, sliced ⅜ inch thick

Marinade
½ cup soy sauce

6 tablespoons sugar

½ cup water

1 tablespoon minced fresh gingerroot

2 tablespoons sake

½ cup mashed papaya

2 teaspoons salad oil

1 teaspoon minced fresh gingerroot

1 cup julienned carrots

½ cup thinly sliced celery

½ thinly sliced onion

1 green pepper, thinly sliced

1 cup thinly sliced cabbage

1 tablespoon oyster sauce

Salt and pepper to taste

Place meat with marinade in a container, and marinate overnight.

Warm oil in a wok at medium-high heat, add ginger and cook for 1 minute. Add carrots, celery, onion, green pepper, and cabbage, and stir-fry until al dente.

Remove rib eye steak from marinade; allow to drip-drain. Lay meat on a flat surface, and scoop stir-fried vegetables into the center of the steak. Add oyster sauce and salt and pepper to taste. Roll the vegetables in the beef, and secure with toothpicks. Broil or grill until done to your preference. Serve hot.

Uncle Jesse's Pulehu Ribs

THIS IS A fast and 'ono (delicious) grill dish that is disaster-proof if you keep an eye on the flames from the grill. In the paniolo (cowboy) town of Kamuela, the ranchers pride themselves on producing the most tender (and hormone-free) meat in the world. One of my paniolo friends says, "This cattle is grass fed, man. They roam the volcano all day. From up here, they have a view of the water that people pay millions of dollars for. They're probably the best-fed, happiest cattle anywhere." This recipe comes courtesy of Uncle Jesse.

SERVES 8

6 cloves garlic, minced
3½ tablespoons Hawaiian or rock salt
¼ cup brown sugar
½ cup canola oil
1 tablespoon sesame oil
4 pounds beef short ribs, sliced ½ inch thick

Mix garlic, salt, brown sugar, canola oil, and sesame oil. Rub mixture on meat, and let stand for ½ hour before grilling. Grill covered (pulehu) over medium heat until done to your preference.

Chicken Long Rice

IN HAWAI'I TODAY, Chicken Long Rice—an Asian dish modified by immigrant workers from Japan—is present at every lu'au, birthday party, or traditional family dinner. This is a delicious low-fat dish that's great for anyone on a soft diet. My granddaughter loves playing with the clear noodles.

SERVES 6

1 pound boneless chicken breast

1-inch piece fresh gingerroot, crushed

4 cups chicken stock

2 cups water

1 medium onion, julienned

2 ounces rice noodles, soaked in warm water for 1 hour and cut into thirds

Hawaiian or rock salt to taste

¼ cup chopped green onions for garnish

In a stockpot, combine chicken breast, ginger, chicken stock, water, and onion; simmer for 25 minutes. Remove the chicken breast and shred. Return the shredded chicken meat to the stock, and add rice noodles. Simmer for 10 minutes. Season with salt to taste. Garnish with green onions and serve.

Lomi Salmon

LOMI SALMON IS a very traditional Hawaiian dish. Whaling ships from the Pacific Northwest traded their stores of salted salmon with the Hawaiians for fresh fish. The word *lomi* means to massage. When my grandmother made this recipe, she would massage the rock salt into the raw salmon, then lightly massage the other ingredients as they were added to the mix. This complements any laulau or pulehu dish.

SERVES 6

1 cup chopped salted salmon
4 medium tomatoes, chopped
1 small Maui (or sweet) onion, chopped
¼ cup thinly sliced green onions
1 cup finely crushed ice

In a large bowl, cover salted salmon with water and soak overnight; drain and rinse. In a large bowl, combine salmon, tomatoes, onion, and green onions; mix well. Chill. Before serving, add finely crushed ice.

Paniolo Cornbread

PICTURE THIS: YOU'RE out in the high pastures of the Big Island of Hawai'i looking out across the channel toward the island of Maui. The sun is setting and lighting up the rounded summit of Haleakala in the distance. Kiawe wood crackles on the fire, and your friends are cooking marinated chicken on a grill. Your contribution is a pan of moist cornbread with chunked pineapple, and flavored with coconut milk. Heaven.   SERVES 8

½ cup cornmeal

1½ cups cake flour

⅔ cup sugar

1 tablespoon baking powder

½ teaspoon salt

½ cup melted butter (1 stick)

1¼ cups coconut milk

2 eggs

1 can crushed pineapple (8 ounces), drained

Preheat oven to 350°F. Spray a 9-inch cake pan with a nonstick cooking spray; set aside.

Sift cornmeal, cake flour, sugar, baking powder, and salt into a medium bowl. In another bowl, whisk the melted butter, coconut milk, and eggs. Combine the wet and dry ingredients, then stir in the drained pineapple.

Pour into the prepared pan, and bake for 35 minutes, or until firm and golden brown. Cool for 30 minutes. Loosen edges, place serving plate over pan, and invert cornbread onto plate. Serve warm with plenty of kiawe honey and butter.

Choy's Chinese Salad Dressing

I MAKE THIS salad dressing all the time. It was my dad's favorite. It's fast and really easy, and takes only a couple of minutes. The best part of the whole process is that it tastes *terrific!*

YIELDS 1 CUP

¼ cup sugar
1 teaspoon salt
1 teaspoon ground black pepper
6 tablespoons white vinegar
½ cup canola oil

Place ingredients in a bowl and mix. Store in the refrigerator until ready to use.

Pineapple Dipping Sauce

THE SWEET-SOUR ASIAN flavor of this dipping sauce adds zest to any deep-fried or stir-fried preparation. I usually use it for Auntie Sarah's Poke Cakes. Fish sauce can be found in most Asian markets.

YIELDS 2½ CUPS

¾ cup fresh pineapple, finely diced, or 8-ounce can crushed pineapple
½ cup white vinegar
½ cup sugar
½ cup water
3 tablespoons fish sauce
2 to 3 teaspoons sambal sauce

Combine ingredients, and chill for 1 hour before serving.

Pineapple-Macadamia Chutney

MY WIFE GIVES bottles of this chutney out at Christmas. I created the recipe after a trip to Fiji. It is great with roasted chicken or sautéed white fish. YIELDS 6 CUPS

8 cups chopped fresh pineapple

3 cups vinegar

1 tablespoon salt

¾ cup chopped red pepper

¼ cup minced garlic

2 tablespoons minced gingerroot

3½ cups brown sugar

1½ cups seedless raisins

1½ cups chopped macadamia nuts

Combine all the ingredients except the raisins and nuts in a heavy saucepan; bring to a boil. Reduce heat, and simmer for about 1 hour. Stir in the raisins and nuts, and cook 20 minutes more. Pour into hot, sterile jars and seal immediately.

Hawaiian Vintage Mocha Cake

I CALL THIS a Hawaiian Vintage Mocha Cake because it has the unmistakable dense texture of a true homemade cake. The coffee flavoring and bittersweet chocolate just add to the wonderful, Old World experience. When you eat this, you'll be taken back to a time when Matson steamer ships glided into Honolulu Harbor beneath the beauty of Aloha Tower.   SERVES 12 TO 16

For cake

1¾ cups freshly brewed, triple-strength Kona coffee

¾ cup unsalted butter

7 ounces Hawaiian Vintage bittersweet chocolate, finely chopped

2 beaten eggs

½ teaspoon vanilla

1½ cups all-purpose flour

½ cup cocoa

1½ cups sugar

1 teaspoon baking soda

½ teaspoon salt

2 tablespoons instant Kona coffee

For glaze

⅓ cup heavy cream

3 tablespoons butter

2 tablespoons corn syrup

1 tablespoon instant Kona coffee

4 ounces Hawaiian Vintage bittersweet chocolate, finely chopped

To make the cake: Preheat the oven to 325°F. Spray a bundt pan with cooking spray, then dust with flour, tapping out the excess. In a large heat-proof bowl, pour the hot coffee over the butter and bittersweet chocolate. Stir until blended, then set aside for 10 minutes to cool.

Add the beaten eggs and vanilla. Sift the flour, cocoa, sugar, baking soda, and salt together, then whisk into the chocolate mixture. Stir in the instant coffee, and pour into prepared pan. Bake for about 55 minutes, or until cake tests done. Cool on a rack, then turn out onto a cake board or plate.

To make glaze: Bring the cream, butter, corn syrup, and instant coffee to a boil in a small saucepan. Put the chopped chocolate in a small bowl; pour boiling cream mixture over it, and let it sit for 5 minutes. Whisk gently until smooth, then pour carefully over the cake. Chill until the glaze sets. Serve at room temperature with whipped cream or ice cream.

Passionate Soufflé Cake

LILIKO'I, OR PASSION fruit, is prized for its sweet, tart flavor and tropical essence. Passion fruit and pineapple are the two quintessential flavors that can transport us to a tropical island with just a sip. I've put the delicate flavor of liliko'i in a soufflé so good that it will, as we say in the Islands, "broke your mouth."   SERVES 8 TO 12

For compote
2 cups sliced strawberries
3 tablespoons sugar
2 tablespoons Grand Marnier (optional)

For cake
⅔ cup sugar
¼ cup all-purpose flour
⅓ cup liliko'i (passion fruit) juice
¼ cup hot, melted butter
1½ cups buttermilk
3 egg whites
¼ cup sugar

For the compote, toss strawberries, sugar, and Grand Marnier together in a medium bowl. Let set at least 1 hour to draw the juices out.

Preheat oven to 350°F. Spray 8 individual soufflé dishes with nonstick cooking spray. Set in a sheet pan with a 1-inch rim. Sift the ⅔ cup sugar and flour together in a medium bowl. Whisk in the liliko'i juice, melted butter, and buttermilk.

In another clean, dry bowl, whip the egg whites until foamy. Beat in the ¼ cup sugar until stiff peaks form. Fold into liliko'i mixture. Divide the egg-liliko'i mixture among the prepared dishes. Place sheet pan in the oven, and pour ½ inch of hot water into the bottom. Bake until the tops are puffed and golden, approximately 20 minutes.

Serve the soufflés warm, with some of the strawberry compote spooned on top.

Traditional Hawaiian Haupia

HAUPIA IS A coconut pudding, and a favorite lu'au dessert. Today, haupia is used as an icing on coconut cake and as a flavoring for gourmet ice cream. It's an instant hit anywhere it's served.   SERVES 16

1½ cups coconut milk
1½ cups milk (water can be substituted)
6 tablespoons sugar
6 tablespoons cornstarch

In a saucepan, combine coconut milk, milk, sugar, and cornstarch. Cook over medium heat, stirring frequently, until mixture thickens. Lower heat, and continue cooking for 10 more minutes. Taste to check that the cornstarch is cooked. It should have a smooth finish when put in your mouth. Pour into a square 8-inch baking pan. Chill. When firm, cut into small squares.

Fresh tropical fruits can be diced and served with the haupia.

Hawaiian Passionate Punch

HAVE YOU EVER been on vacation at a beach resort? You look up, and a hostess is walking toward you with a drink that cools you off just looking at it. This Hawaiian Passionate Punch is just that kind of refreshing and cool summer beverage. Rum or vodka can be added to make it a more spirited punch!

YIELDS 1½ GALLONS

2 cans frozen concentrated passion fruit juice

1 quart water

1 quart pineapple juice

2 quarts ginger ale, chilled

2 cups vodka or rum (optional)

3 kiwi fruit, skinned and sliced

2 fresh oranges, sliced with skin on

1 basket fresh strawberries, sliced

1 bunch mint leaves for garnish

Pour concentrated passion fruit juice, water, pineapple juice, and ginger ale into large punch bowl. Add vodka or rum if desired. Add ice, and stir. Top with fruits and mint leaves. Serve immediately.

Kona Spiced Coffee

YOU CAN GET Kona coffee anywhere these days. I was browsing in a little mom-and-pop store in Kentucky and found small packets of roasted Kona coffee beans. This sweet, aromatic brew is pleasing any time of year. Try it in March, when the snow has melted enough to turn to filthy slush, and you need some warmth and a little ray of hope that summer really is coming.

YIELDS 4 CUPS

¼ teaspoon ground cardamom
½ teaspoon almond extract
½ teaspoon vanilla extract
Dash of cinnamon
4 cups brewed Kona coffee
Cream and sugar to taste

Add the cardamom, almond extract, vanilla extract, and dash of cinnamon to hot brewed coffee. Serve coffee immediately with cream and sugar.

The Marquesas

ON ONE OF MY MANY trips to Tahiti, I took a cargo plane from Papeete to the island of Ua Huka, in the Marquesas, where a friend was meeting me. We'd planned to rendezvous at a remote copra plantation on the north end of the island. After asking many people in the tourist industry and around the airport, I finally got the name of a pilot who transported goods to the area. I TOOK A CAB FROM my hotel in Papeete to a small airstrip at the east end of the city, and met Rémi, a French national who had moved to the Marquesas in the late 1960s. "Bonjour," he said, as I climbed out of the cab and walked into the echoing cavern of the hangar. "I'M SAM CHOY," I SAID, extending my hand.

RÉMI GRABBED MY ARMS, PULLED me to him, and planted a kiss on each of my cheeks. "Comment allez-vous?" he asked. I SMILED, SHOOK MY HEAD, and lifted my shoulders. "AH! OUI OUI. AMÉRICAIN." HE nodded, and blinked knowingly. "Ow arre you?" he asked with pride. He spoke slowly, rounding his mouth to shape the words. When he said "you," it sounded like "zhu."

"We go to Ua Huka," he added. "Five hour only, maybe more. Ready, yes?"

"Yes," I said, "I'm ready." I grabbed my bag from the cab.

As I walked toward him, Rémi looked me over from top to bottom. "Very big man," he said, smiling. He patted his stomach and pointed to mine. His expression made me laugh. "You chef, yes?" he asked.

"Yes."

"Ah." He nodded. "Good chef. Good food."

"Never trust a skinny chef," I told him.

It took a moment, but then he laughed. "Oui, oui!" he said, smiling.

There were two planes in the hangar, a small Piper Cub, and a large cargo plane with four prop engines. "Which one?" I asked, pointing to each aircraft.

"This," he said, *"Mad-o-leen."* He waved his arm like a welcoming maître d' to the large, silver cargo plane. It looked like a salvage job from a World War II U.S. fleet. Plastered to the side of its nose was a worn picture of a reclining woman in a 1940s swimming suit, her legs twice as long as real legs. Steven Spielberg would have loved this plane.

"Will it fly?" I asked, only half joking.

"Oui," he answered. "Short fly to Ua Huka."

At least the trip promised to be interesting—his broken English over the rattle and thumps of antique engines for a thousand miles was going to make for a unique cultural experience.

With the help of a forklift, one of Rémi's friends pushed the plane out of the hangar. Once the relic stood on the tarmac it didn't look so bad. Under the blue sky, in the sunlight, it gleamed all over and I imagined it wanted to fly. The way it was shining seemed like its promise to us that it would take off smoothly, glide through the air like a wise, solid bird, and land safely on that other island, that small green target so far to the north.

We climbed aboard. The hold was packed with wooden crates and metal canisters, all strapped with cargo belts to the interior haul. I sat in the cockpit with Rémi. On the ceiling above and behind us there were a few strings hanging with feathers and shells tied to them. I figured these were good luck charms, but I was afraid to ask.

We clunked down the runway, the ancient propellers chugging with loud sputters and thuds. The short airstrip came to an abrupt end where a stand of ironwood trees rose 30 feet into the air. I wondered if this lump of steel could really lift itself high enough to clear them. "Will we make it?" I yelled.

Rémi just nodded and smiled. A bead of sweat trickled from beneath his Air France baseball cap down the side of his forehead. "You strap in!" he yelled. That wasn't very comforting.

Madeleine slugged along, picking up speed slowly. The end of the runway was getting awfully close. "Rémi!" I called.

He shook his head and concentrated on the trees that were closing fast. I shut my eyes and heard the engines grind as the nose of the heavy plane lifted. We lurched upward. I opened my eyes just in time to see the feathery tops of the ironwoods drop below us. There was a distinct scratching sound as we flew over the trees. "Did we hit them?" I yelled to Rémi. He didn't answer. "Rémi!" I called again.

He turned in his seat and looked at me. "Of course not," he said.

"I heard scratching," I said.

"The trees, they tickle our belly. Nothing to worry." He starting adjusting the dials and gadgets on the control panel. "You rest," he said. "Long flight."

Rémi was right. We flew for hours, no in-flight movies or special beverage service, just me, Rémi, old *Madeleine*, and a blue world: the sky above, and the endless Pacific below.

Sunset was spectacular. There were clouds on the horizon and they lit up like puffy Chinese lanterns, the ones near the sun all yellow but others farther off were reddish and even purple. The sun itself turned light peach, burnt orange, then maroon before it slipped away.

Night settled in. The stars came out. Rémi spent the next two hours showing me the constellations and heavenly phenomena of the Southern Hemisphere, like the Southern Cross, the Magellanic Clouds, the great Nebula of Orion, and Mars and Saturn. He said that you could see Venus only in the day this time of year. He pointed out what he called the "best globular cluster," which was Omega Centauri, and then at the very edge of our galaxy there was a foggy-looking group of distant stars called the Jewel Box. He played connect the dots on the windshield of the cockpit and linked the constellations of Aquarius, Canis Major, Capricornus, and a bunch of others that I'd never heard of. Oh yes, and he showed me the Hydra, the sea serpent.

"How far to the Ua Huka?" I asked when there was a lull in the astronomy lecture.

"About, uh," he paused, "sixteen hundred kilometers, thousand miles."

"But aren't we about halfway by now?"

He smiled again. "Long flight. You rest." He motioned his head toward a small cot near the back of the cabin. It was a great idea. That way I didn't have to worry about whether good old *Madeleine* would stay aloft for the entire trip.

I woke to Rémi's boisterous, off-key rendition of "Yellow Submarine." "Almost there," he yelled between verses. "One hour." We'd flown all night. The sun was high in the sky. I came forward and stood next to him. Below, I could see the outline of a green and brown, crescent-shaped island. "What is that?" I asked.

"Ua Huka. Where we go," said Rémi. "You know, the main islands of Marquesas have names after parts of a house."

"Really?" I studied the island below and wondered what part of a house this shape represented.

"Oh, yes," he said. He explained that Hiva Oa, the main island in the south part, has its name for the long beam that is the peak for the roof. Ua Pou, the second big island in the north part, gets its name for the two support posts that hold up the roof beam, and Nuku Hiva, the largest island in the north, is the corners of the beam. Fatu Iva, in the south, is the nine layers of coconut fronds for the roof thatch. Tahuata, also in the south, means the work is done, and Ua Huka, the island below, means the cleanup.

"There are north and south groups?" I asked. "I'd never heard that before."

"Oh, yes," Rémi said.

Madeleine banked, and we were beginning to descend toward Ua Huka with its single spiked peak and white crescent beaches.

"Nuku Hiva is largest in north group, and Ua Pou and Ua Huka are the smaller," Rémi continued.

Below, resting on the flat center plain of a vast plateau, I could see a small black strip of tar pointed inland toward the mountain, and the arch-roofed Quonset hut of the island airport office.

"Tahuata, Moho Tani, and Fatu Hiva are near main island Hiva Oa in the south."

Madeleine creaked as we turned again to get into position for landing. I made sure my seat belt was secure. Our approach brought us in over the water, heading toward the airfield.

"This is good," Rémi said. "The wind is not bad."

Madeleine's wings tipped, making her flying pattern look like a drunken swagger. In the cockpit, Rémi fought with the controls. I wanted to ask him if he believed in God, but this wasn't the time.

I knew we were coming in low because I could see branches and whorls on the coral heads as we skimmed over the reef. Just as we leveled out and seemed to be heading safely toward dry land, a loud clank shook the bottom of the plane. It sounded like the belly of the fuselage had torn apart. Soon after that, it felt like something dropped out of the bottom of the plane. I must have looked panicked, because when Rémi saw my face he laughed and said, "Wheels!"

The landing was perfect because we settled on solid ground without breaking any bones. When I climbed out I saw my Marquesan friend Yannik. He was sitting in his jeep parked to the right of the Quonset hut. "Bonjour!" he yelled. "Sam, you came with Rémi? You are a brave man, oui?"

Rémi was out of the plane and talking to a man with a clipboard. Rémi looked over at Yannik and waved. I thanked my pilot for all of his help, and asked when he was flying back to Papeete. "Oh," he said. "One, maybe two week."

"Do not worry, Sam," Yannik said as he came to stand beside me. "We go to another island. You take a commercial flight back to Tahiti. No problem."

We got into Yannik's jeep and headed down a dirt road, away from the airport and Rémi and *Madeleine*. "You hungry?" Yannik asked.

My stomach was still in knots from the landing. "No," I said, "I'm fine."

"Good. There will be lots to eat." Yannik gassed the engine, and the jeep took off through dry scrub, and bumped over patches of yellow grass. Mount Hitikau, the tallest point on the island, rose in the distance. "This is a wild place," Yannik said as we drove. "Horses, cows, and goats graze here sometimes. Rémi complains because they are sometimes on the runway when he tries to land. He almost hit a horse once. Then the horse, Rémi, and his precious *Madeleine* would have died. It scares him every time."

We turned and headed downhill to a coast road that hugged the cliffs and dipped into lush valleys steaming with waterfalls.

"I'm glad I didn't know about the horses when we were flying in," I said.

"You were scared, oui?" Yannik laughed. "I will not fly with him. You have such courage."

I had met Yannik many years earlier while doing a "visiting chef" stint in New Zealand. He was one of the vendors who provided the most magnificent variety of shellfish I had ever seen. Most of his catch was taken from the waters off the Marquesan Islands.

I'd made several trips to visit his home on the island of Nuku Hiva (the main island), and had taken deep-sea fishing trips with him, but this, he promised, would be something very different. When he found out I was going to be back in the South Pacific, he planned a traditional Marquesan feast on Ua Huka. We were about 22 miles east of Nuku Hiva and 35 miles northeast of Ua Pou, the second largest island.

"Why is this island called 'cleanup'?" I asked.

"Look at this flat place," he said, making a sweeping gesture with his arm. "I think the people thought the wind and weather cleaned it up. Only one mountain, and many small hills."

It all made sense, I thought. This had to be the most arid terrain I'd encountered in all of my trips through the South Pacific. We drove on, skirting the base of Mount Hitikau, stopping here and there to admire a sweeping view or waterfall. Soon we entered a narrow valley, and at the end of the road, beneath a grove of coconut palms, was a little house. All-terrain vehicles were parked haphazardly around the yard, and guitar music echoed against the valley walls. "Here we are having the feast," Yannik said.

"This is the copra plantation?" I asked. There couldn't have been more than 20 palm trees visible from the yard, and it didn't look like any plantation I'd ever seen.

"Michele, he is the owner. He does not make much money from the copra," Yannik explained as he got out of the jeep. "His family gathers coconuts from trees all over. The whole island is his plantation."

We walked around to the back of the house. The entire population of Ua Huka must have been there. Rémi had somehow arrived ahead of us; he sat with a beautiful Marquesan woman at one of the tables beneath an awning. Three little children fidgeted next to him. "Salut!" he yelled, lifting a cup into the air.

"I think Rémi is already too happy," Yannik said, smiling at his friend. "I will introduce you to Michele and his family. They are very happy to meet you."

Yannik walked me into the house through the kitchen door. A woman standing at the sink turned around and greeted us with a big smile. "Yannik," she said, as she wiped her hands and came to give him a kiss on each cheek. They spoke in French to each other, looking at me the whole time. "This is Hutia, Michele's wife," Yannik said.

"Kaoha," Hutia said in a warm, welcoming voice. She walked over and kissed me on each cheek. She was a rather round woman, very motherly, and extremely kind. I felt at ease instantly. She turned back to Yannik and said something, then motioned for us to go outside.

"Michele is getting the food from the hima'a," Yannik said as we walked down the porch stairs.

I knew from past trips to Nuku Hiva that a hima'a is like an 'imu in Hawai'i, an earth oven. "Don't be surprised if there is a whole cow in there," Yannik said. We rounded the back corner of the house, and there, in the shadow of a cluster of trees, we saw a group of shirtless men working to unearth a large, steaming pile of burlap and banana leaves.

"Michele!" called Yannik. The tallest in the group looked up and waved. After some more hugs and kisses, and a string of French words I didn't understand, Yannik pointed to me.

Michele was a large man, with a smile as big as his belly, which hung over the top of his lavalava. "Sam," he said in a heavy Polynesian French accent. "You eat." He gave some instruction to the men at the hima'a, and led us to the tables.

Hutia was busy telling the many children where to place the food that poured out of her little kitchen. Each dish was served in a wooden bowl or on a rough wooden platter. There were green banana patties coated in coconut flakes, poke (cubed raw fish) with green onions, banana poi, tapioca bread, breadfruit poi, raw oysters, and baskets of fresh baguettes. The group of men from the hima'a soon joined the gathering. They brought with them coconut baskets filled with roasted sweet potatoes, whole breadfruit, and cooked bananas. Then, to loud applause, Michele and his four sons carried in a large, wooden slab piled high with gigantic chunks of roast beef.

The young man playing the guitar strummed the introduction to a *himene* (song) that everyone knew but me. They all raised their glasses and started to sing. I picked up a glass, took a sip of the papaya juice, coconut water, and rum mixture, and almost fell over. The emphasis was definitely on the rum. After a couple of gulps, I was singing, too.

The party lasted into the night, longer than the kerosene in the torches. Almost everyone danced: children bedecked in flowers did an *aparima,* wiggling their little hips and singing along with the guitar and *pahu* (drum); and the men made us all laugh with their competition to see if they could move their legs faster than the drummer could beat the *to'ere* (wooden drum). The women sat and laughed at everything.

About midnight, I crashed. Michele took me into the house and showed me my bed, a mattress on the floor. That was how the entire family slept. In a show of Polynesian hospitality, Michele and Hutia had graciously given me their bed.

The next couple of days were spent touring the island, which was really small enough to be seen in a single afternoon. But Michele wanted to show me all of his favorite fishing reefs, the copra-drying fields, his garden, and a small museum in Vaipae'e, the island's only town. He showed me Ha'atuatua, an archaeological site in Hane.

We ran into Rémi a couple of times. Yannik must have told him that I was scared when we flew over from Papeete, because each time I saw Rémi, he said, "Oh, Sam. I leave soon. You, too, yes? You fly with me. We fly good." Then he'd flash me a toothy grin and throw his head back and laugh out loud.

"He's joking, right?" I asked Yannik. "I thought he was flying in a week or two." Yannik just laughed at me. I wasn't scared, I was petrified.

I left on the afternoon of my third day on Ua Huka. Yannik and I chartered a boat for the 22-mile ride to Nuku Hiva, the main island of the northern group. From there, I caught an Air Tahiti flight back to Papeete. I've traveled back to the Marquesas several times in recent years, but nothing compared to my flight with Rémi, the feast with Michele and Hutia, and my circle-island tour with Yannik.

Food is always better served from a home kitchen and eaten with friends. This is something I strongly believe. The ambience of Hutia and Michele's home combined the smells—valley breezes, ocean spray, drying copra, hima'a steam—with friendly laughter, raucous singing and music, and fabulous food. This experience, more than any other I've had on subsequent visits to the Marquesas, has become my definition of these "forgotten" islands of Polynesia. For me, the magic here doesn't just lie in the cathedral spires and obelisk-shaped columns of Nuku Hiva, or in the misty, rain-filled valleys on Hiva Oa. It is in the easy smiles, incredible food, and generous Polynesian hospitality of Michele's family and friends.

The beauty I saw flying into Ua Huka, coupled with the sensory experiences of feasting with my friends, are sparkling jewels in my treasure box of memories.

Kaoha
(like "Aloha," both hello and good-bye)

Basil-Passion Barbecued Prawns

AQUACULTURE IS A new industry in the Marquesas. The land is very mountainous, so they are experimenting with terraced, freshwater ponds. When I first made this dish I used passion fruit that we'd gathered on a hike in one of the deep valleys on Hiva Oa. You can skewer the prawns or grill them separately. Either way, they are fabulous.   SERVES 4

½ cup frozen liliko'i (passion fruit) concentrate, thawed
1 tablespoon vinegar
1 teaspoon minced gingerroot
1 tablespoon brown sugar
1 tablespoon minced fresh basil
1 pound prawns (16 to 20 count)

In a mixing bowl, combine liliko'i concentrate, vinegar, ginger, sugar, and basil; blend well. Add prawns, and marinate for 1 hour. Skewer prawns on four skewers. Barbecue or broil for 7 to 8 minutes, until prawns are cooked. Baste occasionally with marinade.

Shrimp à la Ua Huka

I LOVE MUSHROOMS and will find any excuse to include them in a menu. While on the island of Ua Huka, we visited a man named Ramon. He lived in a little wood-frame house in the town of Vaipaee. Ramon asked me to help him in the kitchen. He pulled a bunch of ingredients from his refrigerator, including a bag of large mushrooms. "You make," he said, and he walked out the back door. This appetizer is what I came up with. I hope you like it.

SERVES 4

16 large fresh mushrooms (about 1 pound)
2 cups heavy cream
2 tablespoons chopped shallots
¾ cup coconut milk
1 cup cracker crumbs
¾ cup cooked bay shrimp
½ teaspoon salt
¼ teaspoon black pepper
Pinch of dill
½ cup chopped spinach
Paprika for garnish

Preheat oven to 350°F.

Remove stems from mushrooms. In a saucepan, cook 1 cup of the heavy cream until reduced to half. Stir in chopped shallots, and cook for 1 minute. Remove from heat, and stir in ½ cup coconut milk, cracker crumbs, shrimp, salt, black pepper, and dill. Stuff mushroom caps with shrimp mixture. Place in a shallow casserole dish.

In a saucepan, reduce the remaining 1 cup heavy cream to half. Stir in the remaining ¼ cup coconut milk and spinach. Cook for 2 minutes. Heat, but do not boil. Pour sauce over mushrooms in casserole dish. Bake for 10 minutes.

Arrange mushrooms on a serving platter. Pour excess spinach sauce over the top, and garnish with a sprinkling of paprika.

Cinnamon Chicken

I HAD THIS dish in the home of my friend Frank while on one of my trips to the Marquesas. His wife Hetiati is a fabulous cook and creative gardener. She loves to make up dishes using exotic ingredients like raisins, capers, cloves, and cinnamon that arrive in shipments out of Papeete. Most of their staple foods are brought into the Islands on cargo ships, and the Marquesan people are limited by what's available in the imported merchandise. Every once in a while, something fascinating arrives. When this happens, Hetiati says it's like Christmas. SERVES 4

¼ teaspoon ground cinnamon

¼ teaspoon ground cloves

Salt and pepper to taste

4 boneless chicken breasts (skin on)

2 tablespoons vegetable oil

¾ cup chopped onion

Sliced green onions (optional)

2 cloves minced garlic

2 teaspoons minced gingerroot

¾ cup orange juice

2 tablespoons sugar

2 tablespoons raisins

1 tablespoon capers, drained and rinsed

In a large bowl, combine cinnamon, cloves, and salt and pepper to taste. Add chicken breasts, and rub evenly to coat.

Heat the oil in a sauté pan. Cook chicken breasts skin-side down for 3 to 4 minutes. Add onion, green onions, garlic, and ginger. Flip chicken over, and cook an additional 3 to 4 minutes. Drain off excess oil. Add orange juice, sugar, raisins, and capers. Reduce heat and simmer approximately 10 minutes. Serve with hot rice.

Breadfruit Bisque

BREADFRUIT IS A staple starch in the South Pacific. It is fermented, roasted, and mashed into poi. If breadfruit is not available, use russet potatoes and sweet potatoes in equal parts for the recipe.   SERVES 4 TO 6

3 bacon strips, cut in thin strips

½ medium onion, diced

½ cup finely julienned leeks, white part only

¼ cup white wine

6 cups chicken stock

1½ cups breadfruit, cleaned and medium diced

1 cup heavy cream

Salt and white ground pepper to taste

½ cup cooked finely diced breadfruit for garnish

Chopped scallions for garnish

Sauté bacon with onion and leeks in a pot over medium heat until the onions are transparent. Add white wine, and simmer until wine evaporates. Add the chicken stock and breadfruit. Simmer for 35 to 45 minutes. Skim and remove the fat that rises to the top of the soup.

Place the soup in a blender, and puree until smooth. In a separate large saucepan, heat the heavy cream. Add the pureed soup and heat. Season with salt and pepper to taste. Portion soup in bowls, and garnish with diced breadfruit and scallions.

Outrageous Marquesan Beef Soup

THE MOUNTAINS ON Nuku Hiva are steep pinnacles that rise sharply from crashing waves. The wind hits the sea cliffs and roars across the interior plateaus of the island. On one of the plateaus, cattle graze next to the island's landing strip. Pilots are very careful to dodge the cows when approaching the Quonset-hut airport.

SERVES 6

6 pounds beef rib bones

1 pound stew-cut beef, cubed

4 quarts cold water

2 onions, sliced

2-inch piece gingerroot, sliced

3 cloves garlic, sliced

1 stalk lemongrass

1 stick cinnamon

1 teaspoon whole black peppercorns

3 tablespoons fish sauce

Salt to taste

6 ounces rice noodles, soaked 20 minutes in warm water and drained

1 pound seared tender beef, thinly sliced

Put bones and stew-cut beef in a large pot. Add cold water to cover, then onions, ginger, garlic, lemongrass, cinnamon, and whole black peppercorns. Bring to a boil, turn heat very low, cover, and simmer for at least 5 hours. Add fish sauce and salt to taste.

In a separate pot, heat 3 quarts water and bring to a rolling boil. Add the noodles. As soon as the water returns to a boil, drain, and portion noodles into bowls. Add the hot soup, and arrange the sliced beef on the top.

Basil-Lobster Salad with Avocado Mayonnaise

THE COMBINATION OF Basil–Macadamia Nut Pesto and Avocado Mayonnaise is as exotic as it sounds, but it is also great tasting. I prepared this salad for some friends on Hiva Oa after a week of fishing, singing, and basking in the sun. This flavor combination always takes me back to those blissful days in that French Polynesian paradise.   SERVES 4

12 ounces baby greens

Avocado Mayonnaise (see page 131)

Basil–Macadamia Nut Pesto (see page 132)

1 medium cucumber, peeled, seeds removed, and finely diced

½ cup finely diced carrots, blanched

½ cup finely diced French beans, blanched

4 cooked live Maine lobsters (1½ pounds each), shells removed

1 boiled egg, finely grated, for garnish

Portion the greens in the center of 4 dinner plates. Squeeze avocado mayonnaise around the greens. Drizzle the pesto sauce on the mayonnaise. Sprinkle the cucumber, carrots, and beans on the mayonnaise. Cut the lobster into medallions, and place on the greens. Garnish with grated egg.

Shrimp-Spinach Salad
with a Citrus Vinaigrette

I APPRECIATE THE simple style of Marquesan cooking. What they can't grow for themselves they have to purchase off the cargo ships that frequent the harbors. As a result, the people on these fantastically beautiful islands have turned their tropical backyards into gardens of amazing variety. One woman proudly showed me her marvelous spinach patch. She walked out into the middle of the garden and picked a number of delicate, rich green leaves. We sat there, rinsed them, and ate them straight from the ground. What could be simpler and fresher than that?   SERVES 6

2 pounds fresh spinach
1½ pounds medium shrimp, poached, peeled, and deveined
1½ cups fresh hearts of palm, julienned
1 medium sweet onion, julienned
Citrus Vinaigrette (see page 133)
Sections from 2 oranges
⅔ cup crumbled blue cheese

Thoroughly wash spinach leaves. Tear leaves into bite-size pieces, and place in a large salad bowl. Add poached shrimp, hearts of palm, onion, and desired amount of dressing. Toss until ingredients are well coated. Sprinkle with orange sections and blue cheese crumbles.

Baked Snapper with Orange-Coconut Sauce

ANY FIRM, WHITE fish will work in this recipe. It's the Orange-Coconut Sauce that really takes the flavor over the top. There are certain things that trigger memories of places. This dish reminds me of my experiences on the island of Nuku Hiva—picking oranges from a wild orange tree in Taipivai Valley, which was made famous in Herman Melville's novel *Typee*; making coconut milk on the cliffs of Voovii plateau; and sweet green bananas arranged on street vendor carts in the town of Taiohae.   SERVES 4

4 snapper fillets (6 ounces each)
Salt and pepper to taste
4 tablespoons butter
2 bananas, cut lengthwise and in half
4 tablespoons sugar
½ cup orange juice
1 tablespoon lemon juice
½ cup coconut milk

Preheat the oven to 350°F.

Season snapper fillets with salt and pepper. Place fish in a baking pan, and set aside.

Heat a saucepan, and melt 2 tablespoons of butter. Sauté the bananas on both sides to golden brown, and set aside.

Heat the remaining 2 tablespoons of butter with the sugar until the sugar caramelizes. Add the orange and lemon juices, and reduce to half. Add the coconut milk, and season the sauce with salt and pepper.

Place a piece of banana on each fillet, and pour the sauce over the top. Bake in the oven for 10 to 12 minutes or until cooked. Serve hot.

Baked Citrus Crusted Onaga

ONAGA, A RED snapper, has a juicy texture and very mild flavor. This deep-sea fish is a favorite throughout Polynesia. In the Marquesas, where the reefs are rich with sea life, fishermen rarely venture out into the open ocean. When onaga or any other pelagic fish are caught, the open street markets clamor with excitement. If onaga is not available in your area, any firm, white fish will work. For fish substitution suggestions, see page 31.   SERVES 4

2 tablespoons butter
1 lime, juiced
½ orange, juiced
½ lemon, juiced
1 teaspoon Worcestershire sauce
Nonstick oil spray
4 pieces onaga (6 ounces each)
¼ cup fine bread crumbs (or panko)

Preheat oven to 400°F.

In saucepan, combine butter, juices, and Worcestershire sauce; heat until sizzling. Spray a baking pan with nonstick oil spray, and arrange fish skin-side down.

Pour butter mixture over fish, and top with bread crumbs. Bake for 8 to 12 minutes or until done.

Gauguin Chicken

A PAINTING BY Paul Gauguin, which hangs in a house in Puamau Village on the island of Hiva Oa, was the inspiration for this dish. Gauguin used the brilliant light that plays on the colors of the Islands to produce a feeling of languishing beauty. While I stood before his work of art, lost in the way he presented paradise, a chicken ran across my foot. It scared me to death. I thought, "Roasted chicken with a colorful fruit chutney." You never know when inspiration will hit you.

SERVES 4

1 tablespoon roasted fennel seeds
½ teaspoon roasted cumin seeds
2 teaspoons ground turmeric
1 teaspoon chili flakes
¼ cup cilantro leaves
¼ cup chopped scallions
1 stalk lemongrass
3 cloves garlic
1-inch cube gingerroot, sliced
2 tablespoons oyster sauce
⅔ cup coconut milk
Salt to taste
6-pound roasting chicken
Pepper-Papaya-Pineapple Chutney (see page 135)

Grind the fennel, cumin, turmeric, and chili flakes in a coffee grinder. In a food processor, pulverize the ground spices, cilantro, scallions, lemongrass, garlic, and ginger. Add oyster sauce and coconut milk, and season with salt to taste.

Rub the mixture on the inside and outside of the chicken. Let chicken marinate in the refrigerator for 2 to 3 hours. Preheat oven to 300°F. Place chicken on a rack in a large roasting pan, and roast for 2 hours or until done. Let rest for 10 minutes before carving.

Serve on a bed of seasoned rice with Pepper-Papaya-Pineapple Chutney.

Capellini Pasta with Crab Sauce

THERE ARE QUITE a few large crab species in the South Pacific. Coconut crabs are the most common in the Marquesas, Tonga, Tahiti, and Samoa. These large crabs have very powerful pincers, and can be dangerous. Any type of crabmeat will work in this recipe. As always, I encourage the use of fresh, fresh, fresh ingredients.   SERVES 4

8 ounces capellini pasta
1 tablespoon butter
1 garlic clove, minced
½ cup chopped green onions
2 tomatoes, peeled, seeded, and chopped
½ pound cooked and shredded crabmeat
1 tablespoon lemon juice
½ teaspoon celery salt
Cracked black pepper
¼ cup chopped parsley

Cook capellini according to package directions.

In sauté pan, combine butter, garlic, and green onions. Cook for 3 to 4 minutes. Add tomatoes, and simmer for 1 to 2 more minutes. Add crabmeat, lemon juice, celery salt, and pepper; cook an additional 2 minutes. Add chopped parsley.

Place al dente pasta in a serving bowl and top with crab mixture. Enjoy!

Lobster with Magic Coconut Sauce

I LOVE LOBSTER. And on the island of Nuku Hiva I met an old fisherman, affectionately known as Tutu-man, who feels the same way I do about those sea bugs. My vision of heaven is sitting on a beach at sunset after a day of spear fishing with a big pot of boiling water over a beach fire. We cook the lobster, then eat it right there, fresh from the sea. Tutu-man says that he's eaten so much lobster in his day that he really appreciates dressing the meat up a bit. So, Tutu-man, here's a little magic for you.　　　　SERVES 4

4 live Maine lobsters (1½ pounds each)

1 tablespoon olive oil

1 small red chili pepper, chopped

½ teaspoon cumin seeds

2 tablespoons shallots, minced

4 kaffir lime leaves, chopped

½ stalk fresh lemongrass, chopped

3 tablespoons chopped cilantro

3 tablespoons chopped basil leaves

1¼ cups Tutu-man's Lobster Stock (see page 136)

1 cup coconut milk

Lemon juice to taste

4 tablespoons heavy cream

4 tablespoons room-temperature unsalted butter

Salt to taste

Cilantro leaves for garnish

12 cooked asparagus spears for garnish

In a large pot, bring 4 quarts of water to a boil. Plunge lobster into the fast-boiling water for 8 to 10 minutes. Remove lobster, and place in ice-water bath immediately to stop the cooking process.

First, twist legs and tail from body. Using fish scissors, cut around the inside of the shell. Starting from the tail end, peel it back and pull out the meat. For the claws, cut through the joints and open up each section by cracking the ends. Ease the meat out of the shells. Reserve all the meat. The shells and head can be used for making the lobster stock.

For the sauce, heat the olive oil in a saucepan, and add red chili pepper and cumin seeds. Sauté until slightly brown. Add shallots, kaffir lime leaves, lemongrass, cilantro, and basil. Continue to cook for about 2 minutes. Add the lobster stock and simmer for 10 minutes. Pour in coconut milk, lemon juice, and heavy cream; cook for another 3 minutes. Remove from heat and whisk in the room-temperature butter. Add salt to taste. Strain the sauce through a fine strainer.

Warm 4 soup plates. Cut lobster meat into bite-size pieces, and arrange in the center of the plate. Carefully spoon the sauce around the lobster meat.

Garnish with the cilantro leaves and asparagus spears, and serve immediately.

Steamed Prawns in Banana Leaves

YOU ARE GOING to love this one. Like all of my recipes, it's easy to make—just throw things into a bowl, pile the mixture into a cooking vessel (in this case we are using banana leaves or aluminum foil), and cook. This is a very traditional Marquesan recipe with a few added "Choy" flavors.

SERVES 4

8 banana leaves (10 × 10 inches), or aluminum foil
1½ pounds prawns, peeled and deveined
½ cup coconut milk
4 teaspoons lime juice
1 tablespoon honey
2 teaspoons sambal sauce
½ medium sweet onion, finely chopped
1 teaspoon minced gingerroot
2 lemongrass stalks, minced
4 teaspoons fish sauce

6 basil leaves, thinly sliced for garnish
4 tablespoons chopped cilantro for garnish
4 lime wedges for garnish

Soak banana leaves in boiling water to soften. Drain, and clean with a damp cloth. Set aside.

In a large bowl, combine remaining ingredients and marinate for 20 minutes. Divide into 4 equal portions, and place on 4 banana leaves. (More than 1 leaf will be needed for each packet, as they frequently need to be overlapped where they are torn.)

Wrap securely, and fasten with a toothpick or bamboo skewer. Place packets in a steamer, and when the water boils, steam banana parcels for 20 minutes. Put the packets on four plates. Serve with the basil, cilantro, and lime wedges.

Tahuata Lemon Pepper Ono

WE WERE ON a little fishing trip off the island of Tahuata, a tiny island near the coast of Hiva Oa, when my line pulled tight. I'd snagged a fabulous ono. *'Ono* is the Hawaiian word for "good," and this ono was one of the best I've ever seen. To celebrate, I fixed a very simple marinade in my friend's kitchen and grilled the catch. You can substitute any kind of deep-sea fish (if you must) for the ono. Serve these fillets on a hot bed of rice with a little Twisted Tartar Sauce on the side.   **SERVES 4**

3 tablespoons lemon juice

3 tablespoons vegetable oil

1 teaspoon Dijon mustard

Salt and freshly ground pepper to taste

8 ono, wahoo, or sea mackerel fillets (4 ounces each)

Butterhead lettuce leaves

Twisted Tartar Sauce (see page 137)

In a small mixing bowl, combine lemon juice, oil, mustard, and salt and pepper to taste. Add ono, and marinate for 30 minutes. Grill fish for 3 to 4 minutes, leaving the middle pink. (The fish will continue to cook through even after it is removed from the fire.) Remove from the heat.

Serve with hot rice, and Twisted Tartar Sauce on the side.

Orange-Glazed Sweet Potatoes

AS IF THE sweet potatoes weren't sweet enough, I added orange and pineapple and papaya marmalades. This is so much more flavorful than candied yams. The orange juice blends well with the texture and flavor of the potatoes and the creation complements just about any meat dish.   SERVES 4

6 sweet potatoes, boiled with the skins on

1 cup Orange Marmalade (see page 134)

1 cup Papaya-Pineapple Marmalade (see page 135)

½ cup orange juice

1 tablespoon butter

Salt to taste

Additional butter to taste

Boil or steam the sweet potatoes until nearly cooked through. Peel the sweet potatoes and cut into thick slices. Add marmalades and orange juice, and toss to cover potatoes. Butter a casserole dish, make a layer with the potatoes, sprinkle lightly with salt, and dot with pats of butter, then bake in a 325°F oven for 30 to 40 minutes or until browned and candied.

Marquesan Mango Bread

MANGO BREAD IS popular around the world. The people of the Marquesas Islands add coconut to almost everything. This bread is delicious warm, but it slices best when it's completely cooled. It's a mystery. Anyway, serve it up plain or toasted, with cream cheese or butter. Either way, every way, it's very tasty.   YIELDS 12 SLICES

¾ cup butter

1½ cups sugar

2 eggs

1¾ cups all-purpose flour

1 teaspoon baking soda

½ teaspoon salt

1 cup mango puree

¼ cup grated coconut

¼ cup sour cream

2 limes, zest finely grated

Preheat oven to 325°F.

Spray a 9 × 5 × 3-inch loaf pan with nonstick cooking spray. Cream the butter and sugar until light and fluffy; add eggs one at a time. Continue beating until mixture is very light.

Sift the dry ingredients together; stir the mango puree, grated coconut, sour cream, and lime zest together. Alternately add the wet and dry ingredients to the creamed butter. Beat well after each addition, scraping sides often. Beat until smooth.

Pour batter into prepared pan, and bake in the center of the preheated oven for about 50 minutes, or until bread tests done when pierced with a skewer. Cool 10 minutes, then turn out onto a rack to finish cooling.

Mahina's Squid Lu'au

MAHINA IS A little woman who lives on the island of Hiva Oa. We met in the marketplace where she was selecting bunches of taro leaves for a dish she said was better than anything I'd ever tasted. My mother makes the best Squid Lu'au in the world. I'm taking a risk here, but I have to say that Mahina's ties my mom's in every way, except the love I have for my mother. (Whew, I think I made a good save there.)

SERVES 12

2 pounds calamari

3 pounds lu'au leaves (young taro leaves) or spinach

1 tablespoon rock salt

½ teaspoon baking soda

6 tablespoons butter

2 medium onions, diced

3 cups coconut milk

1½ teaspoons salt

1 tablespoon sugar

Clean calamari and slice in rings. Set aside.

Wash lu'au leaves, remove stems and thick veins. In a pot, boil 3 cups of water with the rock salt and baking soda. Add the leaves to the boiling water and reduce heat. Simmer, partially covered, for 1 hour. Drain, and squeeze out liquid.

Sauté onions and calamari in butter until the onions are translucent. Add the coconut milk, cooked lu'au leaves, salt, and sugar. Simmer for 30 minutes.

Avocado Mayonnaise

I USE THIS mayonnaise for everything from salads to sandwiches. I've even used it as a condiment for fish. It's easy to make, fun to eat, and really tastes great.

YIELDS 2 CUPS

¼ cup avocado pulp

½ cup mayonnaise

½ cup chicken or vegetable stock

2 teaspoons lemon juice

2 teaspoons tarragon vinegar

Salt and white pepper to taste

½ cup heavy cream

In the food processor, blend all the ingredients except the cream until smooth. Add the cream, and blend for a few seconds. Chill, and use within a day or two.

Basil–Macadamia Nut Pesto

SWEET IS THE operative word for this pesto recipe. The flavor isn't really "sweet," but the raves you get from your guests are very sweet indeed. Serve this over any fish or chicken, or with a plate of pasta. It's 'ono.

YIELDS 1¼ CUPS

½ cup fresh sweet basil leaves, chopped

3 cloves garlic, minced

¼ cup chopped parsley leaves

1 tablespoon lemon juice

Salt and pepper to taste

1 cup canola oil

½ cup minced roasted macadamia nuts

In a blender, add all the ingredients, except the nuts. Blend. Add the nuts to the mixture, and blend for a few seconds. Keep in the refrigerator, or store in the freezer until needed.

Citrus Vinaigrette

THE SWEET-SOUR FLAVOR of Asian sauces is captured in this dressing: the sour from the red wine vinegar, and the sweet from the orange juice and sugar. I added garlic to bring a little piquant zing to the mix.

YIELDS 1½ CUPS

¼ cup red wine vinegar

½ cup orange juice

1 teaspoon Dijon mustard

2 tablespoons sugar

1 tablespoon chopped fresh basil

1 clove garlic, minced

Salt and pepper to taste

½ cup canola oil

Combine all ingredients, except oil. Whisk until sugar is completely dissolved and mixture is thoroughly blended. Gradually add oil while continuing to whisk. Chill for half a day before using.

Orange Marmalade

MY GRANDMOTHER MADE the best orange marmalade, and gave out bottles of it at Christmas. I use her recipe for many of my dishes. It's one of those "never-fail" recipes that withstand the test of time. I sent a few bottles of this to my friends in the Marquesas, and they still talk about it.

YIELDS 3 CUPS

2 medium oranges
½ medium lemon
⅛ teaspoon baking soda
3 cups water
3 cups sugar
¼ of a 6-ounce bottle liquid fruit pectin

Remove orange and lemon peels; scrape off excess white. Cut peels in very fine shreds. In a saucepan combine ¾ cup of water with the baking soda, bring to a boil, cover, and cook slowly for 10 minutes.

Remove white membrane on fruit; section fruit, working over bowl to catch juice. Combine pulp, 2¼ cups water, reserved juice, and fruit peel; cover, and cook slowly for 20 minutes.

Add 3 cups sugar. Bring to boil, cook 5 minutes. Remove from heat; add fruit pectin. Skim and stir 5 minutes. Pour into hot scalded glasses; seal.

Papaya-Pineapple Marmalade

ONE OF MY favorite marmalades, this papaya-pineapple mixture is wonderful with fruit breads, as a condiment for baked fish, or as a morning spread on toast. Bon appetit.　　　　　YIELDS 1 CUP

½ cup diced papaya
½ cup diced pineapple
3 tablespoons granulated sugar

In a small saucepan, cook the fruit and sugar over medium-low heat for 20 minutes. Serve warm or cold.

Pepper-Papaya-Pineapple Chutney

THE SPICY HOT chili paste can be a little dangerous, so be careful not to use too much. One tablespoon is reasonable to me, but add it a little at a time, tasting with each addition.　　　　　YIELDS 1½ CUPS

1 small fresh pineapple, peeled, cored, and chopped
1 medium fresh papaya, seeded, peeled, and chopped
1 tablespoon minced fresh gingerroot
6 tablespoons sugar
1 tablespoon hot chili paste

In a medium saucepan, combine all ingredients except chili paste. Cook over medium heat for 1 hour or until mixture has a syrupy consistency. Fold in chili paste.

Tutu-man's Lobster Stock

TUTU-MAN IS AN old fisherman who lives on the north end of the island of Nuku Hiva. His rustic little cottage is shaded by tall coconut trees, and the view from the front porch is vast and royal blue. He says that straight out from his beach there's a seamount that is home to thousands of lobsters. He fishes that tall reef once a week, and brings in enough lobster to stew, boil, and sauté. I make this stock using Maine lobster simply because it is so much easier to find.

YIELDS 3 CUPS

4 whole Maine lobsters' shells, heads and tails intact
8 tablespoons olive oil
White of 1 small leek, chopped
½ medium onion, chopped
½ stalk celery, chopped
1 large carrot, chopped
2 cloves garlic, chopped
1 star anise
1 lemongrass stalk, chopped
½ teaspoon crushed white peppercorns
1 large tomato, peeled, seeded, and diced
1 cup white wine
7 cups water
¼ cup chopped cilantro with the stems

Quarter lobster heads, and place with the rest of the lobster shells on a roasting pan. Drizzle with 2 tablespoons olive oil. Heat oven to 400°F and roast lobster shells for 20 minutes in the oven, tossing the shells occasionally.

In the meantime, heat 6 tablespoons of olive oil in a pot. Add leek, onion, celery, and carrot. Sauté until onion is translucent. Add garlic, star anise, lemongrass, and white peppercorns; cook for another 3 minutes. Add tomato and wine. Reduce to one-half.

Add the roasted lobster shells, water, and cilantro stems to the tomato mixture, and simmer for 50 minutes. Strain to skim the stock.

Stock can be kept in a covered container for 2 to 3 days in the refrigerator or several weeks in the freezer.

Twisted Tartar Sauce

ON A WHIM, I added a pinch of coconut to this tartar sauce, and fell in love with it right away. It's just sweet enough, just spicy enough to enhance the flavor of fish without smothering it.   YIELDS 2 CUPS

1½ cups mayonnaise
1 tablespoon capers, minced
¼ cup chopped sweet onion
2 tablespoons chopped green onions
2 teaspoons lemon juice
½ cup finely grated fresh coconut
1 clove garlic, minced
1 teaspoon chili paste
1 tablespoon chopped parsley

Mix all ingredients in a bowl, and serve with your favorite seafood.

Fried Banana Cakes

I LEARNED TO make these delicious little cakes while on Nuku Hiva. A friend of mine who owns a small restaurant picked up a large bunch of very ripe bananas and wanted to experiment a little. I'm most comfortable in the kitchen, so I offered my help, and we whipped up these dessert cakes. Served hot with honey they are fabulous, but covered with ice cream and sprinkled with banana slices, they are incredible.   YIELDS 15 CAKES

4 very ripe bananas, peeled

1 teaspoon vanilla extract

½ to ⅔ cup flour (depending on the size and moistness of the bananas)

¼ teaspoon baking powder

Pinch of salt

1 tablespoon sugar

1 teaspoon grated lime zest

Oil for frying

Cinnamon sugar (1 tablespoon sugar and a few pinches of cinnamon) for garnish

Lime wedges for garnish

In a food processor, pulverize the bananas with the vanilla extract. Sift together the flour, baking powder, salt, and sugar. Add the lime zest and dry ingredients to the food processor. Mix until dough is of a light texture. Rest for a few minutes, then form the dough into 15 patties. Fry cakes in ½-inch-deep oil, turning to brown evenly on both sides. Drain on paper towels, sprinkle with cinnamon sugar, and serve hot with lime wedges.

Steamed Coconut Custard in a Pumpkin

COCONUTS GROW WILD on all of the South Pacific Islands, and the people living in these remote and very exotic places are quite creative in the ways they prepare this versatile fruit. Actually, the rich custard in this recipe is incredible on its own, but I bake it in a pumpkin for added flavor. It looks great, too.   SERVES 6

1 small pumpkin
2 tablespoons cornstarch
1½ cups brown sugar
1¾ cups coconut milk
8 large eggs, well beaten
1½ teaspoons vanilla extract

Cut the top from the pumpkin in a star shape. Remove and discard seeds. Dry pumpkin inside with paper towels.

Mix cornstarch with sugar, then pour in the coconut milk. Mix well. Add the eggs and vanilla; blend well.

Pour mixture into pumpkin shell, replace lid, and steam in a large steamer for 1 hour or until custard sets. Refrigerate until ready to use.

Gingerade

I WAS VERY surprised to find gingerroot growing in backyards and available in the small grocery stores on the larger islands of the Marquesas. But my friends told me that the people of the Islands have grown to appreciate this root because it keeps so well, and the flavor is so appealing. This drink is like an iced tea, but much more refreshing. It has become quite a local favorite among my friends in Vaipaee. YIELDS 12 CUPS

½ cup cubed gingerroot
4 lemons, sliced
2 quarts boiling water
2 cups lemon juice
Sugar syrup (recipe below)
Fresh mint sprigs for garnish

In a large bowl, pour boiling water over gingerroot and lemon slices. Let stand 30 minutes. Strain into large pitcher. Add lemon juice and sugar syrup (to taste). Chill until ready to serve. Serve in a tall glass filled with ice, and garnish with a sprig of fresh mint.

Sugar syrup
2 cups water
1 cup sugar
½ cup corn syrup

Combine ingredients in a saucepan and simmer for 7 minutes or until sugar is completely dissolved. Cool.

Mango Mania

MANGOES GROW WILD in the valleys on Ua Huka and Nuku Hiva. I found juicy "common mangoes" dangling from trees, so many that we filled 6 bags and didn't have to climb once. Now, that's my kind of Eden.   SERVES 4

4 ripe mangoes, peeled and seeded
1 cup fresh orange juice
1 tablespoon lime juice
1 cup yogurt
3 cups crushed ice
4 tablespoons honey or to taste, depending on the sweetness of the mango
Black pepper for garnish

Chop the mango, and pour into a blender with the rest of the ingredients. Blend until smooth, and serve in a tall glass. Garnish with a sprinkling of freshly ground black pepper.

New Zealand

FOR REASONS OF SHEER BEAUTY and extraordinary cuisine, I go to New Zealand whenever I can. The colors in the landscape there are as rich as the food. The pulsing greens of the pine forests, the dark blues in the channels, and the silver white mists that settle over the uplands are surprising to find in the South Pacific, like New Zealand's hybrid sauces and mouthwatering breads. AS WITH ALL THE POLYNESIAN islands, New Zealand was colonized by Europeans in the early 1800s, when explorers and adventure seekers roamed the world. They came to Aotearoa ("Land of the Long White Cloud," the ancient name for New Zealand) and fell in love with its rolling hills, soaring cliffs, and jagged Alpine mountain ranges. They set up farms and ranches, and imported horses, cattle, and sheep. They raised their families, and joined with the native Maori to become a new culture, one rich in Polynesian heritage and European elegance.

IN NEW ZEALAND TODAY, THERE are nearly three million citizens of British descent and only about three hundred thousand native Maori. So naturally the culinary scene is strongly rooted in British tradition.

At one time, the customs and ceremonies of the Maori were near cultural extinction, but the native people are successfully reviving their heritage. There are Maori schools that teach art, language, nationalism, and pride in Maoritanga (the Maori way of life). Along with this cultural resurgence has come a renewed interest in the foods and delicacies that were such an integral part of the lives of Polynesian ancestors.

On one of my early trips to New Zealand, I had the honor of experiencing the warm, but admittedly somewhat frightening, hospitality of the Maori.

While I was in Auckland doing guest chef appearances, Tane Wharlmate, a friend from La'ie, my hometown, rang me at my hotel. "Sam," he said. "You are so lucky. There are some amazing people who want to meet you." He was breathless.

I'd planned to catch up on my rest during this weekend. But Tane insisted. "You'll love it, Sam," he said. "We are driving up north to a traditional village. They want to give you an official Maori welcome."

Early the next morning, we loaded into his Audi. "The drive to Kakohe takes seven hours," Tane said as he picked up the speed to merge with the rushing traffic.

"Great," I said. I was so tired from the appearances and traveling.

"You can sleep on the way if you want." Tane sat to the right of me—they drive British-style, on the left side of the road. The car swerved into the stream of morning drivers. We skimmed along the freeway, a typically modern four-lane thoroughfare, two sets of double lanes moving in opposite directions.

"Aren't you going a little fast?" I asked. The speedometer on the dash read 120. I buckled my seat belt.

Tane laughed. "We're just over the speed limit," he said, pointing to the posted signs that lined the freeway. He was right, each sign read Speed Limit 100 kph. "We always drive between eighty and a hundred. We drive at sixty in residential areas," he added.

"It sounds like every man for himself," I said. Then I realized, of course, that 100 in kilometers equaled about 60 miles an hour. So I was okay, a little; it still seemed like we were going very fast. The traffic glided along smoothly, and the cars were spaced out. "Is this morning rush hour?" I asked.

"The only rush hour is from 3 to 5 P.M. The cars are bumper-to-bumper then," Tane said. "People get rather frustrated. I think in the States you call it Road Rage?"

We took a turnoff, and started driving north. "What is this thing we're going to?" I yawned. I was exhausted. The rock and tilt of the car, as we drove over the blacktop, was lulling me to sleep.

"We are going to the Kakohe Maure for a traditional Maori welcome. It's called a Powhiri," Tane said.

I was too tired to take in the Maori words. I just nodded and drifted off.

A couple of hours later I woke up, freezing. We'd obviously reached a higher elevation—the air pouring through the windows was much colder. We were driving through a forest of kauri trees that looked like giant California redwoods. The bright sunlight filtering through turned everything deep green, and the air bristled with pine scent.

Tane sat back with the driver's seat reclined a bit. He was quietly taking in the beauty of his country. "Every time I make this drive," he said, "I marvel. There's a settlement just beyond these pastures. We can get some petrol and stretch our legs. Are you hungry?"

What a wonderful question. "Hungry?" I asked. "That's a *yes*."

It was another half hour before we saw any buildings. We drove along a very windy road, riding up and down rolling hills, weaving along fences that separated lush pastures dotted with sheep and cows. "There are more sheep in New Zealand than there are people, you know," Tane said. He slammed on the brakes. "Blast," he muttered under his breath. We'd come to a sharp turn in the road, a hairpin as tight as the ones that have made the Hana road on Maui so famous. "I almost didn't make that one," he said with a smile. "Got to be a bit more careful." He smiled again. "Sorry, Sam."

I laughed out loud. "Blast?" I said. "Did you say, 'Blast'? I thought only pirates said that."

I was still laughing when we reached the top of a small hill. Stretching out below us were more pastures. From this vantage point they looked like Chinese rice paddies, square and green. A cluster of small buildings lined the road up ahead. "There is the dairy," Tane said as he accelerated downhill.

We pulled up to a small wooden building with a plank-wood porch and lace curtains in the windows. Signs were plastered all over the double doors advertising meat pies, sausage rolls, Just Juice drinks, and jet plane candies. "Dairies are all along the roads on the North Island," Tane said. He turned off the car and opened the door. "We'll buy lunch here and some munchy things for the road."

I expected to see rows of refrigerators filled with cartons of milk, slabs of cheese, and flats of eggs. They did have those, but there was so much more. It was like a quaint 7-Eleven without the smack of corporate uniformity. As advertised, there were displays of meat pies—steak and cheese, minced meat made with ground beef, and topped with a swirl of mashed potatoes, and sausage rolls that looked like familiar pigs-in-a-blanket. Next to the heated case of these meat pies were chilled sandwiches—things called "filled rolls," long hot dog buns stuffed with a minced meat mixture or egg salad, and sandwiches made with vogal bread, a dense, thickly sliced whole wheat filled with nuts.

While Tane paid for the petrol and filled the car's tank, I browsed the desserts. There were things called Lamington cakes, a yellow sponge cake dipped in chocolate icing and coated with coconut flakes, and Sally Lung's, round cakes with pink icing and coconut on top. The candy case reminded me of my father's store, but these confections were very different. Displayed in neat rows were peanut slabs, pineapple lumps (pineapple marshmallows covered with semisweet chocolate), jet planes (gummy bear–type of candies the New Zealanders call wine gum, shaped like airplanes) in assorted colors, and the famous Cadbury chocolates: maramelos, coconut crunch, raisin and nuts, milky bars, and forest lakes.

I walked to the counter and asked for a cup of coffee to help ward off the chill of the early afternoon. It seemed like it was always cold here, even in the bright sunshine.

The ice chest near the cash register was filled with drinks. Neatly stacked with labels facing front were rows of L & P's, a lemon-flavored soda with an ingredient I'd never heard of: paeroa. Next to them were drinks called Spritz and Fanta Orange Soda in bottles alongside the ever-present Pepsi and Coca-Cola cans. Fruit juices with brand names like Kordials, Raro, and Just Juice sat in a separate case next to the wire shelving that displayed the chips. There was a variety of "crunchy munchies" with names I'd never seen before: Cheezels that looked like Cheetos but heavier; Twisties, that were smaller and crunchier than Cheetos; Corn-Ups, rolled-up corn chips; and wavy potato chips like the ones we use for dipping.

Tane came back into the store and we selected some meat pies, chips, juices, and soda for the next leg of the drive. I bought bags of jet planes and Cadbury chocolates to take home for my sons and my little granddaughter. In moments we were driving over more hills as the road skirted the coast and edged along the sea cliffs. Tane pulled over to a scenic lookout on the roadside. We got out and stood on the edge of a cliff that formed a gorge, dropping 100 feet straight to the ocean below. Fresh mountain runoff poured out in a cascade from beneath a nearby bridge, the wind feathering it as it fell into the sea. The water below was so clear, its color dipping from aqua to deep blue, and you could see fish darting through the shadowy reefs.

"Your country is amazing," I told Tane.

He smiled back proudly. "I know," he said.

Back in the car, we drove for another couple of hours. "Sam, I need to tell you what they are going to do when you get to the marae," Tane said. He looked worried. "You have to pay close attention to what I'm going to tell you," he added. "This is a very serious thing, this ceremony. The Maori people take this ritual very seriously."

"They're not going to kill me?" I laughed.

Tane just looked at me, and drove on quietly.

"You're worrying me," I said. "What am I supposed to do?"

"Well, when we enter the marae," Tane said, "there'll be a young man. Traditionally, when a visiting chief came to the village, a young warrior of the chief class would meet him at the gate. His job is to size up the courage of the visitor. He'll try to scare you. You must never take your eyes off of him."

"That doesn't sound too difficult," I said.

"He'll have a spear. He'll swing the spear around, and if he doesn't like you . . ." Tane paused.

"What?" I said. "What?"

"You'll see," he said. "Just do as I say, and you'll be fine."

"He won't poke me, will he?"

"In the old days, he would kill you if he thought you were disrespectful or scared or cowardly. Just do what I tell you. Don't worry."

"I am worried," I said.

With this little bit of information tucked into my head, the drive seemed to speed up. I wasn't sure I wanted to go to this ceremony. I thought it was going to be fun, a very cultural experience, a welcoming party. I didn't think it would involve pain.

Before the sun began to set, we arrived at the Kakohe Marae, one of many in the small towns of Kakohe on the north tip of the North Island. Shadows stretched along the road as we pulled into a parking lot next to a fenced courtyard. A stylized carving of a fierce Maori face, with a tattooed chin and cheeks, peered at us from the top of the arched gate. Tane and I walked over the gravel to the edge of a grassy area. At the far end of the enclosure were three structures, two smaller buildings flanking a large house adorned with carved panels, all facing the central courtyard. I took a step forward, but Tane grabbed my arm and pulled me back. "It's very bad form to walk across the grass. It's against Maori protocol," he whispered. He was stone-cold serious. "That house to the left is the eating house, the house in the middle is the educational or learning house, and the other house is where the crafts are made. Remember, we are here for an official welcome, a Powhiri. It is very sacred to the Maori people. You are being welcomed as an honored guest. Traditionally, this ceremony would have been performed before a rival chief and his clan were allowed into the marae."

Just as Tane finished his explanation, a woman's shrill voice echoed across the courtyard. *"Haere mai! Haere mai!"* she called.

"Haere mai means welcome," Tane whispered again.

"I know that," I said.

"This is called a *karanga*. She is welcoming us and letting her people know that we have arrived."

There was a long silence, then a woman dressed in a pare, a decorated bodice, and a pupu, or black-and-white reed skirt, appeared from the side of one of the houses. When Tane saw her, he replied, *"He miki!"* He later explained that he was accepting the call and asking for safe entry.

From out of nowhere, a young Maori man wearing a chiefly pupu, with a chest band that ran from his right shoulder to the left side of his waist, sprinted toward us. His chin was tattooed with a moko, signifying his rank. When he got to within 10 feet of where we stood, he started jumping around, yelling, and making faces, sticking his tongue out and going "Baah!" He pulled a long spear called a *taiaha* from behind his back and started twirling it round and round. When he stuck out his tongue its whole length, I noticed it was tattooed as well.

Tane leaned toward my ear. "This is called a *wero*, the traditional welcome. Be careful here." All I could do was look at him and back at the young Maori. "Don't act scared," Tane said.

"I'm not scared," I told him. "What's the name of the tattoo on his tongue?" I'd remembered seeing an old Maori man in La'ie who had a tattoo like that.

"It's called a *pukana*," Tane whispered. "Don't take your eyes off this guy."

Five more young Maori warriors joined the man in the center of the courtyard. They started twirling their spears around as well. "That's his backup," Tane said, "in case you decide to fight. They will defend their marae if they have to."

Just as Tane said that, the front "welcomer" lunged forward. Both Tane and I jumped back. The spear came very close to my shoulder. He then pulled out a token gift— a war club—that he'd lodged in the back of his reed skirt, and placed it on the ground before me. As he stood, he swung his taiaha again, slicing the air beside my head.

Tane whispered, "Pick up the club. Remember to look him in the eyes the whole time."

The young Maori stood back and waited, his taiaha poised to strike.

I bent down slowly, keeping my head up so I could watch the warrior, and picked up the gift. As soon as it was in my hand, the young man jumped back and hooted, sticking out his tongue, and spinning his spear. He and his buddies backed away, still making menacing faces, until they'd reached the other end of the grass near the large house.

The gift was an 8-inch-long bone club with the traditional stylized faces of the Maori ornately carved along its length. The eyes were inlaid with *pala*, abalone shell, and it weighed about 5 pounds. I hadn't noticed, but as I was examining the club, a large group of Maori men and women, all dressed in ceremonial clothing, walked across the grass toward us.

"Well done," Tane said. "This is the official welcome. The man in the center is the high chief. We go to the *wharerunganga* now, the learning house, the big one in the center. Just follow me."

A long line of men stood at the entrance to the wharerunganga; each, in turn, removed his shoes. "It is required that everyone take off their shoes," Tane said. "When a new guest is welcomed, only men are allowed in the *wharerunganga* at first. The women are permitted in later."

The chief and another man entered the building first, then Tane and I were motioned forward. We waited just inside the threshold. Across the room stood our host, an old Maori man, and a young warrior. "The old one is the chief," Tane whispered. "Don't say anything. Let me do all the talking, and I'll tell you when to speak."

I didn't have a problem with that since I had no idea what I would say anyway.

Tane spoke, in Maori. From the expression on the chief's face, I assumed Tane was thanking him for the "warm" welcome, and for his hospitality. The old man held up a *toko*, a genealogy stick, and started speaking very rapidly in Maori. Tane leaned toward me, keeping his eyes fixed on the chief, and said, "He's reciting a *whikorero*, a speech of welcome."

When the old man finished, everyone looked at me. Tane stepped aside, leaving me alone in the doorway. "Say something," he said.

Not having a clue about what was appropriate in this situation, I decided to say what was on my mind. "Thank you," I started. "I'm so happy to meet you all. I feel welcome in your home, and for that I'm grateful. I've already learned so much about your beautiful culture. Thank you." I finished my comments with a slight bow. I don't know why I did that, it just seemed right. When I straightened up, I looked around to see if the warrior was going to charge and hit me with his spear.

Tane took hold of my elbow and moved me aside as the chief and his partner began to chant a *waiata*. The rest of the people entered the house, each smiling at me and Tane as they passed.

The evening rushed by. Groups of people from the marae took turns entertaining us with dances—the stick game, poi balls, and the *haka* (a traditional dance featuring wiggling hands and fierce faces with tongues sticking out). After an hour or so of laughing and clapping and trying to sing along to songs I didn't know, there was a lull in the program. The chief stood up and beckoned me toward the small stage in the center of the room. He spoke in Maori, and Tane translated. "We are honored to have Sam Choy join us in this celebration. It is now time for him to learn to dance in the way of the Maori."

You can't imagine the panic I felt. Two warriors escorted me onto the stage. The entire room of one hundred or more people applauded and laughed, hooting and cheering as I stumbled up the two steps of the raised platform. A group of children came forward, and the musicians started playing the introduction to a song. I was so nervous, it took me a while to recognize the melody to the Coca-Cola jingle, "I Want to Teach the World to Sing." As the audience clapped along with the guitar band, a tiny little girl about five years old walked over and stood next to me. "Just follow me," she said. "The words will tell you what to do."

The audience began to sing, "This is what you have to do, right hand up, and left hand, too. Clap those hands down, clap those hands up—together. Right foot beating, left foot still, swing those hips, it's quite a thrill. Both hands up, and both hands down—together. Together. What is it? It's the real thing!"

The song was repeated twice, and on the third time I did each of the movements without my little friend's help. By then, all the people in the *wharerunganga* were doubled over laughing.

When the song concluded, the chief stood up and invited the entire group to the *kia* hall, the eating house, for the feast. My fierce warrior friend walked the 10 yards from one house to the other with me. "The kia hall is set aside for eating only. There are never meetings or gatherings held here. Only meals," he said. He kept his eyes fixed straight forward. "The men cook the food in the hangi, the outside oven," he said. "I think you call that the imu in Hawai'i. The food in the hangi cooks for 6 to 8 hours and the cooking is timed so that the food can be taken out of the oven when the guests arrive. The older women work in the kitchen, and the teenage girls do the serving. The guest of honor is never left wanting."

With this last bit of information, we entered the great hall. There were rows of tables that ran from one end of the long, cavernous house to the other; complete table settings—plates, flatware, napkins, cups—adorned each table. Along one wall was a very large serving window with a shelf lined with platters of kina, or wana in Hawaiian (sea urchin), mussels or abalone (which I was told were traditionally eaten raw), and pipi (small clams), ready to be distributed to the guests.

"Do you think I could go into the kitchen?" I asked Tane.

"What for?"

"I'm a chef," I said. "That's where I feel most comfortable."

"Of course," he said. I followed him to the chief, whom he asked permission for the "guest of honor" to enter the kitchen. With a smile and a nod, the chief agreed.

There were women everywhere in the kitchen, some tending to large pots the size of vats that were perched on grills over open fires in the middle of the large room. Other women were removing plates, bowls, pots and pans, and cutlery from cupboards that ran the length of a long wall at the far end of the kitchen. I walked over to some older women who were pulling covered pots from the ovens. "What is that?" I asked. "It smells great."

"Maori bread," one woman said in English. Some of the old folks spoke to each other in the ancient Maori language, but most of the members of the marae used a very British-sounding English.

"Why is the bread cooked in those pots?" I asked.

"We make it with flour, water, and yeast. That's all," she said. "Then we put it into these pots after it's had a couple of days to rise."

I heard a large freezer door open, and turned to see two women walking out of a room freezer at the other end of the kitchen. Behind them I saw whole carcasses hanging on hooks.

As I watched the amazing hustle and bustle of the kitchen, the double doors that led to the backyard swung open. A group of men, carrying a length of fencing wire mounded with a large, steaming bundle of burlap, staggered into the room. With a loud thud, the men heaved the bundle onto a 20-foot-long table that lined the wall opposite the cupboards. The women dropped what they were doing, gathered at the table, and began to gingerly peel the burlap back. The room filled with the succulent, woodsy aroma of meat steamed to juicy perfection. It was a whole lamb. As they cut the meat into large steaks and placed them on serving platters, another group of men brought in more burlap bundles, much smaller than the first. The women unwrapped the individual parcels. One contained pounds of potatoes. Another was stuffed with kumara (sweet potatoes). In another, I saw pumpkins, steamed whole, and in still another, cabbage heads that had been chopped into large chunks. There were about five packages of *puha* (fiddleheads) that the women set in piles on serving platters. The pumpkins were cut into sections with the skin left on.

I went back outside to take my place at the men's table. I sat, flanked, with the chief on one side of me, and my warrior friend on the other. Young girls poured coffee and cordials (juice) into our cups, and placed tubs of softened fresh butter before each guest. "For the Maori bread," the chief said. Next came trays and trays of fresh lobster, which the Maoris called crayfish. There must have been 30 or more lobsters just for our end of the table.

The meal progressed from one unbelievable taste treat to another, until I felt like I couldn't eat another thing. I leaned back on my chair. "It is wonderful," I said to the chief.

He smiled. "The best is coming," he said. He nodded to a woman standing next to the kitchen door, and in minutes our young servers came into the room with bowls of fruit salad and ice cream. I watched as the chief scooped a helping of salad into his bowl, then topped it with the ice cream. "You must try this," he said.

I did, and I have to say that Maori ice cream has got to be the richest in the world. The cool, creamy texture seemed to float on my tongue. It was the kind of taste experience that makes you close your eyes and moan.

"Good, yes?" the chief asked.

I nodded.

"The pudding is better," he said.

Another group of girls brought out plates of what looked like steaming slices of cake, and small bowls of custard. "This is called Maori pudding," the chief said. A plate was set down in front of him. He ladled out some custard sauce, drizzled it over the cake, and handed it to me. If you don't believe in heaven, you haven't had Maori pudding. It has every texture—light, dense, coarse, smooth, heavy, creamy—all blended into a most luscious dessert.

I've been to New Zealand many times since that visit (and can't wait to go again), but I'll never forget the flavors I experienced at that amazing feast of welcome, hosted by those kind and friendly people.

There are many beautiful places in the world, but there is no doubt that New Zealand is special, and not just in terms of its breathtaking mountains, forests, and rugged coastlines. The food, cooked plain and dressed down, says it all. It speaks the truth about this stunning land and its people, the glorious variety of landscape, and the gentle boldness of the Maori and all the other races who call these islands home.

Breaded New Zealand Oysters
with Wasabi Cocktail Sauce

WASABI IS A pungent Japanese root that tastes a lot like horseradish. It's available in Asian markets in paste or powder form. Japanese restaurants are very popular in Auckland. They take pride in artfully showcasing the vast array of New Zealand seafood.   SERVES 4

2 cups flour

1½ tablespoons wasabi powder or paste

1½ tablespoons curry powder

Salt and pepper to taste

2 dozen fresh New Zealand oysters

3 eggs, beaten

6 cups panko (Japanese bread crumbs)

Oil for deep-frying

Wasabi Cocktail Sauce (see page 173)

Sift the flour, wasabi powder, curry powder, and salt and pepper together. Start the breading process by placing the oysters, one at a time, in the flour mixture, then in the beaten eggs, and last in the panko. Deep-fry in hot oil. Serve with Wasabi Cocktail Sauce.

Fresh Oyster Shooters with
Wasabi–Water Chestnut Cocktail Sauce

IT'S NO SECRET that I'm an oyster shooter lover. I'm always looking for interesting flavorings to accompany raw oysters. My standard favorites are chili pepper water and limes, but a restaurateur in Auckland suggested the addition of wasabi sauce. Great idea! **YIELDS 12 SHOOTERS**

¾ cup Wasabi–Water Chestnut Cocktail Sauce (see page 174)
12 fresh New Zealand oysters, meat only
Classic Chili Pepper Water (see page 171)
12 lime wedges

Spoon cocktail sauce in 12 shooter glasses. Next, place the fresh oyster meat in each glass. Drizzle some Classic Chili Pepper Water on the oysters. Serve with a wedge of lime.

Grilled Spice Strip Steak
with Honey-Citrus Butter

STRIP STEAKS ARE very thin cuts of tender short loin. New Zealand is known for its grass-fed beef, and this Grilled Spice Strip Steak is a delicious creation inspired by a young ranch hand on the North Island. The Honey-Citrus Butter melts into the hot meat, and adds a tart, buttery coating. 'Ono!

SERVES 4

4 strip steaks (8 ounces each)
2 tablespoons olive oil
Dash of garlic salt
Dash of paprika
Dash of chili flakes
16 slices Honey-Citrus Butter, ¼ inch thick (see page 172)

Prepare a wood or charcoal fire, and let it burn down to embers. To season the steaks, first rub with olive oil, then sprinkle with garlic salt, paprika, and chili flakes. Grill the steaks until done to your liking.

Cut each steak into 4 pieces. Place a tab of Honey-Citrus Butter on top of each piece. Serve immediately.

Lemongrass-Mussel Soup

NEW ZEALAND IS famous for its marvelous green mussels. They are imported to the United States, and sold frozen. Ask your local fishmonger to bring them in if you can't find them. They are definitely worth the asking.

SERVES 4 TO 6

1½ quarts chicken stock
4 stalks lemongrass, sliced diagonally
½ teaspoon crushed red pepper
2 cloves garlic, crushed
1 slice fresh gingerroot
1½ cups straw mushrooms
4 tablespoons Thai fish sauce
2 dozen fresh New Zealand green mussels
Salt to taste
Chopped cilantro for garnish

In a pot, add chicken stock, lemongrass, red pepper, garlic, and ginger. Simmer for 25 minutes. Add straw mushrooms, fish sauce, and fresh mussels. Cook for 10 minutes, or until the mussels open. Season with salt to taste. Garnish with cilantro. Serve hot.

New Zealand Curried Lamb Soup

IN THE SUMMER when we are basking in the sunshine, New Zealanders are in the dead of winter. They make the best soups, chock full of thick chunks of meat and densely flavored stocks. Serve this Curried Lamb Soup with slabs of Maori bread for a satisfying cold-weather meal. SERVES 4 TO 6

4 tablespoons butter
1 small onion, diced
½ cup diced celery
1 medium carrot, diced
1 clove garlic, minced
½ teaspoon fresh thyme
1 tablespoon curry powder
1 bay leaf
½ cup flour
6 cups chicken or lamb stock
½ cup diced tart apples
½ cup cooked long-grain rice
1 cup diced cooked lamb (chicken may be used as a substitute)
½ cup heavy cream or coconut milk
Salt and pepper to taste

Melt butter in a heated pot. Add onion, celery, and carrot. Sauté until the onion is translucent. Add garlic, thyme, curry powder, bay leaf, and flour. Cook for 3 minutes.

Slowly pour in stock, and stir. Simmer for 25 minutes, then add apples, rice, and lamb chunks. Cook for 20 more minutes. Add the heavy cream, and season with salt and pepper to taste. Serve hot.

Cold Rock Lobster Salad

IT IS SO interesting to me that they call lobsters crayfish in New Zealand. I shouldn't be so surprised, because in Hawai'i we call them "bugs," and that's a little strange. In my opinion, it doesn't matter what you call them, they are the most wonderful tasting seafood in the world, and the New Zealand rock lobsters are the best. Substitute any lobster meat in this recipe, they are all great.

SERVES 4

1 cup mayonnaise

1½ cups fresh chopped asparagus, blanched

½ cup green peas

¼ cup diced red pepper

¼ cup diced yellow pepper

2 teaspoons lemon juice

2 tablespoons orange juice

1 teaspoon minced orange rind

1 pound cooked rock lobster meat, shredded

Salt and pepper to taste

1 large butterhead lettuce

Tomato wedges for garnish

Watercress sprigs for garnish

In a mixing bowl, combine mayonnaise, asparagus, green peas, peppers, lemon juice, orange juice, orange rind, and lobster meat. Season with salt and pepper to taste. Clean and dry lettuce leaves, and arrange on a platter. Mound the lobster salad on the greens. Garnish with the tomato wedges and watercress sprigs.

Summer Scallop-Cucumber Salad

NEW ZEALAND IS known for its array of beautiful seafood, from scallops to shrimp, from deep-sea fish to lobster. Sea scallops are much larger, and tend to be a little chewier than bay scallops. While we were preparing for a food demonstration in Christchurch, a local vendor brought in a bushel of fresh sea scallops. I combined a quick list of ingredients, and came up with this. I call it a summer salad because it was December, New Zealand's summer season.

SERVES 6

2 to 3 medium-size Japanese or European cucumbers

1 pound sea scallops, poached

2 tablespoons lemon juice

3 tablespoons rice wine vinegar

¼ cup sugar

1 tablespoon minced fresh gingerroot

½ red pepper, cut in ½-inch dice

½ yellow pepper, cut in ½-inch dice

2 tablespoons minced cilantro

1 to 2 teaspoons sambal sauce

Salt to taste

butterhead lettuce leaves for garnish

Black sesame seeds for garnish

Peel the cucumber, and slice diagonally to a ¼-inch thickness.

In a mixing bowl, add scallops, cucumbers, lemon juice, vinegar, sugar, ginger, peppers, cilantro, sambal sauce, and salt. Marinate salad for 1 hour in the refrigerator. Serve on a bed of lettuce leaves, and garnish with black sesame seeds.

Choy's Soy Roast Leg of Lamb

IN NEW ZEALAND, they prefer their roasted leg of lamb to be rosy pink when done. The meat tends to dry if cooked too long. I've added soy sauce and minced garlic (some of my favorite ingredients) to this marinade for a little Choy flair.   SERVES 4 TO 6

½ cup soy sauce

¼ cup lemon juice

½ cup brown sugar

2 tablespoons honey

2 tablespoons dry sherry

1 tablespoon minced garlic

¼ cup chopped green onions

1 teaspoon chili flakes

1 boneless leg of lamb

Mix the ingredients together and marinate the lamb overnight, turning once or twice to marinate evenly.

Heat oven to 400°F. Place lamb on a baking rack, and cover. Roast in oven, basting every 10 minutes with the marinade, until cooked to your liking.

Remove lamb from rack, and place on a cutting board. Cut into thin slices, then transfer to serving platter. Pour marinade and drippings into a saucepan, bring to a low boil, and pour over the sliced roasted lamb.

Grilled Red Snapper with Spicy Lime Soy Sauce

THERE ARE MANY things I enjoy doing while traveling. The first, of course, is sampling the traditional foods of the countries and talking to the local chefs. The second is golfing the popular courses, and the third is deep-sea fishing. I went fishing with a friend of mine in New Zealand, and made this for him using the fish we caught off the coast near Wellington. This recipe is one of my favorites because the preparation is so simple, and the flavors blend so nicely. SERVES 4

4 red snapper fillets (6 ounces each), scaled with skin on
Cilantro leaves for garnish
4 lime wedges for garnish

Marinade
3 tablespoons lime juice
⅓ cup soy sauce
1 tablespoon oyster sauce
2 tablespoons brown sugar
1 teaspoon chili garlic paste
2 teaspoons minced gingerroot
2 tablespoons chopped scallion
2 tablespoons peanut oil

In a large bowl, combine marinade ingredients. Add fish, and marinate for 2 hours, turning occasionally. Heat the grill to medium-high heat. Grill and baste fish until done. Garnish with cilantro leaves, and serve with lime wedges.

Pork Tenderloin with Blackberries

LAMB AND BEEF are the primary meat products of beautiful New Zealand. So, you'll understand my surprise when my friends Anna and Ricky introduced me to the best pork tenderloin I've ever tasted. Fresh blackberries, picked from their backyard, were the coup de grâce of this incredibly flavorful dish. Serve this with hot rice or mashed potatoes for a rich, filling, and utterly magnificent culinary experience.   SERVES 4

8 pork tenderloins (3 ounces each)
Salt and pepper to taste
2 tablespoons unsalted butter
2 tablespoons shallots
½ teaspoon minced fresh rosemary
½ cup dry white wine
3 tablespoons blackberry vinegar
½ cup heavy cream
⅔ cup fresh blackberries for garnish
Chopped parsley for garnish

Season pork tenderloins with salt and pepper. Heat the butter in a pan, and add pork. Sauté for 4 to 5 minutes on each side, or until done. Remove pork from the pan and set aside.

Place shallots, rosemary, and the wine in the pan, and reduce by half. Add vinegar, and simmer until sauce begins to thicken. Stir in the cream, and cook for 2 minutes.

Return the pork to the pan, and cook for 2 minutes, turning to coat the tenderloin with the sauce. Season with salt and pepper to taste. Place pork on a platter, and pour the sauce over. Garnish with the fresh blackberries and chopped parsley.

Maori Barbecued Salmon Steaks

SALMON FISHING IS a very popular sport in New Zealand, a land known for its sport enthusiasts. I enjoy sharing recipes and cooking ideas with just about anyone who is interested, and while I was in New Zealand, I met many people who had family recipes they wanted to talk about. This grilled salmon recipe was a surprise. It fits so nicely into my style of cooking. Thanks, Roland.   SERVES 4

4 salmon steaks (8 ounces each)
1 tablespoon canola oil
2 teaspoons dry sherry
1 tablespoon chopped cilantro
1 teaspoon minced gingerroot
1¼ cups Roland's Not-So-Secret Barbecue Sauce (see page 173)

Rub salmon steaks with oil, sherry, cilantro, and ginger. Marinate for 30 minutes. Now rub the barbecue sauce on the steaks. Heat the broiler. Place the salmon on a rack and broil. Baste with the sauce and flip over. Continue to cook and baste until done, about 6 minutes. Serve immediately.

Mushroom-Beef Stew with Dark Ale

I LOVE THE ales from New Zealand. This recipe was originally made using one of those hardy ales, but there are so many microbreweries around our country, it'll be easy to find an ale that works for you.   SERVES 6 TO 8

2 tablespoons olive oil
2½ pounds beef chuck, cubed
Salt and pepper to taste
1½ pounds pearl onions
3 carrots, cut in ¼-inch slices
3 cloves garlic, minced
3 bay leaves
1 teaspoon chopped fresh thyme
⅛ teaspoon ground cloves
1½ pounds fresh small- to medium-size button mushrooms
¼ cup flour
½ tablespoon tomato paste
12 ounces dark ale
6 cups beef stock
2 cups chicken stock

Heat olive oil in a heavy pot, preferably made of cast iron. Season the beef with the salt and pepper. When pot is very hot, add the beef, and sear it over high heat until evenly browned. Remove meat from the pan, and set aside.

Lower the heat, add more oil if needed, and sauté the pearl onions, carrots, garlic, bay leaves, thyme, and cloves all together, about 5 minutes or until evenly browned. Add the mushrooms, and sauté for 5 minutes. Mix in the flour, and cook for 2 minutes, then add the tomato paste, and cook for 1 more minute.

Put the meat back in the pot, and add ale and the beef and chicken stocks to cover. Bring to a boil, then reduce to a simmer. Skim the top to remove floating residue and oil. Cook about 1½ hours or until the meat is fork-tender. Season with salt and pepper to taste.

Mushroom Shepherd's Pie

SHEPHERD'S PIE IS a favorite New Zealand dish that originated in the British Isles. Traditionally, it was an economical way to use up leftovers. This recipe was created after an incredible dinner with some friends from Auckland. We had Mushroom-Beef Stew with Dark Ale. The next afternoon, while getting ready to prepare a dinner for her guests, my friend's wife threw last night's stew in a pan, covered it with mashed potatoes, and popped it in the oven. The stew is what makes this well-known dish unique. SERVES 4

4 cups Mushroom-Beef Stew with Dark Ale (see page 164)
3 cups leftover mashed potatoes, room temperature
1 tablespoon vegetable oil or melted butter
1 large egg, lightly beaten
Salt and pepper to taste
Egg wash (1 egg mixed with 1 tablespoon water)
Dash paprika
Chopped parsley for garnish

Preheat oven to 350°F.

Grease individual soufflé dishes or a 9 × 9 × 2-inch gratin dish. Place beef stew in the dish and distribute evenly. In a separate bowl mix mashed potatoes with oil or butter, beaten egg, and add salt and pepper to taste. Spread potato mixture evenly over the stew.

Brush the top with egg wash, and sprinkle with paprika. Bake in 350°F oven for 35 to 45 minutes. Use a meat thermometer—interior temperature should reach 145°F. Remove from the oven, and let sit for 10 minutes. Garnish with chopped parsley.

Roast Rack of Lamb with Honey-Mustard Paste

WHEN ROASTING LAMB, a meat thermometer is the best way to check doneness. If you want your meat rare, internal temperature should reach 125°F. For medium-rare, cook to 130°F, and for medium, cook to 140°F.

SERVES 4

2 racks of lamb, 7 to 8 chops each, trimmed

1 tablespoon olive oil

2 cloves garlic, minced

1 tablespoon chopped parsley

Salt and pepper to taste

Honey-Mustard Paste

1 tablespoon canola oil

3 tablespoons Dijon mustard

2 tablespoons honey

1 tablespoon orange juice

2 teaspoons chopped fresh rosemary

1 teaspoon minced garlic

Salt and pepper to taste

1 cup fresh bread crumbs

3 tablespoons melted garlic butter

1 tablespoon chopped parsley

Salt to taste

Fresh Mint Sauce (see page 171)

Mint leaves for garnish

Marinate the racks of lamb in the olive oil, garlic, parsley, and salt and pepper for 1 hour.

Combine the ingredients for the honey-mustard paste.

Sear the racks of lamb over high heat. Remove from the heat, and cool.

Heat the oven to 450°F. Smear mustard paste on surfaces of the racks of lamb. Roast for 10 minutes.

In a bowl, mix bread crumbs, garlic butter, parsley, and salt to taste. Remove racks of lamb from the oven, and carefully pat with bread crumb mixture. Return them to the oven, and cook to the desired doneness. The crust should be golden brown.

Let rest for 5 minutes before cutting. Serve with mint sauce, and garnish with mint leaves.

Carrots and Cranberries

I LOVE THE combination of cranberries, apples, and carrots. This sweet side dish subtly complements the delicate flavor of roasted lamb. Be sure not to overcook.

SERVES 4

1 cup fresh cranberries
2 apples, grated
4 tablespoons brown sugar
½ cup apple cider
4 cups grated carrots
¼ cup (½ stick) butter

Preheat oven to 350°F.

Wash the cranberries. Mix the grated apples and cranberries, and add brown sugar and apple cider. Add carrots, and place all ingredients in a buttered casserole. Dot with butter.

Cover, and bake for 40 minutes; stir once during baking. Serve immediately.

Fresh New Zealand Sautéed Spinach

NEW ZEALAND SPINACH is a hardy plant, able to grow in colder climates where there is less water. The leaves are thicker than regular spinach, and will hold up better in a sauté. New Zealand spinach is available in specialty markets, or in farmers' markets. Plain old regular spinach works here, too.

SERVES 4

2 pounds fresh New Zealand spinach
½ cup minced garlic
Salt and pepper to taste
Roasted sesame seeds
Butter

Sauté all ingredients quickly, and serve immediately.

Maori Bread

I GOT THIS traditional Maori bread recipe from my friend Riana Mahe. She said that when Maori move away from New Zealand, they sometimes have difficulty finding the correct type of "deep pot" needed to make this delicious bread. As a viable substitute, they use a large coffee can with tin foil for the cover.   SERVES 12

1 tablespoon yeast
1½ cups warm water
1 cup sugar
4 cups flour
Honey-Citrus Butter (see page 172)

In a large mixing bowl, combine yeast, warm water, and sugar. Add flour, all 4 cups at once. Mix, then knead dough until elastic.

Grease a deep pot. Place dough in pot. Cover with a lid, and let rise for 1 hour or until dough has doubled in size.

Preheat oven to 350°F.

After dough has risen sufficiently, place in oven and bake for 45 minutes.

Open oven, remove lid, and let bread brown for the last 15 minutes. Remove bread from oven, and take out of pan. (The loaf will be in the shape of the pot.)

Wrap loaf in dampened cheesecloth to keep the crust moist. Serve hot with Honey-Citrus Butter.

Classic Chili Pepper Water

I TAKE A bottle of my Classic Chili Pepper Water with me when I travel. I know it sounds a little strange, but I'm often called upon to create dishes or do cooking demonstrations while on the road. I use it for spicing up everything from eggs and rice to steaks and stews. It's so much fun to watch people's faces when they taste this concoction for the first time. Try it. It only takes one time to get you hooked. YIELDS 2 CUPS

2 cups filtered water
1 teaspoon salt
1 teaspoon vinegar
1 clove garlic, crushed
6 medium Hawaiian (or locally available) chili peppers

Sterilize a 16-ounce bottle in a hot water bath for 3 minutes, and allow to cool a little. Bring 2 cups of filtered water to a boil. Place salt, vinegar, garlic, and chilies in the bottle. Pour the 2 cups of water into the bottle and stir. Let stand for about 3 to 4 days before using.

Fresh Mint Sauce

MINT IS ANOTHER delicacy that grows wild on New Zealand's hillsides, and it is most plentiful during the summer season (November through February). Mint sauce is traditionally served with roast lamb dishes because it brings out the flavor of the meat so well. YIELDS 2 CUPS

½ cup fresh mint leaves

¾ cup sugar

1½ cups boiling water

½ cup cider vinegar

Place the mint leaves and the sugar in a food processor, and blend. Place in a bowl, and add the boiling water. Steep for 5 minutes. Add the cider vinegar. Heat before serving.

Honey-Citrus Butter

NEW ZEALAND PRODUCES the richest, creamiest dairy products. This butter can be used on breakfast breads, pancakes, and scones, as well as meat dishes. It also freezes well, but in our house there usually isn't enough left over to freeze. YIELDS 2 CUPS

1 cup fresh orange juice

4 tablespoons honey

½ cup unsalted butter, at room temperature

1 teaspoon minced orange rind

Salt to taste

In a small saucepan over high heat, bring the orange juice to a boil. Reduce to the consistency of honey. Set aside to cool.

In a food processor, blend the orange syrup, honey, butter, orange rind, and salt until smooth. Place a sheet of parchment paper or wax paper on a work surface. Pour the butter onto a long side and form into a roll or log about 1 inch in diameter, leaving a 1-inch border of paper. Roll the butter in the paper, and refrigerate for at least 3 hours.

Poisson Cru (TAHITI, p. 225)

Fresh Oyster Shooters with Wasabi–
Water Chestnut Cocktail Sauce

(NEW ZEALAND, p. 154)

Lovo Pork in Roti (FIJI, p. 39)

Auntie Sarah's Poke Cakes

(HAWAI`I, p. 76)

Coconut Crab Cakes

(SAMOA, p. 189)

Shrimp à la Ua Huka

(MARQUESAS, p. 113)

Lemongrass-Mussel Soup

(NEW ZEALAND, p. 156)

South Pacific Gazpacho with

Baby Shrimp (TONGA, p. 263)

Outrageous
Marquesan
Beef Soup
(MARQUESAS, p. 117)

Chilled Minted
Papaya Soup
(TAHITI, p. 228)

Chicken with
Papaya and
Pineapple Salad
(TONGA, p. 264)

Tahitian
Niçoise Salad
(TAHITI, p. 230)

Apia Prawn Salad (SAMOA, p. 194)

left: Deep-fried Calamari Salad
(FIJI, p. 46)   *right:* Summer Scallop-
Cucumber Salad (NEW ZEALAND, p. 159)

Samoan Crab Salad

(SAMOA, p. 195)

Shrimp-Spinach Salad
with a Citrus Vinaigrette

(MARQUESAS, p. 119)

Mushroom-Beef Stew
with Dark Ale

(NEW ZEALAND, p. 164)

Mr. Dean's Incredible

Chicken Pilau

(FIJI, p. 52)

Gauguin Chicken (MARQUESAS, p. 122)

Capellini Pasta with Crab Sauce
(MARQUESAS, p. 123)

Queen Salote's Seafood Pot Pie (TONGA, p. 270)

Pago Pago Snapper

(SAMOA, p. 200)

Cold Trout
in Vegetable
Herb Fumet

(TAHITI, p. 232)

Spicy Suva Fried Fish (FIJI, p. 53)

Kona Oyster Mushroom with Tofu
(HAWAI`I, p. 89)

Roast Rack of Lamb with Honey-Mustard Paste
(NEW ZEALAND, p. 166)

Prawn Curry (FIJI, p. 54)

Fiji Beef Parcel (FIJI, p. 49)

Coconut Lemongrass Baby Back Ribs (SAMOA, p. 197)

Uncle Jesse's Pulehu Ribs (HAWAI`I, p. 92)

Fiji Rum Currant Scones (FIJI, p. 66)

Tropical Fruit with Ginger,
Honey, and Lime (SAMOA, p. 213)

Banana Fritters
(TONGA, p. 280)

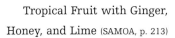

Kiwi Lime Tart

(NEW ZEALAND, p. 175)

Hawaiian Vintage
Mocha Cake

(HAWAI`I, p. 98)

Roland's Not-So-Secret Barbecue Sauce

MY FRIEND ROLAND lives on the South Island in a small town out-side of Christchurch. He is an avid salmon fisherman, and concocted this spe-cial sauce to flavor his catch. Thank you, Roland, for letting me share this great combination of flavors.   YIELDS 2 CUPS

¾ cup hoisin sauce

¼ cup plum sauce

¼ cup honey

¼ cup soy sauce

1 tablespoon tomato paste

1 tablespoon sambal sauce

2 tablespoons dry sherry

1 tablespoon curry powder

1 tablespoon minced fresh garlic

1 tablespoon minced fresh gingerroot

1 tablespoon minced orange rind

In a bowl, combine all ingredients. Store in the refrigerator until ready to use. This sauce can be stored for up to one month in the refrigerator.

Wasabi Cocktail Sauce

ADDING THE SINUS-CLEARING piquancy of wasabi makes a cocktail sauce that will spice up any shrimp, prawn, or lobster. Here's an interesting note: in New Zealand, they have the largest rock lobsters I've ever seen. The local fishermen call them crayfish.   SERVES 4

4 tablespoons wasabi powder

4 tablespoons water

1½ tablespoons fresh lemon juice

2 tablespoons soy sauce

1¼ cups ketchup

Tabasco to taste

Salt and pepper to taste

Mix the wasabi and water to form a paste. Gradually add the rest of the ingredients. Mix well.

Wasabi–Water Chestnut Cocktail Sauce

WATER CHESTNUTS ARE edible tubers that are black-skinned with white flesh and found in Southeast Asia. Canned water chestnuts are available in most national supermarkets. For a spicier sauce, add more wasabi paste to the mix. YIELDS 1½ CUPS

3 tablespoons powdered wasabi

3 tablespoons water

2 tablespoons soy sauce

2 teaspoons lemon juice

¾ cup ketchup

½ teaspoon Worcestershire sauce

½ cup chopped water chestnuts

2 tablespoons chopped onion

2 tablespoons chopped bell peppers

Mix the wasabi and water to form a paste. In a bowl, mix all the ingredients with the wasabi paste.

Kiwi Lime Tart

MY KIWI FRIENDS from the South Island make this tart with straw-berries as a festive dessert for Christmastime—that's their summer season. It looks cool and refreshing, and it's easy to make this dessert look incredible.

SERVES 8 TO 10

Crust

1½ sticks unsalted butter (6 ounces), warmed to room temperature

⅓ cup sugar

Pinch of salt

1 yolk

2 cups sifted all-purpose flour

Filling

1 cup sugar

1½ sticks unsalted butter (6 ounces)

½ cup lime juice

3 eggs

6 yolks

Zest of 2 limes

Topping

4 firm, ripe kiwi fruit

½ cup apricot jam

For crust: Preheat oven to 325°F.

Cream butter with the sugar and a pinch of salt, working just until lump-free and elastic. Do not beat in air. Add the egg yolk and blend. Stir or knead in the flour, mixing until smooth. (You don't want the dough to heat up, so work quickly.) Wrap, and chill for 30 minutes before rolling to a ¼-inch thickness. Fit into a 9-inch loose-bottom tart pan. Roll a little extra dough into the edge for support. Bake at 325°F for about 20 minutes, or until fully baked and golden brown. Cool completely before filling.

For filling: Warm the sugar, butter, and juice together in a stainless steel pot over medium heat. Meanwhile, beat the eggs and yolks well in a stainless steel bowl. When syrup just comes to a boil, add it to the eggs in a slow, steady stream, whisking continually. Return mixture to the pot, and cook on medium heat, stirring constantly until it thickens. Do not boil, or the eggs will curdle. Pour the mixture through a fine strainer into a heat-proof container, and stir in the grated lime zest. You may add a little green food color if you like, but the yellow is more natural. Spread the filling in a baked, cooled shell, and cover the surface with plastic wrap to prevent a skin from forming. Refrigerate several hours or overnight.

To finish tart: When ready to serve, remove the side of the pan. Slide tart gently onto a serving plate. Peel kiwi fruit, and slice thinly. Place fruit out on paper towels to blot excess juices and prevent tart from "bleeding." Arrange fruit in concentric circles from the outside edge to the center. Heat jam in a small pot. When the jam warms, strain, and brush it over fruit. Serve within 2 hours for best appearance.

Traditional New Zealand Trifle

THE BRITISH INFLUENCE is heavily felt in New Zealand, especially on the local cuisine. This traditional dessert showcases the fine fruits and rich cream of the country. There are several components needed to make this dessert. Purchased sponge cake shortens the preparation time. Use a clear glass dish or bowl to show off the layers and colors, and be sure to start 8 hours in advance to allow the flavors to blend.   SERVES 8 TO 10

Sabayon
6 egg yolks
⅓ cup sugar
⅓ cup dark rum
1 cup heavy cream

Strawberry puree

2 bags frozen strawberries, defrosted (juice reserved)

½ cup sugar

Papaya-liliko'i sauce

3 medium ripe papaya peeled, seeded, and coarsely chopped

1 cup liliko'i (passion fruit) juice (from about 12 fruits)

3 tablespoons fresh lime juice

½ cup sugar

Purchased sponge cake layer

2 cups diced tropical fruits (pineapple, mango, kiwi, papaya)

½ cup coconut syrup

¼ cup dark rum

For sabayon: Put the yolks and sugar in a large stainless steel bowl. Whisk until smooth, then add rum. Set over a pot of boiling water, and whisk rapidly until the mixture is thick and mounds when dropped from the whisk. Quickly chill the mixture over an ice bath, whisking until cold. Whip the cream until firm, and fold into the egg mixture. Refrigerate until ready to assemble the trifle.

For strawberry puree: Strain juice from defrosted strawberries. In a small pot, warm with the sugar over low heat until the sugar dissolves. Place strawberries in a stainless steel bowl, and pour sugar mixture over the top. Press the mixture through a fine sieve until most of the pulp and juices are extracted. Scrape any pulp from the bottom of the sieve, but discard the grayish mass inside. This puree is very bright and clear in color. You may also make the puree in the blender, but the color never seems as clear and pretty.

For papaya-liliko'i sauce: Combine papaya with the liliko'i, lime juice, and sugar in a blender. Puree on high speed until completely smooth.

To assemble trifle: Slice the sponge cake into several layers. Toss the diced fruit with the coconut syrup and rum. Spread ¼ cup of strawberry puree over the bottom of the bowl, covering the bottom. Put a slice of sponge cake on top, followed by ½ cup of fruit and juices, then ½ cup papaya-liliko'i sauce, and a ½-inch layer of sabayon. Repeat the layering until the cake, fruit, and cream are used up, ending with a sabayon layer. Refrigerate the trifle at least 8 hours or overnight. Before serving, drizzle a decorative design of leftover puree and sauce over the top.

Kiwi Lemonade

KIWI FRUIT ARE grown in New Zealand and got their name from a flightless bird that lives in the upland plains of both the North and South Islands. This adorable little fruit looks like a brown fuzzy egg but has brilliant green meat with a core of tiny black seeds and a marvelously unique flavor, a cross between melon, strawberry, and pineapple.

YIELDS 2 QUARTS

2 cups peeled kiwi fruit

½ cup fresh lemon juice

1½ cups sugar

5 cups filtered water

Fresh strawberries, sliced for garnish

Fresh mint sprigs for garnish

In a blender, puree kiwi, lemon juice, and sugar until mixed well. Add water, and mix. In a tall glass, add ice cubes and the kiwi lemonade. Garnish with sliced strawberries and a mint sprig. Serve immediately.

Minted Lemongrass Tea

LEMONGRASS GROWS WILD on New Zealand's rolling hills, and is usually used as a hot medicinal tea. I have some friends who live on the South Island. They are originally from Laos, and they combined fresh lemongrass with green tea to make a fabulous drink. I added some mint for a little zip.

SERVES 4

½ cup fresh mint leaves
4 stalks lemongrass, sliced thin
1 tablespoon green tea
6 cups boiling water
Honey to taste

Combine the mint, lemongrass, green tea, and water; simmer for 20 minutes. Strain. Add honey while tea is hot. Serve hot, or chilled on ice.

Samoa

IN THE SAMOAN LANGUAGE, the word *sa* means sacred, and *moa* means center. Look on the maps: the islands of Samoa, sitting halfway between Hawai'i and New Zealand, are believed by their people to be "the sacred center of the universe." TODAY, SAMOANS REPRESENT THE LARGEST existing population of Polynesians. They are very proud that their culture, threatened by the European colonization that nearly wiped out every other Pacific society, has survived virtually intact. Samoans kept their sacred center pretty much sacred. CHIEFS STILL RULE THE LAND. Traditions in song and dance carry on as they always have. Life—especially in the old "Western Samoa"—is still lived rather simply. THIS PLACE OF SPIKED VOLCANIC peaks

and unhurried people is divided into two distinct countries—Samoa (formerly Western Samoa, an independent nation since January 1962), and American Samoa, a territory of the United States. Although culturally and geologically inseparable, the two Samoas display some curious differences.

Samoa is an archipelago of nine islands—Apolima, Manono, Fanuatapu, Namu'a, Nuutele, Nuulua, Nuusafee, Savai'i (the largest island), and Upolu. Only five of these are inhabited. Mostly they are classic Pacific "high islands," meaning they consist of tall mountains rising dramatically out of the sea. The land is covered with dense tropical rain forests and woodlands, broken here and there by lakes and rivers that supply plenty of fresh water. Much of the land in Samoa has been cultivated, creating a strong agricultural community.

The capital city of Samoa is Apia, on the island of Upolu. The people of both Samoa and American Samoa are bilingual, speaking English as fluently as their native tongue.

Six major islands located on the eastern half of the Samoan island group—Tutuila, the Manu'a group, Rose and Sand (two atolls), and Swain—make up American Samoa. More rugged-looking than the islands of Samoa, the high volcanic peaks here jut almost directly skyward from the water, leaving little flatland area for commercial agriculture.

The capital city of Pago Pago, on the island of Tutuila, has one of the best deepwater harbors in Polynesia. Its elbow shape and the surrounding mountains create a protective barrier against the rough currents and high winds that seasonally visit the islands. This natural waterway is the reason American Samoa's main industry is fishing.

An underwater field of sunken fishing trawlers undulates beneath the current in Pago Pago's deep blue harbor. This fleet, once productive in netting huge numbers of tuna and wahoo, was sent to the bottom by a series of hurricanes.

Beyond the wrecks, a large fleet of new fishing boats lines the docks, and hugging the headlands are the massive warehouses and processing facilities of the tuna factories, the major industry of American Samoa. They produce tons of processed fish that are exported to Tonga and other Polynesian islands.

I took my son Christopher with me on this trip to Samoa. He patiently endured three days of scheduled guest-chef appearances at a number of the hotels and restaurants in and around Pago Pago, and on the final day, both Chris and I were exhausted. Our host, a very funny man named Mapusaga Fiamotu, picked us up at the hotel at 8:00 in the morning. Christopher dragged himself into the car, sat down, and quickly fell asleep.

"You have only one presentation today," Mapu said in a whisper.

All I could muster was a nod.

"I was wondering if you and your boy would like to come to my home village for *fa'aipoipoga*. My cousin's getting married this afternoon. My family would be honored to have you folks as our guests." Mapu flashed the smile of a sincere salesman. "Have you ever been to a Samoan wedding?"

"Sure," I said. "We had them back home in Hawai'i. But I'll bet they're different here."

"Oh I'm sure, yes, too," Mapu said. "Very different. They might last for days. Christopher will love to see this one. We have food to go on forever, a party forever, as long as you can think, and there is so much dancing and fun. Everyone comes, everyone. They have to shut the village down."

I remembered Samoan weddings in La'ie. Each was a community gathering involving the whole town; whether you knew the bride and groom or not, you came to party.

I looked at Chris dozing away. "Okay, Mapu," I said. "We accept your gracious invitation."

We finished my last presentation appointment at 10:30, and were on the road to the village of Fagalii, on the northern coast of the island. The highway was paved, but windy and bumpy, and I could tell that Christopher, now fully awake but very tired and grumpy, was about to explode. "How much farther?" he kept asking.

"Just around these mountains," Mapu said. "Another couple of miles." He looked at me and winked.

Samoan weddings are the biggest and best I've ever seen. Each family donates time, talents, money, and food to ensure that everyone has a fabulous time.

On the drive past Leone Bay and around the rugged coves on the western end, Mapu told us that in the past the marriages were arranged. Today, however, the man and woman make their own arrangements. They tell their parents what they want, and Mom and Dad enlist the help of the Talking Chiefs.

The wishes of both families pass through these high-ranking negotiators who are responsible for alerting the extended families of the lovers' wishes. In collaboration with the Talking Chiefs, the happy parents settle the wedding arrangements, when and where the event will take place, how much it will cost, how much and what kind of food to serve, and—most important—the assignments for money donations, the *"Fa'a Toa."*

I was learning a lot.

Christopher, on the other hand, had fallen asleep again in the backseat.

Samoan social obligations are a very complex system of payments and paybacks. Mapu explained to me that the only thing consistent in Samoan weddings is the ever-present competition between the bride's and groom's families to see who would produce the most for the hallowed event. Ultimately, the bride's family is responsible for the basic marital menu, but the Talking Chiefs negotiate what the boy's family will add.

"Talking Chiefs are very high rank and speak slightly different, in better dialect than the common, everyday Samoan language," Mapu said. "It's formal talk. Even I have to ask someone to translate when the negotiations get really fast and heated."

We turned off the paved highway and onto a rutted dirt road that curved off toward a valley. Sharp green ridges rose on either side. "Does it cost a lot to put on a wedding like that?" I asked. "I would think so."

"You know it," Mapu said. "The Talking Chiefs call a planning talk with the men of both families. At this meeting, the bride's family must provide *mea lofa*, the thank-you gifts to honor members of the boy's family. Then the Talking Chiefs discuss what's needed, and give out assignments. The first thing is what we call the *kupe galuenga* or 'working money.' This is what's used to buy food and gifts for the people who donate to the wedding."

"Wow. Wait," I said. "You feed the people who bring donations?"

"Oh, yes, of course," Mapu insisted. "Is it different in Hawai'i or America? I don't know so." He said that, I don't know so, and I understood.

"There are cooks," he told me, "assigned to make plates of chop suey, *fa'i* (cooked green bananas), roasted chicken, noodles, and rice to be handed out as a thank you for the donations. It's only good manners. They bring a gift, you give a gift.

"Anyway," he went on. "About two weeks before the wedding, the Talking Chiefs set a day for the delivery of food, money, other gifts."

"Other?"

"Most are practical, like clothing, household goods, wedding dresses, and things for the bride."

"Wedding dresses?"

"Oh, yeah," he said. "The bride might get three or four wedding dresses, and she has to wear all of them on the day of the wedding."

"Okay," I said, trying to understand. I reviewed the sequence. "First the kids tell their parents they want to get married. Then their parents get Talking Chiefs to make the arrangements. Then the Talking Chiefs call a planning meeting and assign how much money and other gifts people need to donate."

"Right," Mapu said. "And two weeks before the wedding all of the donations are brought to the bride's family's home. On donation day, the Talking Chiefs from each family open the meeting by reciting the family's genealogy. Then the donations are presented."

"So, who keeps track of the donations?"

"The Talking Chiefs agree on a *fai lautusi*. That person, the fai lautusi, is like an accountant assigned to keep track of everything, all the money, food, mats, and thank-you gifts. When each donation is presented, the bride's Talking Chief tells the fai lautusi how many plates of food, cases of corned beef, or fine mats are brought out and given as mea lofa, or thank-you tokens.

"Here's an example: if the gift is small, the Talking Chief says that the host needs to give five plates of food from the kitchen. If the donation is generous, the giver is awarded twenty fine mats."

"Fine mats?"

"Finely woven mats are very valuable in our culture. They are works of art. These mats are given as gifts at funerals and weddings, or any other type of important celebration."

We finally reached the village, and took a small side road that wound past backyards and fields of coconut trees.

"We're almost there. We'll catch up to the wedding party on their way to the church."

As we made another turn, I spotted a large group of people, all dressed in suits and dresses, walking down the middle of the road. "That's them," Mapu said. He parked on the gravel shoulder near a wooden fence, and hopped out.

A young man walked a few steps ahead of this procession, and he was chanting. "That one's the groom," Mapu said. "Listen, he's telling the story of how he courted his bride. He's led these people all the way from his village, and he'll go straight to the bride's house to pick her up."

"Who are the other people?" I asked. I was now helping Chris get out of the car.

"Members of his family. They follow along to show their support."

We trailed behind the procession to the bride's home, a simple stone-walled house with a corrugated tin roof. The young woman emerged, dressed in a stunning white gown, and followed by her own family. Then we kept on past a few more houses, the crowd having doubled in size, and we ended up at a small, white London Mission Society chapel.

The wedding that followed was typically Christian, the I do's and what you'd expect, but after that the entire congregation—bride and groom in the lead—strolled with a lot of fanfare through the village to an open *malae*, or courtyard. A bunch of tents and tables were set up, and all the fabric, linen cloths and canvas, was white.

Coconut fronds draped with garlands of flowers decorated the greeting tent. At the entrance here, on a plain uncovered table of acacia wood, sat a *pusa*, or moneybox, completely unguarded. "All the gifts given at the reception are just for the bride and groom," Mapu said. I dropped two hundred-dollar bills in the pusa.

The scene shifted to the main tent, where the guests of honor and their families, and other distinguished guests, sat on a dais at the head table. As we walked in, the bride's father, a man built like a packing crate, recognized me, got up and came over, and said, "You. Are you Sam Choy?"

"Yes," I said. "Have we met?"

"It's your books," he told me. "I have them all. Please, come and be with us." He put his arm around my shoulder and lead me up. I looked back at Chris and Mapu. A few people applauded, I don't know why. Mapu smiled, but Chris looked abandoned. He got a friendly nudge from Mapu, and then let our guide lead him to the food table. The sight of the rich dishes obviously made Christopher very happy. I think he was as hungry as he was tired.

Costumed waitresses served our table first. This was a group of exuberant young girls dressed in matching *puletasi*. They carried enormous plates piled with roasted pig, *palusami*, fa'i (cooked green bananas), taro, sapa suey (chop suey), corned beef mixed with vegetables, and lima beans.

The food was beyond fabulous. There's really nothing like the smoky flavor of a bounty of greens and succulent meat cooked in an underground oven. It's like a cascade of flavors through smoke—of herbs, leaves, dripping juices, and sun-dried local wood.

In the right-hand corner of the big tent stood two very large wedding cakes. I mean they were huge, like two Towers of Babel redone in frosting.

I was seated next to the village chief, the big authority, so I asked, "Why two cakes?"

He smiled. The sun-bronzed wrinkles got deeper on his face. "One cake is furnished by the boy's family," he said, "and the other by the girl's. There's kind of a competition to see whose is best. Which do you like?"

Each cake had six to eight tiers, glacier-white icing, and tons of sugar flowers and frosting ferns. "They're both amazing," I said.

"Every tier is reserved," the chief explained. "The first is always for the bride and groom. The second tier is for the priest who performed the ceremony, and the others are for distinguished guests, relatives who traveled far to get to the wedding. After the tiers are distributed, the rest of the cake is cut for the guests."

Before the main course was finished, the bride excused herself from the table and disappeared into a makeshift dressing room.

When she came out, she wore a different wedding dress. It dazzled, all ivory-colored and shimmering with shells or diamonds.

I thought the bride seemed newly proud and energized by the fresh dress. She strode regally through the crowd, greeting each relative or friend with a kiss on the cheek, a graceful bow.

"She's displaying gratitude," the chief told me. "She wants everyone to know she's wearing one of the honorific dresses she was given. It's a direct message without words to the family that bestowed the dress."

"How many did she get?" I asked.

We watched the bride, her light-brown skin shining against the clean taffeta and ribbons.

"Five dresses," said the chief. "She is loved in the village."

Our guide was right, the party seemed to go on forever. I left the table and went to sit with Christopher and Mapu. The bride had disappeared again.

The music stopped and the crowd turned expectantly toward the tent entrance. Their attention was drawn by the bride, dressed in a traditional Samoan dancing outfit. A fine mat was wrapped around her, and her hair was pulled up into a bun or *fa paku*. She wore a long wig of human hair, and a headband or *pale* was wrapped around her head. Her skin, doused with coconut oil, shimmered in the torchlight. Around her wrists and ankles she wore bands of croatine leaves, and around her neck was a shark's tooth necklace called a *nifo 'oti*.

"She's beautiful," I said.

Mapu smiled. "She's going to dance the *taualuga*."

The groom let out a loud yelp. He took off his shirt and wrapped a lavalava around his waist. Music started up again, guitars and strong voices, as the bride moved toward the center of the tent.

Her movements were subtle and graceful. Her groom displayed his athleticism and strength by leaping and dancing around her.

"This sometimes lasts for hours," Mapu said. "It depends on how fit the groom is."

A large group of guests approached the couple. As the bride danced, they placed money on her skin, paper bills, and tucked it into her clothing. So many bills eventually fell to the floor that the entire dance area was covered with cash.

Soon, everyone was laughing and dancing. Christopher put his head on my shoulder, a clear sign that he needed to get to bed. Just as we were about to leave, the music stopped. Both Talking Chiefs walked toward the bride and groom from different sides of the tent.

"They are thanking everyone for coming to the wedding and reception," Mapu said.

The chiefs continued on. "Now they are telling the families how the *su'a* will be distributed tomorrow."

"What's a su'a?" I asked.

"Once the wedding is over, the extra food, money, and other items are given back to the people who donated them. The Talking Chiefs meet with the families and distribute the unused items, dividing everything up, depending on the value of the person's original gift."

"The bride and groom don't keep everything?"

"No," Mapu said. We were on our way back to the car. "They only keep the gifts presented at the reception. It's a good thing. That way when other children get married, the families have enough to donate to the other weddings."

The ride back to the hotel was quiet. Christopher slept in the backseat again. Mapu focused on the rugged road to the highway.

It's always amazing to me how traditions that some modern-day people might call savage or backward really have a highly organized, very ancient structure that serves the community, conserves resources, and allows for tons of fun.

The full moon peeked through the clouds as we rumbled down the paved highway and headed toward Pago Pago.

Talofa.

Coconut Crab Cakes

COCONUT CRABS (ALSO called Robber Crabs) climb coconut palms, and using a pair of powerful pincers, they pick the coconuts from the trees, break them open, and eat them. If you've ever tried to open a coconut, you have an idea of how strong these crab claws must be. Coconut crabs can be very dangerous. They grow to a length of up to 16 inches, and can weigh as much as 9 pounds. Substituting Dungeness or Alaskan King crabmeat in this recipe works just fine.   SERVES 4

2 tablespoons canola oil

½ medium onion, finely diced

1 stalk celery, finely diced

1 pound coconut crab or lump crabmeat

½ cup unsweetened shredded coconut

⅔ cup mayonnaise

1 teaspoon Dijon mustard

2 tablespoons finely minced chives

2 tablespoons chopped parsley

5 cups panko bread crumbs

Salt and pepper to taste

½ cup flour

3 large eggs, beaten

Oil for deep-frying

Diced tomatoes for garnish

Chives for garnish

Coconut-Basil Mayonnaise (see page 206)

Heat oil in a sauté pan. Add onion and celery, and sauté until onion is translucent. Remove from heat, and set aside.

In a large bowl, mix crabmeat, coconut, mayonnaise, mustard, chives, parsley, and 1 cup panko with the onion-celery mixture. Add salt and pepper to taste. Form into 2-inch-diameter cakes.

Roll cakes first in flour, then in beaten eggs, then in the remaining 4 cups of panko, each time shaking off excess. Heat oil, and sauté the crab cakes until golden brown. Drain on paper towels.

Arrange on a platter. Garnish with tomatoes and chives. Serve with Coconut-Basil Mayonnaise.

Susanga's Unbelievable Ono

SUSANGA IS A woman who runs a little store on the island of Savaii in "Western" Samoa. She gets fresh ono (mackerel) from the fishing boats that come into the harbor. Then she makes this dipping sauce, and blows people away with how good it tastes. I know I was floored. I asked her to share her recipe. It's amazing. Unbelievable. Worth the price of this book!   SERVES 6

1 pound fresh, raw ono
1½ cups assorted sprouts
½ cup Susanga's Unbelievable Sauce (see page 210)

Thinly slice raw ono. Line a small platter or individual plates with sprouts of your choice. Arrange ono slices on sprouts. Spoon Susanga's Unbelievable Sauce over the raw fish, and serve chilled.

Teletautala Tuna Tartare

WHEN YOU CLEAN just-caught 'ahi, the bones always have a lot of meat. Get a big spoon, scoop out the meat, chop it up, and make a fine poke, like tartare. *Teletautala* is Samoan for "talk a lot." This dish is ideal for those gatherings where people are talking and really enjoying themselves. The flavor is wonderful, the texture moist and tender. The fact that you're eating raw fish in the Samoan fashion is enough to get the conversation going. SERVES 6

1 pound very fresh 'ahi (yellowfin tuna)
¼ cup minced sweet onion
Juice from 1 lemon
2 tablespoons chopped cilantro
1 tablespoon minced fresh gingerroot
1 tablespoon soy sauce
1 teaspoon olive oil
1 teaspoon sesame seed oil
1½ teaspoons grated fresh horseradish
½ teaspoon prepared stone-ground mustard
Pinch red chili pepper flakes
Salt and white pepper to taste

Cut yellowfin tuna into 1-inch cubes.

In a food processor, combine all ingredients and pulse 6 times or until of desired texture; do not puree mixture. If you don't have a processor, mince tuna with a knife to a uniformly coarse texture before combining with other ingredients.

Serve with toast points or crackers and shiso (beefsteak plant) leaves.

Chilled Peppered Mango Soup

WHEN I SAY Chilled Peppered Mango Soup, I mean almost slushy. Samoa is near the equator, and this type of soup is really welcoming on a hot summer day. The pepper will keep things spicy enough to be interesting.

SERVES 6

2 cups fresh, ripe peach mangoes, peeled and cubed

1 cup coconut milk

1 cup ginger ale

⅓ cup honey

1 teaspoon vanilla extract

2 teaspoons lime juice

Coarsely ground fresh black pepper

½ cup diced mangoes for garnish

Mint sprigs for garnish

In a blender, combine mangoes, coconut milk, ginger ale, honey, vanilla, and lime juice. Blend until smooth. Chill. Serve in frozen bowls or in half of a coconut shell. Sprinkle freshly ground black pepper onto the chilled soup. Garnish with diced mangoes and mint sprigs.

Creamy Mussel and Clam Soup

LIKE ALL BASIC seafood chowders, this very creamy, very thick soup is a favorite on chilly evenings. In Samoa they make this soup with coconut milk, but I prefer heavy cream. SERVES 6

4 slices bacon, chopped

2 tablespoons butter

1 medium onion, diced

½ cup diced celery

¾ cup diced carrots

1 clove garlic, minced

½ teaspoon minced fresh thyme

2 bay leaves

6 tablespoons flour

4 cups chicken stock

3 cups clam juice

2 medium potatoes, peeled and cubed

½ cup chopped clam meat

¾ cup diced cooked mussels

1 cup heavy cream

Salt and pepper to taste

Chopped parsley for garnish

In a stockpot, sauté bacon until almost crisp. Add butter, onion, celery, and carrots, and cook until onion is translucent. Add garlic, thyme, and bay leaves. Cook for 2 minutes more. Add the flour, and cook for 2 minutes. Slowly mix in chicken stock and clam juice. Simmer for 35 minutes, and skim soup as needed.

At this time, add potatoes, clam meat, and mussels. Cook for 10 minutes or until potatoes are cooked. Add heavy cream, and simmer for 5 minutes. Season with salt and pepper to taste. Garnish with parsley.

Apia Prawn Salad

AQUACULTURE IS REALLY taking off in the South Pacific Islands. Prawns, a much more easily controlled product than ocean jumbo shrimp, are raised to a consistent, highly marketable size. The chefs in Samoa are having a great time experimenting with prawns and their varied applications in Samoa's eclectic culinary culture.   SERVES 4

½ cup soy sauce

5 tablespoons salad oil

1 tablespoon sesame oil

1 tablespoon minced gingerroot

1 tablespoon minced garlic

2 tablespoons brown sugar

24 whole raw prawns, medium size

1 cup fresh seaweed, chopped

1 cup sliced won bok cabbage

½ cup julienned red peppers

½ cup julienned yellow peppers

1 cup sugar snap peas, blanched

½ pound mixed organic greens

½ pound cooked somen noodles

Citrus Vinaigrette (see page 133)

Cilantro sprigs for garnish

Black sesame seeds for garnish

In a large mixing bowl, blend soy sauce, 1 tablespoon salad oil, sesame oil, ginger, garlic, and sugar. Add prawns (shells on), seaweed, and won bok to mixture, and marinate for 30 minutes.

Heat 4 tablespoons salad oil in a wok. Add the marinated prawns and marinade, and stir-fry for 3 to 4 minutes, or until the prawns are fully cooked. Throw in the red and yellow peppers and sugar snap peas; stir-fry for 30 seconds.

Place salad greens on a platter and top with somen noodles. Remove prawns and vegetables from wok. Arrange cooked vegetables on the noodles, then add the prawns. Drizzle the entire salad with Citrus Vinaigrette. Garnish with cilantro sprigs and black sesame seeds.

Samoan Crab Salad

SAMOAN CRABS ARE known around the world by another name, "mud crabs." They live in the marshes and murky estuaries of Samoa's lowlands. These very large, very agile crabs are black or dark brown in color, and have rich meat. They are quite the delicacy (eaten steamed or baked) in Samoa.

SERVES 4

1 pound cooked Samoan crabmeat, or any lump crabmeat

½ cup thinly julienned sweet onion

½ cup julienned celery

½ cup julienned red pepper

½ cup julienned yellow pepper

1 cucumber, peeled, cut in half, seeded, and sliced

Iceberg lettuce, shredded

Samoan Crab Dressing (see page 207)

Chopped cilantro for garnish

Crispy rice noodles for garnish

In a large mixing bowl, combine crabmeat, onion, celery, peppers, and cucumber. Mix well, then add the shredded iceberg lettuce. Divide salad mixture among 4 chilled serving bowls, and drizzle with Samoan Crab Dressing. Garnish with cilantro and crumbled rice noodles.

Chicken and Coconut Milk

TARO LEAVES (WHAT Hawaiians call lu'au) and coconut milk are staples in Samoan cooking. Combine taro with chicken, and it's the Samoan equivalent to American meat loaf or macaroni and cheese. Working moms come home and whip this dish together very quickly. It's a Samoan down-home favorite. Serve with a bowl of hot sticky rice. Yum!   SERVES 6

2 pounds boneless chicken leg meat
2 cups coconut milk
2 cups cooked spinach or 2 cups canned spinach (or taro leaves)
Salt to taste

Cut chicken into 2-inch cubes. Place chicken in a pot. Add coconut milk, cover, and cook for 30 minutes or until tender. Add the cooked and drained spinach. Salt to taste. Simmer for 5 minutes.

Coconut Lemongrass Baby Back Ribs

BABY BACK RIBS are imported to Samoa from New Zealand and Australia. The normal starch accompaniment for a dish like this is breadfruit that has been baked and mashed—a Samoan-style mashed potato.

SERVES 4 TO 6

4 stalks lemongrass, chopped

2 tablespoons minced garlic

6 kaffir lime leaves

½ medium sweet onion, coarsely chopped

1 tablespoon sambal sauce

¾ cup honey

1 cup coconut milk

1 teaspoon turmeric

4 tablespoons fish sauce

2 tablespoons chopped gingerroot

¼ cup cilantro leaves, coarsely chopped

¼ cup basil leaves, coarsely chopped

¼ cup canola oil

Salt to taste

5 pounds baby back ribs

Blend all the ingredients, except the ribs, in a large mixing bowl. Place ribs, topside facing down, in a large bowl, and pour marinade over top. Cover, and marinate overnight in the refrigerator.

Heat oven to 400°F. Place the ribs on a roasting pan, topside down. Bake for 35 minutes, basting every 15 minutes with the marinade. Turn ribs over so that the topside is up, and continue to baste. Cook for another 35 minutes or more.

Emma's Easy Skillet Pork Chops
with Sweet Potatoes

I GOT THIS recipe in 1984 from a woman who ran a boardinghouse just outside of Pago Pago. We met at a cooking demonstration I was giving for some chefs at a resort. I had just completed a very complicated dish. She raised her hand, and in typical Samoan style told me that she had a much better recipe that took half the time to prepare. I've kept this recipe for years, and I've used it over and over again (changing it a little every time) to great reviews. To Emma, wherever you are, thank you for years of quick, easy, and absolutely fabulous chops and sweet spuds. **SERVES 8**

8 pork chops (4 ounces each)
Salt and pepper to taste
2 tablespoons vegetable oil
1½ medium onions, julienned
1 tablespoon flour
⅛ teaspoon ground allspice
1 cup chicken stock
½ cup apple juice
2 cups peeled and cubed sweet potatoes

Season pork chops with salt and pepper.

Heat a skillet, and add the oil. Fry the pork chops on both sides for 4 to 5 minutes. Remove pork chops from the skillet, and add the onions. Sauté the onions over medium heat until caramelized. Add flour and allspice, then stir for 1 minute. Add chicken stock, apple juice, sweet potatoes, and pork chops. Cover, and simmer for 25 minutes. Season with salt and pepper.

Mango-Spiced Chicken

DON'T BE FRIGHTENED off by the number of ingredients in this recipe. The marinade is easy—just salt, pepper, garlic, and ginger. The cooking liquid is a bit more involved, but still your standard "toss and stir" method. In Samoa, the Chinese influence that has been present for almost 100 years is finally seeping into the culinary mainstream of the country. The flavor and ingredient combinations are extraordinary and 'ono.   SERVES 4

1 chicken, quartered
Sea salt and white pepper to taste
2 tablespoons minced garlic
2 tablespoons grated gingerroot
¼ cup sugar
3 tablespoons water
1½ teaspoons celery seed
½ teaspoon salt
½ teaspoon paprika
2½ tablespoons lemon juice
1 tablespoon Worcestershire sauce
1 tablespoon vinegar
1 cup salad oil
½ cup ketchup
¼ cup grated onion
1 jar mango preserves
1 package onion soup mix
1 cup fresh mango, cubed
¼ teaspoon hot pepper flakes
Samoan Coconut Rice (see page 204)

Marinate chicken by rubbing on mixture of sea salt and white pepper, garlic, and ginger. Cover, and place in the refrigerator for a couple of hours.

Place chicken in a roasting pan. In a large mixing bowl, combine sugar, water, celery seed, salt, paprika, lemon juice, Worcestershire sauce, vinegar, salad oil, ketchup, grated onion, mango preserves, onion soup mix, fresh mango, and hot pepper flakes. Pour over chicken, and bake at 350°F for 45 minutes to an hour. Serve immediately over Samoan Coconut Rice.

Pago Pago Snapper

I PREFER USING red snapper for this dish, but any snapper (red, pink, or gray) or other firm, white fish will work. The harbor at Pago Pago in American Samoa is the hub of the South Pacific deep-sea fishing industry. The factories and processing plants that line the dock are able to select, clean, can, freeze, and ship out an entire catch in a day. This recipe has a definite Choyesque flavor.

SERVES 4

2 large tomatoes, seeded and skinned, finely diced

6 tablespoons seeded and finely diced green pepper

6 tablespoons seeded and finely diced red pepper

6 tablespoons seeded and finely diced yellow pepper

¾ cup skinned, seeded, and finely diced fresh papaya

¼ cup grated gingerroot

Juice from 1 lemon

3 pitted black olives, diced

Freshly ground black pepper and salt to taste

½ cup olive oil

1 to 2 sprigs cilantro

1 to 2 sprigs basil

1 to 2 sprigs tarragon

4 chives

1 to 2 sprigs thyme

4 pieces (4 to 5 ounces each) red snapper

¼ cup vegetable oil

In a large bowl, add the tomatoes, peppers, papaya, ginger, lemon juice, black olives, pepper, salt, and olive oil. Let sit covered for 3 to 4 hours outside of refrigerator.

Remove the stems from the cilantro, basil, and tarragon, and coarsely chop. Cut chives into 1-inch lengths. Add chives to chopped herbs, and set aside.

Remove thyme leaves from stem. Season fish with salt, pepper, and thyme leaves.

Add ¼ cup oil to a large saucepan, enough to cover bottom. Over medium heat, add the fish, and cook for 1 minute on each side.

Place the fish on a serving platter, cover with the tomato-pepper mixture, and sprinkle with the chopped herbs.

Sole's Favorite Peppercorn Rib Roast

IN SAMOAN, THE word *sole* is pronounced "SOH-lay," and it means "man." This hearty rib roast is an absolute favorite among my male friends in Samoa. Since nearly one-sixth of the population in Samoa is of Chinese descent, the ingredients are very easy to find. In the United States, these ingredients can be picked up at any Asian market.   SERVES 6 TO 8

2 tablespoons vegetable oil

8 cloves garlic, minced

2 teaspoons chopped rosemary

4 pounds beef rib roast

2 tablespoons Szechwan peppercorns, coarsely cracked

1 tablespoon cracked black peppercorns

2 tablespoons rock salt

½ teaspoon Chinese five-spice powder

3 tablespoons brown sugar

Star Anise Beef Jus (see page 209)

Honey Mustard–Ginger Sauce (see page 208)

Heat oven to 350°F.

In a small mixing bowl, combine oil, garlic, and rosemary, and rub onto rib roast. Place meat into roasting pan.

In a separate bowl, combine peppercorns, salt, five-spice powder, and brown sugar. Firmly pat spice mixture on top of the rib roast. Roast for 1½ hours or until done to your preference.

Transfer meat to a cutting board, and let it stand for 15 minutes before slicing. Serve with Star Anise Beef Jus and Honey Mustard–Ginger Sauce.

Palusami

PALUSAMI IS ONE of my favorite Samoan dishes. It is a mixture of onion, salt, and coconut cream wrapped up in taro leaves, then baked. In Polynesia, taro leaves are used in many different types of dishes. This culinary staple can be steamed, roasted, or boiled with any combination of meat or vegetables. Substituting spinach leaves for taro leaves works fine. Be careful not to overcook the spinach.   SERVES 8

20 taro leaves (or 2 pounds of fresh spinach leaves), cleaned and patted dry
2 medium onions, diced
Salt and pepper to taste
2 cans coconut milk (8 ounces each)

Preheat oven to 350°F.

Line the bottom of a 9 × 13-inch pan with taro (or spinach) leaves. In a large mixing bowl, combine onions, salt and pepper, and coconut milk. Stir for 15 seconds, or until blended. Pour coconut milk mixture into pan, covering taro leaves. Cover pan with aluminum foil, and place in 350°F oven for 15 to 20 minutes or until tender.

Samoan Coconut Rice

I CONCEDE THAT this is a very rich side dish, and that it would take a special type of main dish to blend well with the combinations here. But once you taste this fabulously exotic recipe, you'll do what I did. I went out looking for something that would match well. This is truly 'ono-licious.   SERVES 4

2 cups Basmati rice
1 cup coconut milk
1 cup chicken stock
½ cup diced onion
Shredded unsweetened coconut for garnish
2 tablespoons Ginger Pesto (see page 206)

Rinse rice, and drain. In a rice cooker, combine rice, coconut milk, stock, and onion. After rice is cooked, sprinkle with shredded coconut, and dollop with a little Ginger Pesto.

Slaw from Samoa

GERMAN SAILORS, LURED by the call of Samoa's beautiful islands and warm climate, immigrated there in the 1800s. Of course, they brought with them their love for stout beers, spicy sausages, and tart cole slaw. Here's a recipe from an old German/Samoan family I met in Samoa. This cole slaw is always a hit at my barbecues.   SERVES 4

4 cups cabbage, shredded
8 stuffed olives, sliced
¼ bunch watercress
1 tablespoon chopped pimiento

¼ cup chopped green pepper

1 teaspoon salt

¼ teaspoon pepper

½ teaspoon dry mustard

1 tablespoon celery seed

2 tablespoons sugar

3 tablespoons salad oil

⅓ cup vinegar

Place cabbage, stuffed olives, watercress, pimiento, and green pepper in a large bowl. Cover, and chill. Place salt, pepper, dry mustard, celery seed, sugar, salad oil, and vinegar in a jar. Cover. Before serving, shake jar, and toss vegetables with sauce. (For crunchy cole slaw, cut cabbage in half and soak it in salted ice water for about 1 hour; drain well. Chill cabbage, and slice into thin strips.)

Umala Wild Rice

LIKE MOST OF the food in Samoa, wild rice and long grain rice are imported from Australia. I am always drawn to interesting texture and flavor combinations, and this one is really unique. The grainy texture of rice, the crunchy, nutty wild rice, and the soft texture of the sweet potatoes are really intriguing.   SERVES 6

½ cup chopped onion

2 tablespoons butter

1 box long-grain and wild rice (6 ounces)

2¼ cups chicken stock

½ pound sweet potatoes or yams, cooked and cubed

In a medium saucepan, sauté onion in butter until translucent. Stir in long grain and wild rice. Add chicken stock. Bring to a boil. Cover tightly, reduce heat, and simmer for 25 minutes or until liquid is absorbed. Stir in sweet potatoes, and serve.

Coconut-Basil Mayonnaise

THIS SAUCE HAS the consistency of a rich tartar sauce, but the flavor of sweet basil, coconut, and garlic. It's great as a dipping sauce for any white fish, shrimp, or crab. 			YIELDS 1½ CUPS

1 cup mayonnaise
½ cup unsweetened shredded coconut
1 tablespoon lime juice
1 tablespoon basil, chopped
1 teaspoon chili garlic paste
Salt and pepper to taste

Combine all ingredients in a mixing bowl, and whisk until smooth. May be prepared a day ahead, covered, and refrigerated. Bring to room temperature before serving.

Ginger Pesto

IN SAMOA, A fascinating regional cuisine is emerging. It is a combination of traditional Samoan with English, German, and Chinese. All of these cultures have successfully blended into the landscape of this beautiful island country. Young chefs are finding new and innovative uses for ingredients like ginger. This is one of my favorite pesto recipes. 			YIELDS 2 CUPS

½ cup vegetable oil

½ teaspoon salt

¼ cup minced gingerroot

¼ cup minced green onions

¼ cup lightly packed minced cilantro

⅛ teaspoon white pepper

Place all ingredients in a food processor; pulse until blended.

Samoan Crab Dressing

I AM A crab lover, and if crab is on the table, I'm ready to start cracking, right then. It's too hard to wait for a complicated dressing to be made. So here's a really quick, really simple recipe for crab salad dressing that takes no time— measure, toss, and mix.   YIELDS ¾ CUP

3 tablespoons rice wine vinegar

¼ cup peanut oil

2 tablespoons lemon juice

4 tablespoons sugar

2 teaspoons finely grated gingerroot

1 tablespoon roasted sesame seeds

3 tablespoons light soy sauce

Combine all ingredients. Mix well. Bring on the crab.

Honey Mustard–Ginger Sauce

THE NATURAL SWEETNESS of honey and orange provide an interesting counterpoint to the mustard and ginger flavors in this sauce. Its sweet-sour piquancy is great with any meat dish, and delicious as a sandwich spread.

YIELDS ½ CUP

¼ cup Chinese mustard

3 tablespoons honey

1 tablespoon orange juice

1 teaspoon juice from fresh grated gingerroot

Mix all ingredients together in a small mixing bowl. Store in the refrigerator until ready to use. Serve at room temperature.

Star Anise Beef Jus

THE JUS CAN be thickened slightly with cornstarch and water. The consistency of the jus should be on the thin side, just slightly coating a ladle. This jus can be stored in the freezer for up to 6 weeks. YIELDS 4 CUPS

2 tablespoons vegetable oil

½ medium onion, diced

¼ cup diced celery

½ cup diced carrots

1 clove garlic, crushed

1 teaspoon black peppercorns

2 bay leaves

1 teaspoon fresh rosemary leaves

1 sprig fresh thyme, about 3 inches long

2 parsley stems

2 pieces star anise

1 tablespoon tomato paste

½ cup dry sherry

5 cups beef stock

1½ cups chicken stock

Salt to taste

Heat oil in a pot, and add onion, celery, and carrots. Sauté until onion is slightly golden brown. Add garlic, peppercorns, bay leaves, rosemary, thyme, parsley, and star anise. Sauté for 2 minutes, then add tomato paste. Cook for 2 more minutes, then add the sherry, beef stock, and chicken stock. Simmer for 1 hour and 15 minutes. Skim the top of the jus occasionally. Strain jus in a cheesecloth-lined fine strainer. Season with salt and pepper to taste.

Susanga's Unbelievable Sauce

THE CHILI PEPPER really spices up this dipping sauce. Use it when serving any raw fish sashimi-style. It brings out the best flavor of the fish, and adds a little zing.

YIELDS ¾ CUP

½ cup vegetable oil
½ teaspoon salt
1 clove garlic, minced
¼ cup minced gingerroot
¼ cup minced green onions
¼ cup minced cilantro, lightly packed
⅛ teaspoon white pepper
¼ teaspoon minced chili pepper

Heat oil in a small saucepan. Add salt, and cook for 2 to 3 minutes. Cool. Stir in garlic, ginger, green onions, cilantro, white pepper, and chili pepper. Serve chilled.

Mary Jane's Killer Pineapple Pie

MARY JANE ESERA teaches high school math, and we all know what a difficult job that can be. In her spare time, she comes up with outstanding recipes like this Killer Pineapple Pie that is just as juicy and tasty as those found in vendor carts on the streets of Pago Pago. Be careful with the juices. They get really hot.   SERVES 8

1 can sweetened crushed pineapple with juice (8 ounces)
1 can sweetened pineapple chunks with juice (8 ounces)
1 cup sugar
¼ cup butter
1½ teaspoons cinnamon
½ teaspoon nutmeg
¾ cup water
¾ cup flour
Preformed 2-crust pie shell

Preheat oven to 375°F.

Combine crushed pineapple and pineapple chunks in nonreactive saucepan over medium heat. Add sugar, and stir until dissolved. Stir in butter until melted. Add cinnamon and nutmeg, stirring continuously until spices are completely incorporated into the mixture.

In a separate bowl, whisk water and flour together. Strain if mixture has lumps. Add to pineapple mixture, and cook over medium heat for 10 to 15 minutes, stirring constantly, until thick. Place mixture in 2-crust pie shell. Bake for 45 minutes.

Traditional Samoan Fausi

FAUSI, A SAMOAN dessert, is traditionally made from steamed taro. But outside of Samoa, pumpkin is commonly used. Look for Japanese Kabocha or sugar pumpkins. They are remarkably sweet, with lower moisture content than many commercial varieties, and produce a smooth, creamy puree.

SERVES 6

1 medium pumpkin, preferably Kabocha or other sugar variety

1 tablespoon canola oil

1 cup sugar

¼ cup water

1 can coconut milk (14 ounces)

Preheat the oven to 375°F.

Cut the pumpkin in half, and scoop out the seeds. Lightly oil a baking sheet, and put the pumpkin halves on it, cut sides down. Bake until very tender. Time will vary depending on the size of the pumpkin.

While the pumpkin bakes, put the sugar in a medium-size heavy-bottomed pot with ¼ cup of water. Stir just to blend, then bring to a boil over high heat. Cook until sugar caramelizes to a rich golden brown. Add coconut milk all at once, making sure to stand back as the mixture will bubble up and spatter violently. *Be careful of steam vapors!* Swirl mixture until bubbling subsides, then stir over heat for a minute or two to dissolve any remaining bits of hard caramel on the bottom. Set sauce over ice, whisking occasionally to cool. Set aside at room temperature until ready to serve. (Any leftover sauce may be stored in the refrigerator and used later or with other desserts.)

When pumpkin is tender, scrape the pulp into the bowl of a mixer or food processor. Pulse to mash or puree until smooth. Serve warm with some caramelized coconut sauce. Bring to room temperature to serve.

Tropical Fruit with Ginger, Honey, and Lime

A TRIP TO the farmers' market will inspire you when making this dessert compote. Be sure to look for fruits that provide contrasting color and texture when making your selection, and don't be afraid to try something new! Choose at least five different fruits like sunrise papaya, white pineapple, star fruit, red grapefruit, kiwi, apple banana, or mango. You can serve the compote with a scoop of frozen yogurt, a slice of angel food cake, or simple cookies if desired, but it is both beautiful and delicious alone.   **SERVES 8**

6 cups peeled, seeded fresh tropical fruits cut into bite-size pieces
½ cup honey
½ cup water
1-inch piece of peeled gingerroot, crushed
¼ cup fresh lime juice, or to taste
Strips of fresh coconut for garnish (optional)

About 1 hour before serving, combine the fruit in a nonreactive bowl.

In a small saucepan, bring the honey, water, and ginger to a boil. Simmer for 1 minute, remove from heat, and add lime juice to taste. Pour the hot syrup over the prepared fruit, and fold very gently with a rubber spatula, being careful not to break up the soft fruits. Cover, and let stand at room temperature for no less than 1 hour, but no more than 3 hours. Garnish with coconut strips.

Kalofai Coffee Shake

THE SAMOAN SLANG *kalofai* means "Oh, too bad. I'm sorry for you." This great-tasting drink is comforting in texture and flavor, and it has the nice little kick of Kahlùa and rum. Even without the "hard stuff" it's a winner.

SERVES 2

½ cup coffee, double strength

2 tablespoons rum

1½ tablespoons Kahlùa

1½ cups milk

3 cups vanilla ice cream

2 tablespoons chocolate syrup

Whipped cream for garnish

Chocolate sprinkles for garnish

Mix all ingredients in a blender and whip until thick. Serve in a hurricane glass, topped with whipped cream and chocolate sprinkles.

Sparkling Guava Punch

GUAVA TREES GROW on many of the South Pacific Islands. The guava fruits are usually eaten raw. Everything but the stems is edible. The pink flesh is sometimes scooped out and strained to make guava nectar. Fresh guava is wonderful for this drink, but commercially produced guava juice will do the trick. YIELDS 6 CUPS

2 cups guava juice
1 cup pineapple juice
½ cup orange juice
1 tablespoon lemon juice
½ cup sugar
1 teaspoon grated orange rind
3½ cups chilled ginger ale
Lime slices for garnish

Combine the juices and the sugar. Chill. Before serving, fill glass pitcher with ice. Pour in chilled fruit juices, orange rind, and ginger ale. Stir to blend. Garnish glasses with lime slices.

Tahiti

THE ISLAND OF TAHITI is the largest in French Polynesia, with a surface area that covers 402 square miles. Mountain peaks as high as 7,353 feet rise into wisps of drifting clouds, and deep green tropical valleys pulse with rain-forest flora and steaming waterfalls. Whenever people talk about "paradise," they picture Tahiti. **THE ORIGINAL POLYNE-SIANS WHO SETTLED** these islands are the Maohi, who were part of the thousand-year-long migration that slowly spread from Southeast Asia to all the islands of the Pacific. Over the past hundred or so years many other nationalities have come to the beautiful islands of French Polynesia, and today with the help of interracial marriage Tahitians claim French, Chinese, European, and Polynesian ancestry. Many believe that this mingling of bloodlines is the reason Tahitians are so 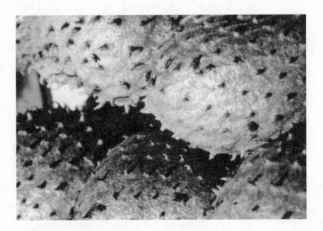 beautiful. I think it's because they are friendly and fun-loving, habitually taking in the relaxing, tropical atmosphere of their island. **TODAY, ABOUT 70 PERCENT OF TAHITI'S** population are Polynesian (Samoan, Tongan, Fijian, Hawaiian, and Tahitian), 12 percent European,

10 percent a Polynesian-European mix, 5 percent Chinese, and 3 percent Polynesian-Chinese. All are citizens of France.

The official languages of French Polynesia are French and Tahitian, and English is taught in most of the schools.

I travel to Tahiti whenever possible, but my favorite season to visit is the temperate months from May through October. Tahiti is one of the Windward or Iles du Vent islands within the Society Island group that includes Moorea, Bora Bora, Huahine, and Raiatea.

Before the arrival of people, the island of Tahiti and the other Society Islands had plenty of freshwater, captured by the porous volcanic rock, and funneled into mountain streams and pools. Vegetation was limited to plants carried as seeds by the ocean currents and sea birds. The surrounding reefs and ocean were, and are today, filled with angelfish, bonito, butterfly fish, eels, groupers, harp fish, jacks, mahimahi, mullets, parrot fish, sharks, soldier fish, stingrays, surgeonfish, swordfish, trumpet fish, tuna, and countless more.

Polynesians were great voyagers. They sailed to Tahiti on double-hulled canoes, steering with huge paddles and pandanus sails. With them they brought pigs, dogs, chickens, lizards, taro, sweet potato ('umara), coconuts (miti), bananas (fe'i), and breadfruit ('uru). Later, missionaries and settlers from Europe and America introduced cattle, chickens, pigs, corn, cotton, sugarcane, citrus fruits, tamarinds, pineapples, guavas, figs, coffee, avocados, mangoes, papayas, custard apples, bananas, pamplemousse (a kind of grapefruit), oranges, and other vegetables. Even later, other trees and plants were introduced: kauri from New Zealand, red cedar, eucalyptus, rubber, gum, and jack trees.

I scheduled a trip to Papeete so I would arrive on the morning of July 13, the day before Bastille Day, a French national holiday celebrating the storming of the Bastille in 1789, and the overthrow of Louis XVI. Here in Tahiti they call it Fete du Quatorze Juillet, or the Celebration of July 14, but it really lasts the entire month of July. I'd heard so much about Bastille Day in Tahiti, with parties that rivaled Mardi Gras in New Orleans. It was one of those experiences you should feel with all your senses.

I arrived as the sun was setting. Lights were gleaming yellow, romantically taking over the fading sunlight. I took a cab—an elaborately decorated, open-air jeep bristling with purple dinker-balls—to a hotel on the other side of town. We drove past the harbor, where international cargo freighters, copra ships, and sailing ships bobbed in their moorings, then we traveled along a tree-lined waterfront promenade for a few miles. This marina is popular with the yachting community. Tethered to a string of floating docks, million-dollar boats rock gently in the harbor swells.

At the hotel, I asked the man at the front desk about local restaurants, and which were his favorites. He said he had many favorites (a very French response). "There are several excellent places to eat," he said. "You can have French, Italian, Chinese, Vietnamese, Japanese, and American. Whatever you like. You can go downtown and eat at one of the roulottes. The food is good. Many people like it."

I later learned that roulottes, small food trucks, lined the streets of downtown Papeete at one or two o'clock (after naps), then again after dark. They look a lot like the lunch wagons we have in Hawai'i. But my friend at the front desk assured me they didn't serve lunch. "There are no lunch wagons here," he said. "At lunchtime, people sleep. It is hot. Everyone leaves their offices and goes home for a nap. What is it they say, 'Only dogs and crazy Englishmen go out in the hot sun'?" He laughed at his joke.

I asked about the Bastille Day celebrations, and he handed me a brochure. The fold-out pictures were scenic shots of the island of Tahiti. "You are from Hawai'i, yes?" he asked, leaning over the counter to point at the photo. "The island of Tahiti looks like your island of Maui."

It did. There were two bulbous mountain regions on either end of the island, with an isthmus, but a very narrow one, connecting them. "I see," I said.

"Yes," he said. "We have a road that goes all the way around. It is 113 kilometers (or 71 miles) long and it runs between the mountains and the sea. The big section of the island is called Tahiti-Nui." It was obvious he was very proud of his country.

"Big Tahiti," I offered.

"Correct," he said. "And the small part is called Tahiti-Iti."

"In Hawai'i we would call it Tahiti-Iki, for little Tahiti."

"Yes," he said, grinning and nodding. "Are you planning to travel the island?" he asked.

"I'm only here for a couple of days. Maybe I should focus on the celebration."

"You can go to the interior of the island," he said. "You will see many beautiful places. There are dairy farms and citrus groves, and fantastic views from the Plateau of Taravao between Tahiti-Nui and Tahiti-Iti. You would like it very much."

"I was told to ask for a street view," I said. "I heard that in the morning, the parade comes down this road. I'd like to watch it from my room."

"I am so sorry, sir," the clerk said. "We have no more street view rooms." He looked sincere. "I do have tickets to the black tie dinner and ball tomorrow night, though. It is the best in all Tahiti. It is the best part of the celebration. I take my wife. We will see you there."

In the morning, I joined the crowds that packed the boulevard. The parade was fabulous, with flower-decked floats, South Pacific–style marching bands, floats with dancers and drummers and some with guitar-playing musicians. I always knew that music was a big part of Tahitian life, but the sounds of the rapid *toere* drum and happy singing made me love it too. It was the whole experience that captured my heart, the morning heat, the children walking along the sidewalk with shaved ice cones and cotton candy, the harmonies in the air, and the smell of sweet *tiare* flowers. I was glad after all that my room had a mountain view, and I was forced to come out and be a part of such a scene.

Returning to the hotel, I stopped for a late lunch at a little café. I ordered their Tahitian Niçoise Salad, a colorful combination of fresh peppers, tomatoes, sweet potatoes, and greens, topped with 'ahi (yellowfin tuna) steaks and Niçoise olives. I'm not a drinker, but I looked over a wine menu. Tahitians import wines from France, and the selection in this little café was surprisingly sophisticated.

Across the street from the café was a little park where a group of musicians performed as part of the Bastille Day festivities. They played reggae music with a Latin flair, French lyrics, and Tahitian subject matter. They sang of the mountain streams, their love of the sea, and their love of life. I commented on the music when the waitress brought my food. She said, "Oh yes. They are very good, but the best place to listen to Tahitian music is the festival grounds."

So I made the fair my next stop. I could hear the music a street away. Then I saw the lights. The fairgrounds featured typical carnival scenes, with rides of every kind, folks waiting to play games or get food from vendors, and children in shorts and scruffy T-shirts walking with their *nunu* (nannies).

At the far end of the grounds stood an open-air pavilion where a band made up of eight musicians played guitars, a bass, and lots of drums. A troupe of female dancers, about twenty or thirty of them with the traditional bright headdresses and low-slung grass skirts on their hips, danced in single file from both sides of the makeshift stage, and spread out into lines in the grassy field in front of the musicians. The dancers did the fast-moving Tahitian *tamure*, that most famous exotic dance of gyrating hips. With a shout from one of the male singers, a large group of men, also wearing grass skirts, ran into the middle of the dancing women. They whooped and yelled, doing a kind of "funky chicken" around the women.

A young flower girl approached me. "You like buy?" she asked, holding up a basket of fragrant tiare.

"Sure," I said. I selected one of the delicate blossoms, and placed it behind my right ear. The little girl laughed. "You are available?" she asked, pointing.

"What?" I said.

"A flower behind the right ear means you are available. You are?"

"No." I laughed. I took the flower and placed it behind my left ear. "I'm married."

The Tahitian people love flowers and leis of all kinds. They wear them all the time. It's not unusual to see a man dressed in a business suit walking down the street with a flower tucked neatly behind his ear, or a woman in a Sunday dress with a wreath of flowers around her head.

The fairgrounds opened to a broad beach where canoe races were in progress. It was now late afternoon, the sky turning yellow. A small kiosk stood between the fairground crowds and the race spectators. "Soixante-dix franc!" called the ticket clerk. I did some quick figuring, and it cost less than a dollar to watch the races. I paid my money and walked through the gate. Canoes painted in striking reds and blues lined the beach, one-man, two-man, three-man, and teams of up to sixteen men waited their turns to get into the water. It was a sprint to the finish line marked by colored flags bobbing on buoys anchored offshore.

On the other side of the fairgrounds the *Course aux fruit,* a race where people sprint to a finish line with 20-pound baskets of fruit on their backs, was about to begin. And later, a javelin-throwing contest was scheduled. I walked to the competition grounds and saw the javelin target, a red-painted coconut tied against the trunk near the top of an 80-foot-high coconut tree.

I picked up a brochure (written in French) that described the other Bastille Day activities: more canoe races, a Tahitian dance competition, more javelin contests, and a bicycle race through Papeete, à la the Tour de France. The brochure also gave the rules for the government lottery, which was held each day. The lottery was simple and modest. With the spin of a roulette wheel, people could win a new *pareu* (cloth wrap), a blanket, or a stuffed animal. Even small children were invited to enter.

Evening settles in early this close to the equator. At 6 P.M. I was in a cab, dressed in my finest, and on my way to the Pavilion for the Bastille Day dinner and ball. This was an adults-only affair at a cost of $100 (American) per couple. There isn't a discount if you go it alone.

I got out of the cab and walked up the stairs of the grand building. Lively music blared out of the opened double doors. Inside, against the walls were tables covered with serving platters of every kind of food. I guess I was easy to pick out among the other guests, because as soon as I entered the room, my hotel clerk friend sauntered up to meet me. "Bonsoir," he said with a big smile. "You made it."

I smiled back. "I guess I did," I said. "What do we have here?"

"This is the first course," he explained. "The dinner is much like a traditional French meal." We walked around and looked at all of the tables. "In a little while the platters will be taken away, and the second course will be set out. Would you like something to eat?" He was a great host. He took my elbow and led me through the crowd, introducing me to people along the way. The first course was made up of appetizers: shrimp, oysters, and clams. He picked up an oyster. "This is my favorite," he said. He grabbed a Tahitian lime from a plate, pried open the oyster, and squeezed the lime juice inside. He then scooped out the meat, and with a grin, slid it into his mouth. "You try," he said. "It is the best."

After we'd made our rounds, sampling sautéed shrimp and steamed clams sautéed in garlic butter and served with slices of baguette, a group of waiters whisked the platters away, and replaced them with the next course: the Main Dish.

There were slabs of filet mignon, Cuire au Poisson (a white fish steamed in Tarragon-Mustard Vinaigrette), and Chicken Fafa (slices of chicken breast steamed in an earth oven with onions, sweet potatoes, and taro leaves). Everything was "broke the mouth" tasty.

After the main course came the salad, then the cheese (always imported from France and New Zealand), then the wine, and finally the dessert.

When the last platters were taken away, the light dimmed, and the band started up. The highlight of the evening is always the introduction of Miss Tahiti and Miss July. Traditionally, Miss Tahiti and the mayor of Papeete start the ball with a waltz.

"How do you eat all of the stuff and have enough energy to dance?"

"That is why we eat," he said. His smile was infectious. "So we have strength to dance all night." And he did. As soon as the floor was open, he took his wife's hand, and they went out to the middle of the room. That was the last I saw of them. I assume they tripped the light fantastic into the next morning.

I stayed for over an hour, and when I had just decided to leave, the lights came on and a large group of Tahitian dancers swirled into the room. I couldn't believe my luck. I love to watch Tahitian dancing. It's so exciting and beautiful, just like the islands. I could only stay a little while longer because my ship was leaving early in the morning, and I had to get some sleep. But the colorful dancers—their hips wobbling about a hundred miles an hour, the grass skirts making S-shapes with the motion—left me with a great sendoff.

That was my only experience with Bastille Day in Tahiti. I had wanted to go back some other July and give it a good shot with more time to spend, maybe take my family down there, but my schedules never worked out. Then a couple of years ago, I heard that the Tahitians, in an effort to distance themselves from the French government, stopped celebrating Bastille Day altogether. There are still parties beginning in late June and lasting through July 14, however. Instead of Bastille Day, the Tahitians celebrate Te Heiva or Te Tau'urua Tiurai. Leave it to the spirit of the place to keep the parties going, no matter what the occasion is called.

Tahiti will always be a place of sumptuous revelry, and I can't wait to get back.

Adieu, mes amis du gastronomie.

Oyster Poor Boy

RAW, FRESH OYSTERS are a favorite appetizer in Tahiti. Usually, they are pried open, drizzled with lime juice, scooped out, and swallowed. To those who would like their oysters a little more refined, I offer my Oyster Poor Boy recipe.

SERVES 4

7 fresh large oysters
Cajun spice, to taste
½ teaspoon Tabasco sauce
White pepper to taste
1 cup flour and cornmeal mixture
1 quart peanut oil
French bread
Spicy Poor Boy Sauce (see page 242)
Sliced green onions, tomatoes, and lettuce, as desired

Season oysters with Cajun spice, Tabasco, and white pepper. Dust lightly with flour and cornmeal mixture. Deep-fry in peanut oil. Set cooked oysters on paper towels to drain.

Cut the French bread in half, and scoop out the center. Spread Spicy Poor Boy Sauce over bread, and fill with oysters. Add green onions, tomatoes, and lettuce.

Poisson Cru

POISSON CRU IS a traditional Tahitian dish with a French name. Raw fish cooked with the acid in Tahitian lime juice is mixed with cucumbers, tomatoes, onions, peppers, and coconut milk. For those with a weak stomach, fear not. This isn't raw fish, and it tastes wonderful. Don't let the name scare you. Try it.

SERVES 6

1½ pounds fresh 'ahi (yellowfin tuna), cut into ½-inch cubes
½ cup lime juice
1 medium onion, diced
½ bell pepper, diced
1 medium tomato, seeded and diced
½ peeled and diced cucumber
1 cup coconut milk
Salt to taste
Chopped scallions for garnish

Place the cubed fish into a bowl. Mix with lime juice. Marinate the fish for 5 minutes, then spoon out half the juice. Add the onion, bell pepper, tomato, cucumber, and coconut milk, and season with salt. Garnish with chopped scallions.

Tuna Carpaccio with Confit Cabbage and Avocado

CONFIT IS A traditional French method of preserving meat. First, the meat (usually duck, pork, or goose) is salted, then slowly cooked in its own fat. The word *confit* has since been used to describe the method where hot oil is poured over vegetables for flash cooking.

SERVES 6

1 medium Napa cabbage, shredded

1 quart canola oil

1½ pounds fresh 'ahi (yellowfin tuna), thinly sliced

1 large avocado, diced

Horseradish Vinaigrette (see page 240)

1 vine-ripened tomato, diced for garnish

Radish sprouts for garnish

Place the cabbage in a stainless steel pot. Heat the cooking oil in a saucepan over high heat until it starts to smoke. Pour the hot oil over the cabbage. Mix and drain immediately, and cool to room temperature.

On a platter, arrange paper-thin slices of fish on a bed of the confit cabbage and avocado. Pour the Horseradish Vinaigrette over the top, and garnish with tomato and radish sprouts.

Tahitian Shrimp Soup

TAHITIAN SHRIMP SOUP is a favorite with the guests who frequent my restaurants. It's hearty enough to serve as a complete meal on a cold
evening. I created this recipe in theory first. I was flying from Honolulu to
Papeete and I sketched this on a United Airlines napkin. The flavors just
seemed to be made to blend. And they really do.   SERVES 4

1½ pounds fresh saltwater shrimp, with heads on
4 tablespoons cooking oil
¼ medium onion, chopped
1 leek with green leafy part, chopped
½ celery stalk, chopped
1 carrot, diced
1 clove garlic, sliced
4 kaffir lime leaves
1 branch fresh thyme
1 teaspoon paprika
1 tablespoon tomato paste
1 cup dry white wine
5 cups chicken stock
2 tablespoons fish sauce
1 cup coconut milk
½ cup heavy cream
Salt and cayenne pepper to taste
Blanched julienned leeks, turnips, and carrots
1 tablespoon finely sliced fresh basil leaves for garnish

Peel shrimp, and remove heads. Reserve heads and shells.

Heat cooking oil in a heavy skillet over high heat. Sauté shrimp heads and shells to flavor oil. Remove heads and shells, and discard. Add onion, leek, celery, carrot, garlic, kaffir lime leaves, thyme, and paprika. Sweat vegetables, then strain mixture through a cheesecloth-lined strainer. Return to heat and add tomato paste and wine. Cook for 5 minutes until alcohol has evaporated. Pour in chicken stock and fish sauce, then add shrimp meat, coconut milk, and heavy cream. Bring to a simmer. Season with salt and cayenne pepper to taste. Simmer for 3 more minutes. Add blanched vegetables, and serve immediately. Garnish with basil leaves.

Chilled Minted Papaya Soup

I LIKE TO call this my "fruit gazpacho." It's a sweet, cool soup designed to quench the heat of a Tahitian summer. Served in a large soup tureen, this soup brings back memories of sparkling bays viewed from covered lanais.

SERVES 6 TO 8

2 medium papayas, seeded, skinned, and cubed

1½ cups fresh pineapple, cubed

12-ounce can pineapple juice

2 teaspoons fresh lime juice

4 sprigs spearmint

12-ounce bottle ginger ale, chilled

Mint leaves for garnish

Place papaya, pineapple, and pineapple juice in the blender. Cover, and blend well. Pour into saucepan, and stir as the mixture comes to a boil. Remove from the heat, and add the lime juice and mint. Stir, and chill. Before serving, remove the mint sprigs, and mix in the ginger ale. Place soup in chilled soup cups. Garnish with fresh mint leaves.

La Crevette Pochée with Green Papaya Salad

IN TAHITI, THEY call papayas *pawpaw*, and use them in many of their fruit salads, desserts, and dinner salads. I truly believe that this recipe of Tahitian lime, green papaya, and cilantro vinaigrette, coupled with poached shrimp, is one of those dishes that will make you famous. SERVES 4

1½ pounds green papaya, seeded and peeled

Juice from 2 limes

2 cups water

3 tablespoons rock salt

2 medium tomatoes, seeded and cut into strips

⅓ cup Cilantro Vinaigrette (see page 59)

Lettuce leaves

12 poached large shrimp, peeled and de-veined

Chopped cashew nuts for garnish

Cilantro leaves for garnish

Grate papaya with a Japanese grater.

In a large bowl, mix lime juice, water, and salt, then add the grated papaya. Soak for 10 minutes, and drain thoroughly.

In a large salad bowl, toss papaya, tomatoes, and vinaigrette together. Place a bed of lettuce leaves on each of 4 salad plates. Mound papaya on the lettuce, and top with poached shrimp, 3 per plate. Garnish with nuts and cilantro leaves.

Tahitian Niçoise Salad

NIÇOISE IS A French word that means "prepared in the style of Nice." A typical Niçoise salad contains the key elements of onions, tomatoes, black olives, French beans, tuna, and hard-boiled eggs. In Tahiti, this very traditional French salad is served in the finest restaurants as a bow to their colonial history.

SERVES 4

8 'ahi (yellowfin tuna) steaks (3 ounces each)
2 tablespoons olive oil
Salt to taste
1 tablespoon cracked black pepper
½ pound mesclun mix or any salad greens
½ pound French beans, blanched
1 medium European cucumber, julienned
½ red bell pepper, julienned
½ yellow bell pepper, julienned
2 sweet potatoes, cooked and sliced
1 vine-ripened tomato, cut into wedges
4 hard-boiled eggs for garnish, quartered (optional)
Niçoise olives for garnish
Soy-Balsamic Vinaigrette (see page 241)

Heat a skillet over high heat. Lightly oil tuna, and season with salt and cracked black pepper. Sear 'ahi steaks on both sides, leaving them medium-rare in the center.

Arrange mesclun mix on a platter, and place the 'ahi steaks on the greens. Garnish with the French beans, cucumber, bell peppers, sweet potatoes, and tomato. Garnish with eggs and olives. Serve the Soy-Balsamic Vinaigrette on the side.

Chicken Fafa

CHICKEN FAFA IS a Tahitian dish that is usually cooked in an *ahi-ma'a*, or earth oven. Served at traditional Tahitian feasts, it is most attractive when each serving is presented in a half green coconut, adding coconut milk at the last moment. As with other exotic dishes, it's unwise to judge a food unless you've tried it first. Serve it warm with a side of hot rice.   **SERVES 4**

3 tablespoons butter
¼ cup chopped onion
8 chicken breasts
1¼ cup cooked fafa (taro top), or spinach
1 cup coconut milk
2 garlic cloves, chopped
Salt and pepper to taste

In a frying pan melt 1 tablespoon of butter, brown the onion, and set aside.

In a separate pan, lightly fry chicken breasts in 2 tablespoons of butter, then add the onion, and continue cooking for about 10 minutes. Add precooked fafa, and lightly stir to mix.

Strain off any liquid, and fry gently for a few minutes. Add coconut milk, chopped garlic, and season with salt and pepper to taste

Cold Trout in Vegetable Herb Fumet

AQUACULTURE HAS PLAYED a large part in supplying Tahiti and the islands of French Polynesia with a variety of fish and prawns. Trout, usually imported from New Zealand, is a favorite, light-tasting freshwater fish in Tahiti. Served either cold or hot, this is a fabulous entrée. **SERVES 4**

4 fresh trout (12 ounces each)
6 cups clear fish or chicken stock
½ cup dry white wine
2 bay leaves
6 branches fresh thyme
2 stalks lemongrass, thinly sliced diagonally
2 cloves garlic, thinly sliced
2 teaspoons black peppercorns
1 medium onion, cut into thin round slices
1 medium carrot, sliced ¼-inch thick
2 tomatoes, peeled, seeded, and sliced
Salt to taste
4 lemon wedges

Wash, clean, and fillet the fish, removing the thin veil of skin, the bones, and the head. Refrigerate fish until ready to use.

In a saucepan, add the rest of the ingredients, except the lemon wedges. Simmer for 45 minutes, and skim top occasionally. Add fish, and poach until cooked. Remove from heat. Can be served warm or cold. Portion into 4 wide-mouth soup bowls. Serve with lemon wedge on the side.

Cuire au Poisson

TI LEAVES ARE very important to all of the South Pacific cultures. They are used in religious rites, as vessels for steaming food, and as ornamental dress when performing traditional dances. Ti leaves are available from most florists, but aluminum foil is an acceptable substitution. SERVES 4

4 large ti leaves, trimmed

4 fillets red snapper (6 ounces each), or other firm, white fish

Salt and white pepper to taste

½ cup Tarragon–French Mustard Vinaigrette (see page 243)

8 slices tomatoes

¼ cup chopped chives for garnish

Lemon wedges for garnish

Preheat oven to 375°F.

Place each ti leaf on a square of aluminum foil. Place fish on ti leaf, and season with salt and white pepper. Pour 2 tablespoons Tarragon–French Mustard Vinaigrette over each fish fillet, then top with 2 tomato slices. Wrap in the ti leaf. Seal the aluminum foil, and transfer wrapped fish to a baking pan.

Bake at 375°F for 20 minutes. Fish will be slightly pink. Serve hot, and garnish with chives and lemon wedges.

Fresh Prawns in Coconut Milk

FRESHWATER PRAWNS ARE found in most rivers and streams of Tahiti. The locals prefer to cook prawns, as they do most of their seafood, by marinating them in the citric acid of Tahitian limes. When you prepare your prawns, be sure to carefully remove the black tube that runs down the back of each, then rinse thoroughly.

SERVES 6

1½ pounds fresh, large peeled and de-veined prawns, cubed
Juice of 4 limes
Salt to taste
1 medium onion, diced
2 tomatoes, diced
2 tablespoons chopped parsley
1 cup coconut milk
Pepper to taste
Chopped scallions for garnish

Place fresh prawns in a bowl, and squeeze lime juice over them. Add a pinch of salt, and marinate for 5 minutes. Remove half of the juice, and add the onion, tomatoes, parsley, coconut milk, and pepper to taste. Garnish with scallions, and serve.

Tahitian Cold Lobster

IN TAHITI, THEY call lobster crayfish. Halfway between a salad and a light summer entrée, my Tahitian Cold Lobster will water the mouth of any guest. This dish is best served cold as the evening is settling in, and the heat of a hot August day is subsiding.

SERVES 1

4 cups water

Juice of 1 lemon

1 teaspoon cracked peppercorns

2 bay leaves

1 clove garlic, crushed

1 12-ounce bottle of beer

1½-pound Tahitian crayfish or lobster

2 tablespoons asparagus, parboiled 3 minutes, then chopped

2 tablespoons green peas

2 tablespoons carrots, parboiled 2 to 3 minutes, then diced

½ teaspoon minced cilantro

½ teaspoon snipped fresh dill

½ cup chopped fresh spinach (or frozen cooked spinach, squeezed)

2 tablespoons diced water chestnuts

Salt and pepper to taste

1 cup mayonnaise, or to taste

½ teaspoon curry powder, or to taste

Finely chopped lettuce

Lemon wedges for garnish

Fresh dill sprig for garnish

Place water, lemon juice, cracked peppercorns, bay leaves, garlic, and beer in the bottom of a steamer. Place crayfish (lobster) in a steamer basket, and steam for 6 to 8 minutes. Remove lobster from steamer when cooked, and immediately submerge in ice water to stop the cooking process. Keep lobster in ice water until chilled, about 15 to 20 minutes.

While lobster cools, mix all remaining ingredients, except for the mayonnaise, curry powder, lettuce, lemon wedges, and dill sprig.

Blend mayonnaise and curry powder together, then mix thoroughly with vegetables. Set aside.

Split lobster in two, remove tail meat, discard innards, and reserve shell. Fill shell about half full with vegetable mix, reserving about ½ cup of the mix. Slice tail meat into 3 or 4 sections and place in tail shell over vegetables, leaving gaps between sections to be filled with reserved mix. Crack claws, and use for garnish.

Arrange stuffed lobster and cracked claws on a bed of finely chopped lettuce. Garnish with lemon wedges and a sprig of fresh dill.

Sautéed Snapper with Soy Butter Sauce

YOU CAN USE any kind of snapper in this dish: red, pink, or gray. They all work well. I got this recipe from my friend Philipe, a cab driver in Papeete. He makes the best snapper in the world. Merci beaucoup, mon frère.

SERVES 4

4 snapper fillets (6 ounces each)
Salt and pepper to taste
¼ cup flour
3 tablespoons vegetable oil
6 tablespoons unsalted butter
4 teaspoons soy sauce
½ teaspoon garlic, minced
Juice from ½ lemon
Chopped scallions for garnish

Season snapper fillets with salt and pepper, then dust in flour. Heat a sauté pan with oil. Add snapper, and sauté on both sides until cooked. Remove fish from the pan, and set aside. Discard excess oil, and return to medium-high heat. Melt butter until golden brown, then add soy sauce, garlic, and lemon juice. Season with salt and pepper to taste. Pour sauce over snapper, and garnish with the scallions.

Tahitian Fish Stew

THIS IS A typical fish stew that is served in households throughout French Polynesia. I created the recipe after tasting a dish like this in a small café in Papeete. I know you'll like it. It's a favorite at our house.

SERVES 6 TO 8

½ cup olive oil

1 teaspoon fennel seeds

1 chili pepper, minced

2 medium sweet onions, diced

2 cloves garlic, crushed

1½ teaspoons paprika

¾ cup dry white wine

½ cup tomatoes, peeled, seeded, and diced into ½-inch cubes

3 quarts fish stock

Salt to taste

2½ pounds fresh white fish, cut into 1-inch cubes

½ pound fresh spinach, chopped

Chopped chives for garnish

Chopped parsley for garnish

Lime wedges for garnish

In a pot, heat oil, fennel seeds, and chili pepper. Sauté onions until transparent, then add garlic and paprika; cook for 2 minutes. Add dry white wine and tomatoes, and simmer until one-half of the liquid has evaporated. Add fish stock, and simmer for 35 minutes. Add salt to taste. Add fish and spinach, and cook for 5 minutes or until fish is cooked.

Serve immediately. Garnish with chives and parsley. Serve lime wedges on the side.

Le Calamar Fafa

WE HAVE A dish like this in Hawai'i that we call "Squid Lu'au." Le Cala-mar Fafa is a traditional Tahitian accompaniment to any seafood meal. The fafa or taro leaves are cooked until they have a creamy consistency. This is a Tahitian comfort food that is very tasty and gloriously filling. I know you'll like it.

SERVES 12

2 pounds calamari

3 pounds fafa leaves (taro leaves), or fresh spinach leaves

1 tablespoon rock salt

½ teaspoon baking soda

2 medium onions, diced

6 tablespoons butter

3 cups coconut milk

1½ teaspoons salt

1 tablespoon sugar

Clean calamari, and slice in rings, then set aside.

Wash fafa leaves, remove stems and thick veins. In a pot, boil 3 cups of water with rock salt and baking soda. Add the leaves to the boiling water and reduce heat. Simmer, partially covered, for 1 hour (reduce time for spinach leaves). Drain, and squeeze out liquid.

Sauté onions and calamari in butter until the onions are translucent. Add the coconut milk, cooked fafa leaves, salt, and sugar. Simmer for 30 minutes. Serve hot.

Tahitian Coconut Bread

I REMEMBER HAVING these tasty loaves of hot coconut bread when I was young. My friend's mother was Tahitian, and she made this bread every day. It's very easy. I love it as a breakfast bread, but it's also great as a side to any Tahitian dish. Next to the omnipresent baguette, this bread is the other favorite accompaniment to a meal.   YIELDS 4 LOAVES

5¾ to 6 cups white flour
⅔ cup brown sugar
2⅔ cups flaked coconut
½ teaspoon salt
1 can coconut milk (14 ounces)
4 large ti leaves, cleaned and deboned (or use aluminum foil)

Combine flour, brown sugar, flaked coconut, salt, and coconut milk in large mixing bowl, and knead for a few minutes to blend. Mixture will be stiff. Shape into 4 loaves about 6 inches long and 2 inches in diameter. Wrap each loaf in a buttered ti leaf, using toothpicks to tie and seal.

Place loaves in pan, and bake at 350°F for 1½ hours. Remove ti leaves. Serve warm.

Horseradish Vinaigrette

HORSERADISH, THE ROOT of a mustard plant native to Eastern Europe, is frequently found in supermarkets during the Jewish Passover holidays when it is used to represent the "bitter herb" in the traditional Seder observance. Although my motto is "Fresher is always better," it is sometimes difficult to find fresh horseradish. If this is the case, feel free to use the bottled variety. It is grated and packed in vinegar and spices, and there is little difference in taste. But remember, "Fresher *is* always better." YIELDS 1½ CUPS

1 tablespoon grated fresh horseradish

1 teaspoon minced garlic

2 teaspoons Dijon mustard

1 teaspoon sambal sauce

3 tablespoons honey

4 tablespoons soy sauce

3 tablespoons lime juice

¾ cup peanut oil

Salt to taste

Combine first seven ingredients in a bowl. Stirring constantly, drizzle oil until blended. Season with salt to taste.

Soy-Balsamic Vinaigrette

I LIKE THE pungent sweetness of balsamic vinegar and the way it brings out the flavors of a salad when added to the dressing. I've had wonderful results when I've used this preparation to steam fish.   YIELDS 1½ CUPS

1½ tablespoons minced shallots

½ cup olive oil

2 tablespoons balsamic vinegar

2 tablespoons soy sauce

1 tablespoon lemon juice

2 teaspoons Dijon mustard

½ cup orange juice

2 tablespoons honey

2 teaspoons minced orange rind

Salt and pepper to taste

Sweat shallots briefly in a sauté pan with a small amount of olive oil.

In a bowl, combine balsamic vinegar, soy sauce, lemon juice, Dijon mustard, orange juice, honey, orange rind, and shallots. Whisk in the oil in a slow, steady stream to emulsify. Season with salt and pepper to taste.

Spicy Poor Boy Sauce

THIS SAUCE WAS created to complement the deep-fried oysters and French bread in the Oyster Poor Boy appetizer. But its spicy flavor also goes nicely with lobster, firm white fish, mussels, clams, or shrimp, and it makes a wonderful spread for sandwiches.   YIELDS 1½ CUPS

1 cup ketchup

1 tablespoon horseradish

2 tablespoons mayonnaise

2 teaspoons shoyu

1 teaspoon Worcestershire sauce

Hot pepper flakes

1 teaspoon chili paste

Combine all ingredients in a small bowl. Blend well.

Tahitian Caramel-Vanilla Syrup

THIS SYRUP CAN be used for any coffee drink. Tahiti produces wonderful vanilla beans that have achieved worldwide acclaim. You can find Tahitian vanilla in most specialty food shops. Get it if you can, it's well worth the hunting.   YIELDS 1½ CUPS

6-inch Tahitian vanilla bean

1 cup sugar

1¼ cups water

Split the vanilla bean in half and scrape the seeds into the sugar. Caramelize the sugar in a copper or stainless steel pan. When golden brown, add the water. Simmer for 7 minutes. Cool, and store in the refrigerator until ready to use.

Tarragon–French Mustard Vinaigrette

TARRAGON, A DARK, pointy-leafed aromatic herb, is often used in French cooking. This herb, like many others from the "old country," was brought to Tahiti during colonization in the late 1800s. Today, the Tahitians use it to season many of their sauces, stews, soups, and dressings. It is best to use this dressing a few hours after it is made to allow the infusion of flavors.

YIELDS 1 CUP

⅔ cup olive oil
2 tablespoons wine vinegar
2 tablespoons lemon juice
2 teaspoons French mustard
1 tablespoon chopped parsley
2 teaspoons chopped fresh tarragon
Salt and pepper to taste

Combine all ingredients in a large mixing bowl, and beat vigorously. Season with salt and pepper to taste.

Baked Banana Vanilla Custard

I LOVE GOOD custard. On one of my trips to Tahiti, the woman who ran a small hotel on the island of Moorea served this dessert for breakfast. The rich, creamy texture is fabulous any time of day. I call it a well-deserved treat.

SERVES 6

4 large eggs

1 cup brown sugar

1½ cups coconut milk

2 teaspoons vanilla extract

Dash nutmeg

Pinch of salt

3 ripe bananas

Heat oven to 350°F. In a large bowl, beat the eggs until light colored. Gradually beat in sugar and coconut milk, a little at a time. Whisk in vanilla extract, nutmeg, and pinch of salt.

Slice bananas about ½ inch thick, and fold into custard. Pour custard into a deep, well-buttered soufflé dish. Place dish in a pan with enough water to come 2 inches up the side of the dish. Bake for 45 to 50 minutes, or until a tester comes out clean. Cool, and refrigerate until ready to use.

Tahitian Po'e

PO'E IS WHAT I call an "imu-style" dessert, a dish steamed in an earth oven and typical of the Polynesian islands. Don't be put off by the amount of fruit called for; most varieties have a lot of peel and pit weight to discard. I've tried hot fudge with this dessert. It works for me, but I'm a bit adventurous. It's worth a try.   **SERVES 12**

2 tablespoons butter, room temperature

2 vanilla beans, split

10 pounds whole assorted tropical fruit (use at least 4 varieties, particularly bananas, papaya, pineapple, mango, and poha)

½ cup cornstarch

1 cup packed brown sugar

Tahitian Vanilla Ice Cream (see page 246)

Shredded coconut for garnish

Preheat oven to 375°F. Butter a 12 × 9 × 2-inch baking pan, set aside.

Scrape the seeds from the vanilla beans into a large bowl; also add the pods. Peel, seed, and cut the fruits into chunks. In a food processor, coarsely chop them, then set them in a strainer over a bowl to drain. Stir occasionally until all liquids are drawn. Pour into prepared pan and spread evenly. Mix 1 cup of the juice with cornstarch and brown sugar, and add to the bowl with the vanilla beans and seeds. Toss to mix, then pour into the prepared pan; smooth the top. Bake in the center of the oven for 1 hour, turning the fruit once or twice to bake evenly.

Remove from oven, and cool. Then cover, and refrigerate several hours before serving. Scoop into bowls and top with Tahitian Vanilla Ice Cream. Sprinkle with shredded coconut.

Tahitian Vanilla Ice Cream

LIVING IN TAHITI means getting used to the intense summer heat and humidity that exists so close to the equator. A friend who lives on the island of Moorea gave me this recipe after I raved about the intense vanilla flavor. I have to share it with you. It's fantastic!

YIELDS APPROXIMATELY 1 QUART

2 Tahitian vanilla beans, split

⅔ cup sugar

½ cup water

2 cups heavy cream

6 egg yolks

1 cup half-and-half

Scrape the vanilla bean seeds into a heavy, 2-quart saucepan. Add the pods, sugar, and water, and stir to dissolve the sugar. Bring to a boil over medium heat, and cook without stirring until the mixture just begins to caramelize.

Meanwhile, warm the cream. When the sugar mixture is ready, add the cream all at once, standing back from the pot, as the mixture may steam and spatter. Swirl the mixture until the bubbling subsides, then stir over medium heat to dissolve any lumps of sugar. Return to boil.

Have yolks ready in a heat-proof bowl. Whisk hot cream mixture into yolks. Whisk thoroughly and fast. This process cooks the yolks, and eliminates the need to stir on the stove. Add the half-and-half to stop the cooking process. Strain through a fine sieve and refrigerate, stirring now and then to prevent a skin from forming. When cold, freeze in an ice cream maker according to manufacturer's instructions.

Tahitian Caramel-Vanilla Coffee

THE TAHITIAN CARAMEL-VANILLA Syrup adds creamy sweetness to this hot, zesty drink, but a little splash of Kahlùa really zips things up.

SERVES 4

Tahitian Caramel-Vanilla Syrup (see page 242)
4 cups freshly brewed coffee
Whipped cream

Add the Tahitian Caramel-Vanilla Syrup to the coffee. Serve whipped cream on the side.

Tahitian Vanilla Colada

THE CRUSHED VANILLA bean in this recipe adds a grainy texture to this icy, tropical drink. If that doesn't appeal to you, add a teaspoon of pure vanilla extract to the mix, and you'll be fine. I really like the texture, and I think you'll like it, too.

SERVES 1

Ice
2 tablespoons (1 ounce) white rum
1 inch Tahitian vanilla bean
2 tablespoons (1 ounce) coconut syrup
2½ tablespoons (3 ounces) pineapple juice
2 tablespoons (1 ounce) half-and-half
1 quarter slice of pineapple for garnish
1 Tahitian vanilla bean for garnish

Fill one-third of a blender container with ice. Add ingredients, and blend until slushy. Pour into hurricane glass. Garnish with a quarter of a pineapple slice and a Tahitian vanilla bean.

Tonga

IN RECENT YEARS I've enjoyed the good fortune of traveling to the South Pacific as a Crystal Cruise Lines celebrity chef. My duties are always the same. I offer an introduction to South Pacific foods and ingredients, do cooking demonstrations, and share my culinary insights on the countries we visit. I know it sounds like a dream job. AND IT IS. I GET to travel on a luxury liner, create fantastic dishes, visit the stunning islands of Polynesia—and the best part is they pay me for doing it. It's fabulous. A HIGHLIGHT OF THE CRUISES is Tonga, one of the smallest nations in the world.

Close your eyes and think of treasure, and Tonga would be a scattering of emeralds. YOU COME TO IT OVER miles of open ocean, a vast cobalt setting that gets azure as the sea floor and reefs start to rise. Then these rather modest islands show up. What

catches your eye is the way they almost glint this fantastic green in the sunlight—yes, like emeralds. Maybe it's because Tonga doesn't include any high islands so typical of the Pacific, what you find in Tahiti or Samoa. These are just rain-forest-covered mounds in the middle of nowhere. But after you've spent days at sea, the sights of Tongatapu and 'Eua seem as rare and beautiful as living jewels.

You know just by looking that this is a special place, a welcome landfall filled with the promise of good fish and hospitable people.

The kingdom of Tonga is known as "The Friendly Isles." I can only begin to say how friendly. The finest example of Tongan hospitality I've experienced came on one of my earliest visits, and it started long before we reached the islands themselves.

The first destination of this particular Crystal cruise was the main island of Tonga-tapu. Located near the southernmost tip of the country, Tongatapu is home to two-thirds of the population. We flew to Auckland, New Zealand, boarded the cruise ship, and headed northeast on the long journey.

Growing up, I had lots of Tongan friends. Their fathers were master craftsmen who came with their families as labor missionaries to our little town of La'ie to help build the Polynesian Cultural Center and the Mormon churches and temple. I was always welcome in their homes, welcome to stay for dinner. I loved their style of cooking. It was so clean and simple. I think it must have been the simplicity in preparation that caused the flavors to blend just right. There was definitely something about the harmony of ingredients that kept me coming back for more. I remember hanging out with my friends even after my mom and dad had called our family in for dinner, in hopes of being invited for a Tongan meal.

On this trip, I realized that although I knew the stories my friends told me about Tonga, all about their food, and their dances and traditions, I had yet to really "experience" their islands. My previous trips had been too brief or unfocused. I resolved to change that.

It's really funny how serendipity takes a hand when you're determined to do something. About three hours out of Auckland, I took a walk on deck, to catch some fresh air. I was unpacked, and my stateroom made me a little claustrophobic, so I took in the full tour of the ship. I walked past couples reading on lounge chairs, past the swimming pool where children screamed and giggled as they jumped into the water; I looked down from the bow to see dolphins speeding below the surface. I'd just finished my stroll and headed for my room, when I rounded a corner and ran smack into an elderly Polynesian woman walking with a cane. She staggered back, about to lose her balance and fall into a bulk-head. I lunged and grabbed both her arms. "I'm so sorry," I said. "I didn't see you."

She was a little shaken, but regally composed. "It's perfectly all right," she said. She smiled, fixed her grip on her walking stick, gave me a slight nod, and glided away in a long blue dress, her white hair pulled into a tight bun on top of her head. I'd never met such a gracious person.

It was almost dinnertime, and I needed to complete the evening's cooking presentation, which would take place a half hour after our meal. I always bring an assistant chef with me to handle all of the rough prep, but I did a last-minute check before leaving for the dining room to join the captain at his table.

Dinner that evening was typically elegant. There was lobster from Tahiti, asparagus, beets, and summer peas drenched in artichoke sauce, and crystal goblets filled with the finest wines from New Zealand. The guests at my table were well into their appetizers when I was finally seated, across from the captain. One seat at the table remained empty. "Who's missing?" I asked.

"Madam Tupou," the captain said with his thick Australian accent. "She is quite old, and it takes time to get down from her stateroom."

As he said this, the dining room's main double doors opened, and an elderly Polynesian woman—the one I almost bowled over on deck—walked into the hall, assisted by the maître d'. It was Madam Tupou. She wore a black skirt that flowed to her ankles. Around her waist was a *ta'ovala*, a finely plaited pandanus-leaf mat that was securely tied with a *keikei* (a pandanus waistband with dangling strands of seeds).

"She's a member of the Tongan royal family," the captain said. "Her daughter passed away in Auckland. Madam Tupou attended the funeral, and is now on her way home. She's a very nice woman."

"Is that why she's wearing black?" Mrs. Talbot, one of the captain's guests, asked.

The captain nodded, then turned his attention to Madam Tupou. Everyone at the table stood up as the maître d' pulled out her chair. The old woman slid gracefully into her seat.

"Good evening, Madam. I am Captain Richards." He occupied the head of the table. "Please let me introduce everyone." He went around the table: "This is Mr. and Mrs. Talbot, retirees from Cincinnati; Mr. Adolpho, a businessman from Western Samoa; Miss Lopez, a schoolteacher from upstate New York; and Mrs. Augustus, a widow from Germany. And seated over here is Sam Choy, a chef from Hawai'i. I present to you all Madam Tupou."

The regal lady nodded to each of us.

"Excuse me, Madam," said Miss Lopez. "I'm a teacher, and am very interested in your country. The good captain said that you were of royal birth. Is there still a monarchy in Tonga?"

"Oh, yes," Madam Tupou said. As we took our seats, she launched into a fascinating lecture about the royal history of her islands. It lasted through the salad course and into the soup service. "But I am only a very distant relative to His Majesty King Taufa'ahau Tupou, the son of the late Queen Salote Tupou the Third. He lives in a great palace on the island of Tongatapu, in the city Nuku'alofa, the capital of Tonga."

"Could you tell us a bit about the country?" Mr. Talbot asked.

"It is very beautiful," Madam Tupou said. "Of all of the countries in the South Pacific, mine is the most isolated. Tonga consists of 171 islands and atolls, but only 45 are inhabited. It is divided into four island groups, each centered around a major, populated island—Tongatapu in the south, the volcanic and coral islands of the Ha'apai group in the middle, the Vava'u archipelago, and finally the remote volcanic islands of the Niuas in the far north."

Captain Richards added, "The most wonderful thing about Tonga is her people."

Madam Tupou smiled. "This is true," she said. "My people are kind and friendly. It is easy to be proud of them."

After dinner, I had a few moments before my scheduled evening cooking demonstration, so I went straight to the ship's library—my curiosity piqued by Madam Tupou—and pulled out a book on Tonga. It lies about two-thirds of the way from Hawai'i to New Zealand, and is just west of the international dateline where it meets the Tropic of Capricorn. From the island Niuafo'ou in the north, Tonga stretches nearly 1,000 miles to the Minerva Reef in the south, with a total population of about 100,000.

I arrived at the presentation suite five minutes before I was scheduled to begin. The room was filled with guests. Usually, I don't have many people the first night, when we're scheduled right after dinner. Madam Tupou sat in the front row. She smiled at me as I took my place at the table. My assistant was completing the final setup, so I took the time to introduce myself. When the cooking demonstration began, I realized that Madam Tupou was probably much better suited to deliver the section on the natural ingredients of her country. So I changed my format, and talked about general ingredients used in the South Pacific like coconuts, taro, breadfruit, and reef fish. After the lecture, I cornered Madam Tupou, and asked if she would spend some time with me the following day, so I could talk to her about the cooking of her country.

"I'd be delighted," she said. "I'll tell you everything I know about Tongan cuisine."

I have many philosophies about cooking, but only one about life. I believe that the ability to learn is the most important skill a person has, and this skill needs to be practiced. I could tell I would learn a great deal from Madam Tupou.

The next afternoon, I met her on the aft deck for tea, and we chatted for hours. She made the point that since of all the South Pacific nations Tonga is the most distant from Westernized countries, it has avoided much of the commercialization inflicted on other Polynesian islands. "We hold tight to the traditions of our ancestors." She also said, "We are the first to see the new day. We're right on the international dateline, and the days, months, years, decades, and centuries begin for us first." Her smile really had the power to light up your heart.

I spent my evenings with food demos and presentations, but most of those first days talking to Madam Tupou. She told me about her favorite Tongan dishes—*lupulu* (taro leaf–wrapped corned beef in coconut milk), *faikakai* (breadfruit pudding), and *'ota 'ika* (like a poke with coconut milk)—many of them my childhood favorites in La'ie.

We also talked about the pace of life in Tonga. It's slower than anyplace in the world. "You will see," she said. "When we enter Queen Salote Harbor, you will feel your pulse slow down."

"I think I'd like to introduce some Tongan dishes in one of my demonstrations," I said.

Madam Tupou looked distracted. She was gazing over the railing toward the pool below. "My people are very modest," she said.

I strained to see what she was looking at. All of the children, teens, and adults basking in the sun were clad in swimming suits and bikinis.

"My people, men, women, and children, would never be seen naked like that in a public place. It is against the law. The passengers will discover our laws when they get to Tonga. We are completely modest." She lifted her pandanus fan and cooled herself with it. "I'm sorry," she said. "You wanted to know about food?"

Slightly nonplussed by the distraction, I returned to my original thought. "Do you think I should introduce lupulu, faikakai, and 'ota 'ika in my demonstrations? I want to give the people a taste of where we're going."

The old woman smiled. "It is a very different taste, you know? They may not like it."

"I'll add a Choy flair," I said.

But the next evening I presented lupulu and kept it quite traditional, using New Zealand corned beef, taro leaves, and coconut milk. It might have been the exotic perspective most of the guests were experiencing, but the dish was a smash.

The next day, we did the dessert breadfruit pudding faikakai. I made it two ways, first with breadfruit, and next with yams. Again, people were clamoring for the recipe.

This was the easiest crowd I've ever had. They adored everything.

We were at sea for five days, each evening a new demonstration, each time a big success. We had so many people attending the lectures that we had to move to a larger room. Madam Tupou came to the first two demos, but near the end of the trip, she vanished. She even missed some dinners in the grand dining room.

"Madam Tupou is ill," Captain Richards announced one night. "She will be taking her meals in her stateroom."

After dinner I made my way to her suite, and knocked on the door. "Come in," a sweet young voice answered. I opened the door, walked through the narrow walkway to the sitting room, and was greeted by a young Tongan woman. She motioned me to a settee near the large cabin window, and there sat Madam Tupou, gazing through the glass into the darkness.

I sat down and reached over to pat the old woman's hand. "I've missed you," I said.

She smiled, but didn't look at me. "I will be fine," she said. "I can only handle crowds for so long. It tires me. Soon we'll be home, and all will be well."

In this elegant cabin, listening to Madam as she stared into the night, I felt like a character in one of the fantasy novels my son reads.

"Have you a place to stay in Nuku'alofa?"

"On the boat," I said. "I've got some day trips planned."

"I want you to come to my home for dinner. Come early, so I can show you the town. I will take you to the palace."

"Thank you," I said. "I'd love that. I'm worried about you, though."

"I am fine, just a little tired. It has been a hard journey." She closed her eyes and let her head rest on the back of the chair. "You go now," she said without opening her eyes. "I will nap."

At dawn the next morning I was on the bow of the ship watching the wondrous green of Tonga come into view.

We put into Queen Salote Harbor under a thin cover of clouds. A Tongan band and choir, dressed in traditional outfits, greeted the boat with the most jubilant song I had ever heard. The men wore white shirts with ties, black *vala* skirts that hung to midcalf, a plaited pandanus ta'ovala around their waists, and sandals. The women wore white shirts, vala, ta'ovala, and sandals as well.

I'd forgotten how beautiful the Tongan harmonies sounded. The blending of voices is unlike any other Polynesian singing. To me, the sound spoke of remote atolls and aquamarine lagoons, coconut palms casting shade on deserted white sand beaches, and warm, South Pacific breezes. I stood at the railing and listened to the musicians and singers, and wished I could bottle the music and take it back home. This was the feeling I wanted to give guests in my restaurants, to readers of my books, and to my TV show audience. I wanted them all to feel this perfect harmony of soul, culture, and environment.

"You are happy?" It was the calm, resonant voice of Madam Tupou. She stood with her attendant at her side, ready to disembark. "I will send for you tomorrow evening. I will show you the real way to cook Tongan style." She smiled, and turned to leave.

I spent my day exploring the capital city of Nuku'alofa, with its Victorian government buildings and the royal palaces. I didn't realize there were actually two palaces, the original one built in 1867, and a newer palace where His Majesty King Taufa'ahau Tupou lives today. I visited both. They aren't open to the public, but these and the residences of the crown princes are magnificent, even from the street. We saw the Tongan War Memorial, the House of Parliament building, the Treasury Building, the British High Commissioner's Home, the Royal Tombs, and the Basilica of St. Anthony of Padua. Modern Tongan culture is heavily influenced by the British.

We had lunch at a small place called Angela's Restaurant. It was our guide's favorite lunch hangout. The menu offered the regular hamburger and fries lunch fare, with the interesting addition of casava curry and rice. That was my choice. It was fabulous.

Dinner that night was at the best upscale restaurant in Nuku'alofa, the Seaview Restaurant, west of the palace. The red snapper was wonderful, cooked just beyond raw, and served with delicious tropical fruit chutney.

When we returned to the ship, a message from Madam Tupou was waiting. On the following day, I was to meet her "carriage" on Vuna Road at 10:00 A.M. It would take me to her home.

I arrived early, and waited at the corner. The business traffic was light, cars and bicyclists courteously sharing the narrow street. I watched as a black Mercedes sedan slowed to a stop in front of me. It was an older model, kept in prime condition, and obviously meticulously cared for. The driver leaned across the front seat to yell out of the passenger window. "You the Choy man?"

"Yes."

"You come wit me," he said with a thick Tongan accent. "Madam Tupou wait for you in Nakolo." We headed east out of the town on a broad street that turned into a narrow two-lane road. We drove for over an hour, weaving through the center of the island of Tongatapu, to the little town where Madam Tupou lived. The driver explained that the name "Tongatapu" means sacred Tonga, and that the name "Nuku'alofa" means house or place of love.

My driver's name was Solomone, Tongan for Solomon. It was a biblical name, and it reminded me of Madam's reference to Tongan modesty. They are a very religious people.

We arrived at the gate to Madam Tupou's home, a wooden Victorian mansion that looked older than the tall trees lining the drive to the front porch. The young attendant greeted us, and escorted me into a large entry hall with a vaulted ceiling.

"She will meet you in the library," the young woman said, and she led the way down a corridor appointed with antiques and portraits. It was like walking back in time. Everything was tidy and extremely clean, vases polished, every tassel on the Oriental hall runner in place.

The library was huge and dark, with shelves of old books filling every available wall space. Madam Tupou sat in a large chair at the other end of the room.

"Hello, my friend," she said. "Thank you for making the trip."

I greeted her with a kiss on both cheeks, and sat in the chair next to her. "You look well," I said.

"Thank you. Dinner will be early this evening. I'm not feeling very well, but I wanted you to come. I've asked my people to prepare a sampling of our traditional foods. I think you will like it."

She gave me a tour of the house and compound. We walked through rooms that looked like museum displays: bedrooms with four-poster beds covered with brocade spreads and decorative pillows; a large dining room with a table to seat ten people; and a parlor reminiscent of an English country house. We strolled through the garden, where coconut palms swished in the wind overhead. The flowerbeds were filled with tropicals she'd gathered in her travels to New Zealand, Hawai'i, Tahiti, and Samoa. It was a spectacular place, filled with the calm, quiet elegance that characterized my hostess.

Dinner was served at 4:00 P.M. A table had been set on the patio on the east side of the house. The meal began with a bowl of crabmeat and coconut milk soup. Its light creamy color and soothing flavor made me feel right at home.

The main entrée was lupulu. The most amazing lupulu I'd ever tasted. We also had 'ota 'ika, with a side of steamed *kumala* (sweet potato). And, of course, dessert was faikakai made from baked breadfruit, coconut cream, and sugar.

A few were "acquired taste" items, like the raw *fingota* (shellfish) and veihalo, but the experience of tasting such treasured cultural comfort foods was priceless. I haven't included these more esoteric dishes in my collection. So, if you want to try them, jump the next flight to Tonga. The ambience of the islands will greatly enhance the taste.

It amazed me how well the flavors blended, even the ones that caught me off guard.

This reminded me of the voices on the dock the day before, harmonizing into a sound that was so uniquely Tongan. It's the same with their food: a perfect harmony.

Dinner went by too fast, and around 7:00 it was time to leave. "Don't let your journey of Tonga take you to this island only. There are lots more to see," Madam Tupou said as I climbed into her car. "There is so much to learn here."

She was a very private woman. Before I left her home, she gave me a kiss on each cheek, then looked me in the eye and made me promise that if I ever wrote a book about her islands, I would keep her name and the location of her home a secret. At that time, I had no intention of writing cookbooks, but true to my word, her name and the location of her home are changed.

That was the last time I saw the grand old woman. She had been too ill to take me to the palace. On my next trip to Tonga, I was told that she'd passed away. To my mind, the spirit of Madam Tupou still embodies the essence of her country—the elegance of her people, their strong ties to their culture, and the harmony of their song and their food.

So let me introduce you to the cuisine of Tonga, Choy-style, keeping in mind the memory of my kind friend.

Maloelele to all, and Ha'u 'o kai.
(Come and eat.)

Tongan Caponata

THIS CAPONATA, A flavorful vegetarian spread, can be used with pasta or any kind of grilled meat dishes. Not all caponatas are sweet and sour to taste, but this one is, and it has the consistency of chutney. I first sampled it at a dinner while visiting friends in Tonga. It works well as a filling *pupu* (appetizer), or as a light meal.

SERVES 6

¾ cup canola oil

1 small chili pepper, minced

½ teaspoon cumin seeds

2 teaspoons mustard seeds

2 medium sweet onions, diced

2 tablespoons minced garlic

2 medium eggplants, ½-inch diced

4 large tomatoes, peeled, seeded, and chopped

½ cup roasted red peppers, peeled, seeded, and chopped

¼ cup red wine vinegar

¼ cup brown sugar

2 tablespoons capers, chopped

¼ cup pitted, chopped black olives

3 tablespoons chopped basil leaves

4 grilled chicken breasts

Salt and freshly ground pepper for garnish

Heat the oil in a pot. Add chili pepper, cumin seeds, mustard seeds, and onions. Cook until onions are brown on the edges. Add garlic, and cook for 1 minute. Add eggplant, and cook for 5 minutes. Add tomatoes, roasted red peppers, vinegar, and brown sugar. Simmer until the mixture is slightly thick, then add capers, olives, and basil. Cook for another 5 minutes. Dilute with water if the mixture is too thick.

Season with salt and pepper to taste. Cool, and refrigerate the caponata for up to 1 week.

Cut grilled chicken breasts into 2-inch pieces. Serve with caponata and slices of French or sourdough bread.

Crab Cakes with Cucumber Relish

I LOVE CRAB cakes, any type of crab cakes. These take a little longer to make than usual, but they are well worth the effort. I had these while visiting some Maori friends who now live in Tonga. They adapted a traditional Tongan raw crab recipe to one more suited to their tastes. It is 'ono. I know that you and your guests will love it.   SERVES 4

1 dried chili pepper (optional)
1 cup fresh crabmeat
1 shallot, finely chopped
Zest of ½ lime
1-inch piece fresh gingerroot, finely grated
¼ red pepper, seeded and finely chopped
2 teaspoons fish sauce or 1 tablespoon fish stock
2 tablespoons chopped fresh cilantro
1 small egg, beaten
½ cup panko, or dried bread crumbs
2 tablespoons oil
¼ cup chopped fresh cilantro for garnish
Cucumber Relish (see page 278)

Crush the chili with a mortar and pestle or with the back of a metal spoon on a board. Put the crushed chili in a bowl with the crabmeat, shallot, lime zest, ginger, red pepper, fish sauce or stock, and cilantro.

Add beaten egg, and mix well. Mixture should be soft, but not wet. Divide mixture in four parts.

Spread panko on a plate. Place one part of crabmeat mixture in the middle. Shape the mixture into a cake, and spoon bread crumbs over the top. Be sure to press crumbs in until cake is completely coated on all sides. Repeat with all four parts.

Chill the cakes in the refrigerator for 30 minutes.

Heat oil in a frying pan, and fry the cakes over medium heat for 7 minutes on each side. Drain cakes on paper towels, then place on serving dish. Sprinkle with chopped cilantro, and dab Cucumber Relish on the top of each one.

Serve immediately.

'Ota 'Ika

IN TONGA, TRADITIONAL 'ota 'ika is made from any type of firm-fleshed fish. Cooked with the acid from the limes, the tender meat is flavored with the sweetness of the coconut milk and onion, and spiced up with chili peppers. I've adjusted the original recipe for added flavor and texture. I know you'll love it. Ha'u 'o kai.   SERVES 8

1-pound block very fresh 'ahi (yellowfin tuna)

1 tablespoon rock salt

Juice of 2 limes (about 2 tablespoons)

1 cup diced cucumber, seeds removed

½ cup finely chopped sweet onion

2 cups coconut milk

½ tablespoon peeled and grated fresh gingerroot

3 chili peppers, seeds removed (optional)

Cut 'ahi into ½-inch cubes and place into a glass bowl. Add together rock salt and lime juice. Fold the fish mixture to allow the salt/juice marinade to coat all the 'ahi pieces. Cover the bowl and refrigerate for 30 minutes.

Fold the diced cucumber and onion into the marinated fish. Add more lime juice if the fish has soaked up the marinade completely. Add coconut milk and grated ginger. If you like "hot" seasoning, the chili peppers can be added at this time.

Stir to incorporate the remaining ingredients. Refrigerate for at least 1 hour to allow flavors to mix to full effect.

Ha'u 'o kai Crabmeat Soup

HA'U 'O KAI means "come and eat" in the Tongan language. And once
you've served this delicious soup to your family and friends, they will understand how exciting that phrase can be. It will become part of their vocabulary.
So, Ha'u 'o kai, it's an experience you won't forget. SERVES 4

2 cups diced onions

¼ cup butter

2 tablespoons flour

2 cups heavy cream

1½ cups chicken stock

2 cups coconut milk

2 cups frozen chopped spinach, thawed, or 3 cups chopped fresh spinach, washed
and steamed

1½ cups crabmeat

Salt and white pepper to taste

In a large saucepan, sauté onions in butter until translucent. Stir in flour; blend well. Add
heavy cream and chicken stock. Simmer for 5 minutes, stirring frequently. Stir in
coconut milk, spinach, and crabmeat. Cook for 3 minutes, stirring frequently. Season to taste with salt and white pepper.

South Pacific Gazpacho
with Baby Shrimp

A COOL SOUP originally from Mexico, this South Pacific Gazpacho can cool the hot, near-the-equator afternoons in Tonga. I served this soup to some friends on the veranda at an old Victorian home on the island of Tongatapu.

SERVES 6

2 vine-ripened tomatoes, peeled and seeded

¼ cup diced onion

½ stalk celery

¼ cup diced red pepper

⅓ cup peeled, seeded, and diced cucumber

1 clove garlic, minced

2 tablespoons lemon juice

¼ cup olive oil

2 cups tomato juice

2 slices good-quality white bread

2 teaspoons Classic Chili Pepper Water (see page 171)

Salt and pepper to taste

Diced avocado for garnish

Cooked baby shrimp

Cilantro sprigs for garnish

In a food processor, puree tomatoes, onion, celery, pepper, cucumber, garlic, and lemon juice. Remove, and place in a bowl. Next, place olive oil, tomato juice, white bread, and chili pepper water in food processor, and puree.

Pour liquid into the bowl with the pureed vegetables, and mix. Season with salt and pepper, and chill. Divide the soup among 6 bowls. Garnish with avocado, baby shrimp, and cilantro. Serve chilled.

Chicken with Papaya and Pineapple Salad

TRADITIONALLY, TONGAN CUISINE does not include salads. I created this layered salad to accompany a Tongan-style meal for some friends in New Zealand. This recipe serves one guest as a cool, entrée salad. It can be divided into four equal parts to be served to guests at a dinner. SERVES 1 TO 4

6 ounces sliced chicken meat

1 tablespoon soy sauce

1 tablespoon oyster sauce

1 teaspoon minced garlic

1 teaspoon minced gingerroot

Salt and pepper to taste

2 tablespoons salad oil

2 flour tortillas (fried)

1 handful of mixed salad greens

¼ cup diced pineapple

¼ cup diced papaya

Curls made from carrot, daikon, and beets

Choy's Chinese Salad Dressing (see page 96)

Combine chicken with soy sauce, oyster sauce, garlic, ginger, salt, and pepper. Allow to marinate for 10 minutes.

Heat oil in a wok. Add marinated chicken, and stir-fry 4 minutes or until the chicken is just cooked. Remove from heat.

Place one tortilla on a plate. Top with salad greens, then cover with other tortilla. Pour cooked chicken on top, then top with papaya and pineapple. Garnish with vegetable curls and Choy's Chinese Salad Dressing.

Spicy Shrimp Salad

I LOVE SHOPPING in open markets when I travel. In Tonga, the vendors allow you to taste their wares before purchasing. I found the most beautiful shrimp at one of the markets on Tongatapu. It is next to impossible for a chef to pass up food that looks that good. I bought a bagful, hurried back to a friend's house, and whipped up my Spicy Shrimp Salad. It has just the right amount of refreshing zing to make a lunch or early dinner sizzle. SERVES 2

¼ cup shoyu
1 teaspoon chopped garlic
1 teaspoon chopped cilantro
1 teaspoon chili sauce
1 teaspoon chopped green onion
1 tablespoon sugar
1 tablespoon sesame oil
1 teaspoon roasted sesame seeds
8 pieces 16/20 shrimp, butterflied with shell on
1 teaspoon salad oil
1 flour tortilla, cooked
8 ounces mixed tossed greens
2 ounces somen, cooked
Horseradish Vinaigrette (see page 240)

In a large mixing bowl, combine shoyu, garlic, cilantro, chili sauce, green onion, sugar, sesame oil, and sesame seeds. Add shrimp, and allow to marinate for 10 minutes.

Heat oil in wok. Remove shrimp from marinade. Stir-fry shrimp three-quarters of the way cooked. On a large plate, layer flour tortilla, tossed greens, and somen. Add shrimp last.

Serve with Horseradish Vinaigrette.

Chicken Lupulu

I CALL THIS dish Chicken Lupulu because it resembles traditional Tongan lupulu that is made with corned beef. Spinach leaves may be substituted for taro or lu'au leaves. Once you've had this dish, you'll understand what I mean about Tongan harmonies. The flavors are blended, but distinct.

SERVES 4

1 pound lu'au leaves (young taro leaves) or spinach, cooked

2 tablespoons butter

½ medium onion, chopped

1 clove garlic, minced

¾ pound boneless chicken breast, cubed

1 cup chicken stock

1 cup coconut milk

Salt to taste

Hot rice

Drain, and squeeze out excess liquid from cooked lu'au or spinach leaves. In a large saucepan, heat butter. Sauté onion and garlic until translucent. Stir in cubed chicken, and cook 4 minutes, stirring frequently. Add chicken stock, coconut milk, cooked lu'au leaves, and salt; simmer for 20 minutes. Serve hot over rice.

Coconut Fish

SEA BASS IS imported from New Zealand to Tonga. The combination of lemon, garlic, and ginger was brought to Tonga by Chinese immigrants who arrived to work in the copra and fishing industries. The coconut milk tenderizes the fish, and creates a truly South Pacific flavor.   SERVES 4

4 sea bass fillets (6 ounces each)
½ cup lemon juice
1 medium onion, cut into rings
2 teaspoons minced gingerroot
1 clove garlic, minced
4 tablespoons butter
2 cups coconut milk
Salt and pepper to taste
2 medium tomatoes, sliced
Chopped scallions for garnish

Preheat oven to 350°F.

Marinate fillets briefly in lemon juice for 15 minutes, and drain. Arrange on bottom of greased baking pan.

In a sauté pan, cook onion, ginger, and garlic in butter for 2 to 3 minutes. Add coconut milk, and simmer for 2 minutes. Season with salt and pepper.

Pour coconut sauce over the fish, and top with the sliced tomatoes. Bake in 350°F oven for 25 to 30 minutes. Garnish with scallions, and serve immediately.

King's Shrimp Pasta

IN TONGA, THERE are three predominant cuisines: Tongan, of course, Chinese, and Italian. The capital of Nuku'alofa features three Italian restaurants. Even the fine dining establishments offer Italian fare. I love this dish because of the crossover blending of national flavors. I believe someday soon we will become a global people, appreciating and enjoying a world cuisine that takes the best regional flavor combinations and creates something better.

SERVES 2

2 tablespoons olive oil

8 large shrimp

1 medium onion, diced

1 tablespoon minced garlic

2 cups chicken broth

1 cup cooked lu'au leaves (or spinach), chopped

8 ounces cooked penne pasta

½ cup coconut milk

1 tablespoon grated Parmesan cheese

Heat oil in pan. Add shrimp and onion. Cook shrimp about 1 minute on each side. Add garlic, chicken broth, then lu'au leaves. Cook 2 more minutes, or until shrimp are almost cooked.

Add pasta, coconut milk, and cheese. Cook about 1 more minute, just enough to heat pasta through.

Pour into bowl, and sprinkle with more cheese.

Mango and Brown Sugar–Glazed Pork Chops

AUCKLAND, NEW ZEALAND, is the closest major Pacific port to the royal seat of Tonga. As a result, trade between the two countries has been brisk for decades. Imported New Zealand pork is a favorite meat in Tonga. I got the idea for this recipe while traveling on the island of Ha'apai. We'd stopped in at a restaurant there, and they served us broiled pork chops sprinkled with brown sugar. The unique flavor addition of a mango glaze has made this one of my family's favorites. Enjoy! **SERVES 4**

4 pork chops (3 ounces each)
Salt and pepper to taste
2 tablespoons garlic, minced
Hot, cooked rice
Mango and Brown Sugar Glaze (see page 278)
Chopped cilantro, for garnish

Season pork chops with salt and pepper, and pan-fry in wok. Add garlic, and let simmer until cooked.

Place pork chops atop a bed of rice. Pour Mango and Brown Sugar Glaze over pork chops, and garnish with cilantro.

Queen Salote's Seafood Pot Pie

I CREATED THIS recipe in honor of Her Royal Highness Queen Salote of Tonga. On one of my trips, I was told of her love for seafood, and thought I would make something that she might have liked. The broth in this pie tends to run a bit thin. I choose not to thicken it because the thickening agent mutes the flavors. As always, it is your choice. I like to decorate the pastry top with images of the sea.

SERVES 4

Pot pie broth

1 tablespoon minced garlic

1 tablespoon grated gingerroot

1 cup sliced onion

1 cup sliced celery

2 cups stewed tomatoes

2 cups clam stock

Salt and pepper to taste

3 tablespoons butter

Pot pie filling

2 ounces fresh spinach

3 ounces shiitake mushrooms, stems removed and sliced

4 ounces crabmeat

3 each shrimp, scallops, and clams

2 ounces fresh 'ahi (yellowfin tuna) or red snapper

Salt and pepper to taste

Cilantro, finely chopped, add to taste

1 tablespoon chopped green onion

1 sweet potato, cooked and chopped

Ready-made puff pastry or pie dough

Preheat oven to 350°F.

Pot pie broth: In a wok, brown garlic and ginger. Add onion, celery, and stewed tomatoes. Add stock, and bring to a boil. Season with salt and pepper to taste. Top off
with butter, and reduce mixture to half.

Pot pie filling: In a baking dish, layer spinach, mushrooms, and mixed seafood. Add salt
and pepper to taste. Scatter in cilantro, green onion, and sweet potato. Pour in prepared broth to cover pie filling.

Cover dish with ready-made puff pastry or pie dough, sealing sides of dough to baking
dish. With a sharp knife, slice a diagonal vent near the center of the pie to allow
steam to escape. Bake at 350°F for 30 minutes or until pie top is golden brown.

Red Snapper with
Tamarind-Pineapple Sauce

TAMARIND, WITH ITS tart, tangy essence, has become a popular flavor in Tonga. Tamed by the sweet taste of pineapple, tamarind is commonly found in many recipes that identify modern Tongan cuisine.   SERVES 4

8 ounces tamarind pulp

1½ cups water

2 tablespoons melted butter

2 cups diced fresh pineapple

1 onion, diced

3 green onions, minced

1 tomato, diced

1 clove garlic, minced

2 tablespoons brown sugar

½ teaspoon black pepper

½ teaspoon thyme

¼ teaspoon ground cloves

1 teaspoon minced cilantro

¼ teaspoon ground allspice

¼ teaspoon salt

1 whole snapper

1 cup all-purpose flour

Oil for frying

Combine tamarind pulp and water in saucepan, bring to a simmer, stirring frequently. Cook for 5 minutes, then drain, reserving liquid. Discard pulp.

Add butter, pineapple, onion, green onions, tomato, and garlic to saucepan. Sauté over medium heat for 8 to 10 minutes.

Add tamarind liquid, brown sugar, pepper, thyme, cloves, cilantro, allspice, and salt to pan. Simmer for 15 minutes. The mixture should be thick, similar to chutney consistency.

Dredge red snapper in flour, and shake off excess. Heat oil in wok, and cook fish until done. Place fish on a bed of hot rice and spoon tamarind-pineapple sauce over top.

Salote Harbor Stew

A FISHING BOAT captain, outfitting his boat in Queen Salote Harbor, once told me, "You know, during Tonga's winter months (June, July, and August), cold winds whip in from the ocean out there. If you can come up with an easy-to-make beef stew that an old salt like me could make, I'd really appreciate it." He gave me his address, and when I'd perfected the flavors of this stew, I sent him a copy.

SERVES 4

2 pounds lu leaves (taro leaves), or spinach leaves

3 cups water

2 teaspoons sea salt

½ teaspoon baking soda

1 tablespoon vegetable oil

1 cup chopped onion

1 pound stew beef

1 pound beef short ribs

3 cups beef stock

2 cups water

Hot, cooked rice

Rinse lu leaves, and trim off stems and thick veins. In a stockpot, bring water, 1 teaspoon of the sea salt, and baking soda to a boil. Add lu leaves; reduce heat, and cook, partially covered, for 1 hour.

Drain and squeeze out excess liquid.

In a stockpot, heat oil, and sauté onion until translucent. Brown stew beef and short ribs. Add beef stock, water, and the remaining 1 teaspoon sea salt. Cook until meat is fork tender. Add lu leaves, and simmer for 30 minutes.

Serve hot over rice.

Traditional Tongan Lupulu

AS ALWAYS, YOU may use spinach leaves as a substitute for taro or lu leaves. This recipe calls for the meat mixture to be wrapped in the leaves. Since taro leaves are large and sturdy, you will need to double the amount of spinach you use.

SERVES 4

2 pounds lu leaves, cleaned, stems removed, or large spinach leaves
4 squares aluminum foil (about 10 inches each side)
½ can corned beef
½ onion, diced
1 tomato, sliced
½ can coconut milk (7 ounces)
Hot, cooked rice

Preheat oven to 350°F.

Spread leaves onto a 10-inch square of foil. Spread some corned beef on leaves, then add a layer of onion, then a tomato slice.

Gather foil into a bowl shape, and pour coconut milk over onion and tomato to soak. Carefully bring foil edges together to make a tight seal. Place the 4 foil packets on a baking sheet, and bake for 1 to 1½ hours.

Scoop rice onto serving plates. Open baked packets, and empty lupulu onto rice. Serve immediately.

Kumala Polenta

SIDE DISHES IN Tonga usually consist of roasted sweet potatoes, taro, yams, tapioca, or breadfruit. For something a little more refined, combine sweet potatoes with chicken stock and cornmeal to add a little Italian flair. This polenta is very tasty, and can be served hot, as a mashed potato substitute, or chilled, cut, and fried. *Kumala* is Tongan for sweet potato.   SERVES 6

3 cups chicken stock

5 ounces cornmeal

4 ounces unsalted butter

½ cup grated Parmesan cheese

½ cup chopped scallions

2 cups cooked sweet potatoes, peeled and cut into small cubes

Bring chicken stock to a rolling boil. Whisk in cornmeal, stirring constantly to avoid lumps. Mixture will thicken quickly. Reduce to medium heat, and continue stirring with wooden spoon. Cook for 8 to 10 minutes.

Mix in the rest of the ingredients until combined. Serve hot.

Tongan Fry Bread

I HAD TONGAN fry bread when I was a little kid. My friends had it for breakfast, and again as a snack after school. Serve it with Tongan Stew, or any of the soups in this book, for rave reviews. It's *faka Tonga,* the Tongan way.

SERVES 6

1 cup flour
¼ teaspoon baking soda
½ teaspoon cream of tartar
½ teaspoon salt
⅓ cup shortening
⅓ cup shredded coconut
6 tablespoons milk

Lightly grease a large, thick-based frying pan or griddle. Sift flour, baking soda, cream of tartar, and salt into a bowl. Cut shortening into dry ingredients, until mixture resembles fine bread crumbs. Add coconut and milk. Stir with a fork until mixed to soft dough.

Place frying pan over low heat.

Turn dough out onto a floured board, and knead lightly. Roll out into a circle about 8 inches in diameter. Place dough in heated frying pan, and cook until golden brown on underside, about 15 minutes.

Turn, and lightly press down the edges. Cook on the other side for 8 to 10 more minutes.

Remove from pan, and split in half with a sharp knife. Spread half with butter, and sandwich together. Cut into wedges, and serve hot.

Uila's Rice Dish

UILA, A FRIEND from Nuku'alofa, calls it a "throw together" dish, one that tastes great anytime. I prefer to serve this as a cold side to fish and meat dishes. Uila prefers to serve it hot.   SERVES 4

1 cup long-grain and wild rice, cooked and cooled
1 red pepper, seeded and finely diced
12 pitted black olives, quartered
1 bunch green onions, freshly sliced
2 tablespoons freshly chopped basil
Salt and freshly ground black pepper
3 tablespoons Cilantro Vinaigrette (see page 59)
Basil leaves to garnish

Place rice, pepper, olives, green onions, basil, and seasoning in a bowl. Mix well. Just before serving, stir in Cilantro Vinaigrette, and serve garnished with fresh basil leaves.

Cucumber Relish

THE LAST LINE of instruction for this recipe is very important. Be sure to make the relish just before you serve it. Cucumbers, especially when grated, have a tendency to become soggy. SERVES 4

½ cucumber, grated
1 teaspoon white malt vinegar
1 teaspoon sugar

Place grated cucumber in cheesecloth, and gently squeeze out excess juices. Mix cucumber with vinegar and sugar. Serve immediately.

Mango and Brown Sugar Glaze

I'VE USED THIS sweet, fruity glaze on ham, pork chops, and ice cream. Substitute lime juice for orange for a tart-sweet twist. SERVES 4

½ teaspoon cinnamon
¼ cup orange juice
3 tablespoons brown sugar
2 cups julienned fresh mango

Combine all ingredients in a large bowl. Stir to blend.

Pane Po Po Coconut Sauce

THE COCONUT SAUCE soaks into the Pane Po Po yeast bread rolls, giving them a sweet, pudding-like texture. I also like to use this sauce as a topping for bread puddings.

YIELDS 2 CUPS

⅔ cup granulated sugar
¼ cup flour
1 can coconut milk (14 ounces)

Sift together sugar and flour. Add coconut milk and mix until blended.

Banana Fritters

BANANAS ARE A common ingredient in South Pacific and East Asian cuisine. These batter-fried treats are served in fine restaurants and humble homes alike throughout Tonga. Although they're usually made with green bananas, I've chosen ripe apple bananas for their tart flavor and firm texture. I've also added a little extra sweetness to the mix for that distinctive Choy touch.

SERVES 6 TO 8

1½ cups all-purpose flour

2 tablespoons sugar

½ teaspoon baking soda

¼ teaspoon salt

1 egg

1 (generous) cup buttermilk

8 apple bananas, peeled and split

Oil for deep-frying

1 cup granulated sugar for dredging fritters

Sift dry ingredients into a medium bowl. Combine egg and buttermilk, and stir into dry ingredients, mixing until well combined. Place bananas carefully in batter. (They can rest in the batter, covered, until you are ready to fry them.)

Heat the oil to 350°F to 390°F, or until the oil gives off a slight haze. Make sure bananas are well coated with batter before setting them in oil. Using a fork, place coated bananas in oil, and fry for 2 to 4 minutes, or until golden brown. Remove from oil with tongs, and drain on several layers of paper towels. Dredge drained fritters in sugar, and serve hot with ice cream or sorbet, caramel or chocolate sauce.

Faikakai

FAIKAKAI IS A traditional Tongan dessert. This is a very simple recipe, but as is true with simple dishes, it's important to practice to get it just right. Add sugar to taste, and play with the coconut milk amounts to find a texture you prefer. I like it very soft. I pour the pudding into custard dishes, heat thoroughly, and serve with vanilla or coconut ice cream. If breadfruit is not available, substitute with 4 yams.　　　SERVES 6 TO 8

1 breadfruit, roasted, peeled, and mashed
2 cups sugar
1 cup coconut cream
Coconut or vanilla ice cream

To roast breadfruit, place in a 350°F oven for 1 hour. Remove from the oven, then peel and mash flesh. This makes about 2 cups.

Place sugar in saucepan over medium heat, and melt, stirring constantly to prevent burning. When sugar has melted, remove from heat and add coconut cream, stirring continuously until mixture thickens.

Place mashed breadfruit in large bowl. Add sweetened coconut cream in a thin stream, stirring constantly until mixture is smooth and all lumps disappear.

Serve hot, and top with coconut or vanilla ice cream.

Pane Po Po

PANE PO PO is a traditional Tongan dessert that resembles an English cobbler. The biscuits in pane po po are made with yeast, and are much larger than those generally used in cobblers. The rich and very creamy coconut sauce is what sets this dessert apart. Pane po po brings back many good memories of old-time La'ie, my hometown.

SERVES 4

1 package dry yeast
½ cup warm water
2 cups hot water
1 stick unsalted butter
8 to 10 cups flour
¾ teaspoon salt
2 eggs
½ cup granulated sugar
Pane Po Po Coconut Sauce (see page 279)

Dissolve yeast in ½ cup warm water. Place hot water in mixing bowl. Add butter, and let stand until butter is melted. Combine yeast with butter-water mixture. Set aside.

In a large bowl, sift together flour and salt. Add eggs, and mix until blended. Add liquid mixture to dry, and blend thoroughly. Let rise for 1½ hours, then pound down. Let rise again, and work down again. Shape dough into 24 balls, and place in a baking pan.

Preheat oven to 400°F.

Pour coconut sauce over bread balls, and bake at 400°F for 35 minutes. Serve hot.

Malo e Tau Lava

MALO E TAU lava is a Tongan phrase that defines happy hour. It means "I'm glad we've made it this far." So, bottoms-up, a toast to you and your friends. Malo e tau lava. Omit the rum and you have a refreshing "virgin" cocktail.   SERVES 1

1¼ ounces light rum
2 ounces pineapple juice
1 ounce sweet and sour mix
¼ ounce Grenadine
Dash of milk
Pineapple slice for garnish
Umbrella for garnish

Mix ingredients and serve over crushed ice in a 12-ounce cocktail glass. Garnish with pineapple slice and umbrella.

Malohi Sling

MALOHI IS THE Tongan word for "strong." This combination of rum and Kahlùa makes for a blasting tropical drink.   SERVES 1

1 ounce rum
¾ ounce Kahlùa
½ ounce coconut syrup
1 ounce milk
Back scratcher for garnish
Pineapple slice for garnish

In blender, whip rum, Kahlùa, coconut syrup, and milk with 1 cup small ice cubes until smooth, and serve in chimney or hurricane glass with back scratcher and pineapple slice.

Mahalo

Acknowledgments

IT'S A POLYNESIAN TRADITION to thank everyone who helps on a project. In the old days, before a feast or the launching of a canoe, the chief of the village would take a moment and say *mahalo* to the craftsmen and artists who created the event. **I HAVE MOST OF MY** favorite people to thank for this book, the many kind and generous friends who contributed greatly to the experiences and information you see in these pages. **FIRST, I SAY MAHALO TO** my photo shoot team for bringing such outstanding beauty to film: Faith Ogawa for her persistence toward excellence as the stylist for the photos; Doug Peebles for his expertise and skill as our photographer; and Leo Gonzales for his imaginative artistic talent in arranging the perfect shot. **A SPECIAL MAHALO TO NEIMAN** Marcus Hawai'i for allowing us the honor of using their exquisite merchandise to showcase the dishes. And to the other corporate contributors: the Polynesian Cultural Center for loaning their Island crafts, Host-Marriott for providing props, and Aloha Airlines for their assistance in shipping all of the artwork from Honolulu to my restaurant in Kona. **THANK YOU TO MY FAMILY,** my wife, two sons, and granddaughter Tini for their unwavering support; to my mother and sisters for allowing us the use of the restaurant photo studio, and to the staff and chefs at my restaurants for preparing and testing these recipes.

Also, mahalo nui to my agent Laurie Liss for her professionalism and advice, to Will Schwalbe and Mark Chait for their unparalleled editorial skills, and to U'i and Steven Goldsberry, who helped me say what I wanted to say.

Listed below are some more wonderful people, members of my "ohana" who contributed artwork, flowers, and produce for the shots, helped me in my travels, provided valuable insight into their culture, and always extended their warmest aloha. Mahalo for your *kokua* (help), and for demonstrating your love for your countries, cultures, and cuisine.

Alex Lui-Kwan, Hawaiian Airlines
Alison Beddow, artist
Charlene Tashima, artist
Clark Crabtree, artist
Dietrich Varez, artist
Doug Doi, artist
Ed Enomoto
Erhard Autrata, artist
Eric Workman, Polynesian Cultural Center
Gerald Ben, artist
Hetiate Pane'e (information on Tahiti)
Hina Lei, artist
Jackie Cabebe, American Restaurant Supply
Janice Gail, artist
Jennifer Pontz, Tropical Art Glass
Joe Jones, artist
Joel Park, artist
Junko Weeks, artist
Karen Ehart, Art Glass artist
Karen Lee Thrasher, artist
Kathleen Kam, Volcano Art Center
Kathy Long, artist
Kazumi Koike, Amaury Saint-Gilles Gallery
Kenny Bruner (information on Tahiti)
Leimana Pelton, Volcano Art Center

Lora Akase, Lora's Tropical Designs
Cynthia Wilson, Mamo Howell, Inc.
Mary Jane Esera (information on Samoa)
Momi Greene, Greene Acres
Nancy 'Iwalani James, Host-Marriott, Polynesian Cultural Center
Naoki Hayashi
Noelani, Noelani Gallery
Pauline Warshim, Public Relations, Neiman Marcus, Hawai'i
Peggy Chesnut, Chesnut & Co.
Phillip and Andrea Bruner (information on Tahiti)
Renee Fukumoto-Ben, Chesnut & Co.
Rhonda Valeri, Volcano Art Center
Riana Mahe (information on New Zealand)
Rick Clark and Tim De Peralta, "Hapa Happy Leis"
Ronald Y. Hanatani, RYH Pottery
Sina Kaluhiokalani (information on Samoa)
Steve Nadalin, Tropical Clay, Hawai'i
Tane and Maureen Datta, Adaptations, Inc.
Terry Taube, artist
Tulani Uale (information on Samoa)

And thank you to my many guides and friends mentioned throughout the book. *Mahalo nui. Aloha nui ka kou.*

Photo Credits

Apia Prawn Salad (Samoa—Salads): Platter (Tropical Clay), placemats (Neiman Marcus), napkin (Neiman Marcus), flowers (Marc Kinoshita Farms)

Auntie Sarah's Poke Cakes (Hawai'i—Appetizers): Vintage salt and pepper shakers (Rick Clark of Hapa Happy Leis), small bowl (Charlene Tashima of Noelani Galleries), platter (Kyle Ino), Tiles (Kyle Ino), flowers (Roen Hufford and Marie MacDonald)

Banana Fritters (Tonga—Desserts): Glass platter (Karen Ehart of Art Glass), glass candies (Beatrice and Burt Block)

Capellini Pasta with Crab Sauce (Marquesas—Main Dishes): Ceramic bowl (Tropical Clay), chopsticks (Tropical Clay), popcorn orchids (Yamaguchi Farms)

Chicken with Papaya and Pineapple Salad (Tonga—Salads): Lauhala mats (Faith and Friends), bamboo tray (Peggy Chesnut and Company), square tray platter (Faith and Friends), napkin ring (Neiman Marcus), napkin (Faith and Friends), flowers (Roen Hufford and Marie MacDonald)

Chilled Minted Papaya Soup (Tahiti—Soups): Pareu (Hina Lei Hawai'i), wooden bowl (Faith and Friends), shells (Host-Marriott, Polynesian Cultural Center Shops)

Coconut Crab Cakes (Samoa—Appetizers): Triangle plates (American Restaurant Supply), coconut cup (Faith and Friends), chopsticks (Faith and Friends), leis (Koike of Amaury Saint-Giles Contemporary Fine Art)

Coconut Lemongrass Baby Back Ribs (Samoa—Main Dishes): Pareu (Hina Lei Hawai'i), wooden platter (Faith and Friends), handmade paper (Susan O'Malley)

Cold Trout in Vegetable Herb Fumet (Tahiti—Main Dishes): Plate and bowl (Faith and Friends), block prints (Dietrich Varez of the Volcano Art Center)

Deep-fried Calamari Salad (Fiji—Salads): Plate (American Restaurant Supply), fabric (Hina Lei Hawai'i).

Fiji Beef Parcel (Fiji—Main Dishes): Kava bowl (Polynesian Cultural Center Museum Shops), bird of paradise (Yamaguchi Farms)

Fiji Rum Currant Scones (Fiji—Desserts): Plate (Tropical Clay), bowl (Tropical Clay), pareu (Lora's Tropical Designs), poha berries (Yamaguchi Farms)

Fresh Oyster Shooters with Wasabi–Water Chestnut Cocktail Sauce (New Zealand—Appetizers): Wooden forks (Faith and Friends), etched shot glasses (Gary Wagner of Cane Road Gallery, Inc.), blue plate (Tropical Glass), glass beads (Beatrice and Burt Block), New Zealand limestone carvings (Alan Wehipeihana)

Gauguin Chicken (Marquesas—Main Dishes): Platter (Edmond Enomoto of Ahinahina Haleakala), placemats (Peggy Chesnut), breadfruit leaves (Adaptations, Inc.)

Hawaiian Vintage Mocha Cake (Hawai'i—Desserts): Gold plate (Neiman Marcus), flowers (Green Point Nursery and Kilauea Flowers), tablecloth (Neiman Marcus)

Kiwi Lime Tart (New Zealand—Desserts): Plates (Neiman Marcus), leis (Blanche Leiolani Batchelder of Elegant Flowers), handmade paper (Susan O'Malley)

Kona Oyster Mushrooms with Tofu (Hawai'i—Main Dishes): Serving bowl (Ronald Y. Hanatani Pottery), flowers (Green Point Nursery)

Lemongrass-Mussel Soup (New Zealand—Soups): Plate (Neiman Marcus), bowl (Neiman Marcus), scarf (Junko Weeks of the Volcano Art Center), lei (Roan Hufford and Marie MacDonald)

Lovo Pork in Roti (Fiji—Appetizers): Blue platter (Neiman Marcus), flowers (Yamaguchi Farms), hand-painted silk (Aelbert C. Aehegma)

Mr. Dean's Incredible Chicken Pilau (Fiji—Main Dishes): Ceramic platter (Edmond Enomoto), protea flowers (Yamaguchi Farms)

Mushroom-Beef Stew with Dark Ale (New Zealand—Main Dishes): Ceramic casserole (Edmond Enomoto), placemats (Neiman Marcus), flowers (Deborah DeBoer)

Outrageous Marquesan Beef Soup (Marquesas—Soups): Plate and bowl (Neiman Marcus), flowers (Green Point Nursery), handmade paper (Susan O'Malley)

Pago Pago Snapper (Samoa—Main Dishes): Wooden platter (Faith and Friends), black pearls (Moses Thrasher of Mountain Gold Jewelers), vintage ceramic fish (Rick Clark of Hapa Happy Leis), handmade paper (Terry Taube)

Poisson Cru (Tahiti—Appetizers): Ironwood bowls (Rene Fukumoto-Ben), Tahitian clubs (Alex Lui-Kwan), handmade paper background (Susan O'Malley)

Prawn Curry (Fiji—Main Dishes): Stone bowl with silver bowl (Neiman Marcus), lei (Tim DePeralta of Hapa Happy Leis)

Queen Salote's Seafood Pot Pie (Tonga—Main Dishes): Tongan tapa cloth (Polynesian Cultural Center Museum Shops), canoe paddle (Alex Lui-Kwan), maile lei (Blanche Leilani Batchelder of Elegant Flowers)

Roast Rack of Lamb with Honey-Mustard Paste (New Zealand—Main Dishes): Plate (American Restaurant Supply), napkin (Neiman Marcus), flowers (Deborah DeBoer), pareu (Rhonda Valerie of the Volcano Art Center)

Samoan Crab Salad (Samoa—Salads): Plate (American Restaurant Supply), pareu (Hina Lei Hawai'i)

Shrimp à la Ua Huka (Marquesas—Appetizers): Glass platter (Karen Ehart), triangle plate (American Restaurant Supply), glass beads (Beatrice and Burt Block), zigzag cup (Neiman Marcus)

Shrimp-Spinach Salad with a Citrus Vinaigrette (Marquesas—Salads): Glass bowl (Jennifer Pontz)

South Pacific Gazpacho with Baby Shrimp (Tonga—Soups): Glass bowl (Tropical Glass), flowers (Green Point Nursery), ferns (Green Point Nursery)

Spicy Suva Fried Fish (Fiji—Main Dishes): Plate and sauce dish (Neiman Marcus), lei (Rick Clark and Tim DePeralta of Hapa Happy Leis)

Summer Scallop-Cucumber Salad (New Zealand—Salads): Glass bowl (Paul Hathcoat of the Volcano Art Center), tablecloth (Neiman Marcus)

Tahitian Niçoise Salad (Tahiti—Salads): Plate (Neiman Marcus), napkin (Neiman Marcus), napkin ring (Neiman Marcus), fish print ("Catch of the Day" by Naoki Hayashi)

Tropical Fruit with Ginger, Honey, and Lime (Samoa—Desserts): Glasses (Jennifer Pontz of Tropical Art Glass), scarf (Karen Thrasher), flowers (Momi Greene), handmade paper (Terry Taube)

Uncle Jesse's Pulehu Ribs (Hawai'i—Main Dishes): Wooden platter (Joseph Jones of the Volcano Art Center), gourds (Momi Greene), lei (Roen Hufford and Marie MacDonald)

Glossary

'Ahi Hawaiian name for yellowfin tuna, bigeye, or albacore tuna.

Ahima'a Tahitian name for "earth oven."

Alofa Tongan for "aloha."

Aloha a hui hou Hawaiian phrase meaning "Good-bye. Until we meet again."

Aotearoa the ancient name for New Zealand.

Aparima Tahitian/Marquesan word for slow, rhythmical dance.

Apple banana small, tart variety of banana. Available in Asian and specialty markets.

Baby Lu'au celebration and party in honor of a baby's first year.

Banana leaves leaves from the banana tree used for steaming and roasting meats and vegetables in the South Pacific. Available in Asian markets and florist shops.

Bonjour French for "Good day."

Bonsoir French for "Good evening."

Breadfruit a lumpy-skinned, bland-tasting fruit of the South Pacific. Available in most Asian and specialty markets. Substitute with equal amount of potatoes.

Bula vinaka Fijian greeting.

Butterhead lettuce has soft, round, loosely formed heads with soft, buttery-textured leaves. Available seasonally in most supermarket produce sections.

Cabbage

Napa also called Chinese cabbage.

red the red variety of head cabbage. Generally used in slaws.

won bok Chinese cabbage, also called Napa cabbage.

Calamari octopus, also called squid by many Pacific Islanders. Available in most supermarkets. When buying, look for calamari that are small and whole, with clear eyes and an ocean (not fishy) smell.

Capellini thin pasta that is slightly thicker than angel hair pasta. Substitute with angel hair pasta. Available in most supermarkets.

Capers flower bud of Mediterranean bush. Sold dry, or bottled in "brine." Always rinse before using to remove excess salt.

Caponata a flavorful spread of mixed vegetables.

Carpaccio an Italian-style raw meat dish, usually made with beef, olive oil, and lemon juice, and topped with capers and onions.

Cassava variety of tapioca found in the South Pacific.

Celery seed seeds of the celery plant. Sold in the spice sections of most supermarkets.

Chicken and bonito broth a broth that is half chicken and half fish. Available in powder form, in Asian and specialty markets.

Chicken fafa Tahitian dish; slices of chicken breast steamed in an earth oven with onions, sweet potatoes, and taro leaves.

Chicken hekka a light, stir-fry mixture of vegetables, chicken, and noodles. Recipe can be found on page 198 of *Sam Choy's Island Flavors*.

Chili flakes dried, red chili pepper flakes found in the spice sections of most supermarkets.

Chili garlic paste commercial preparation made of red chili peppers and sometimes garlic. Also called "sambal oelek" or Chinese garlic-chili sauce. Sold in bottles in most Asian sections of supermarkets, or in Asian and specialty markets.

Chili pepper small, potently hot chili peppers. Known in Hawai'i as "Hawaiian chili peppers."

Chili sauce made from cayenne pepper. Very popular in Latin America and India. Substitute with Tabasco sauce.

Chinese five-spice powder pungent spicy Asian licorice flavoring made with Szechuan peppercorns, cinnamon, cloves, fennel seed, and star anise. Also called five-star powder.

Chutney spicy, East Indian condiment made of fruit, vinegar, sugar, and spices. Used as an accompaniment to curried dishes.

Cilantro the green leaves and stems of the coriander plant. Also called "Chinese parsley."

Clam juice seasoned juices of cooked clams. Sold canned, in most supermarkets.

Clam meat cooked, canned meat from clams in cooking juices. Available in supermarkets.

Coconut, flaked dried coconut meat sliced into flakes. Available sweetened or unsweetened in the baking section of most supermarkets.

Coconut milk rich, creamy liquid extracted by squeezing the grated meat of a coconut. Available fresh, canned, or frozen in most supermarkets, and in Asian and specialty markets.

Coconut, shredded dried coconut meat shredded into coarse or fine textures. Available sweetened or unsweetened in the baking section of most supermarkets.

Coconut syrup a sweet, thick syrup made from coconut milk and sugar. Available in supermarkets near the maple and fruit syrups.

Compote fruit stewed or cooked in a syrup.

Confit a French dish of salted meat cooked in its own fat.

Coriander, ground powder made from the ground seeds of the coriander plant. Available in the spice section of supermarkets.

Coriander leaf also known as cilantro, or Chinese parsley.

Crab

coconut crab common name for a large tropical land crustacean found on the islands of the South Pacific and Indian Oceans. Also called robber crab. Substitute with crabmeat from Alaskan King crab, spider crab, or Dungeness crabs.

crabmeat commercially cooked and canned meat from either spider, King, Dungeness, or soft-shell crabs. Available in most supermarkets and specialty shops.

King crab giant crab found in the North Pacific. Available fresh from fishmongers, or sold frozen in most supermarket meat sections.

Samoan crab a variety of mud crab found in the estuaries of rivers in the South Pacific. Substitute with any other crabmeat, preferably fresh.

Cranberries tart, red berries, sold fresh, canned, or dried at most supermarkets.

Crevette French word for shrimp.

Cucumber

European cucumber also known as "English" or "hothouse" cucumbers. Sold wrapped in plastic in the produce section of most supermarkets. Substitute with any other cucumber.

Japanese cucumber very similar in texture to the "English," "hothouse," or "European" cucumber, but smaller in size. Available in the produce section of most supermarkets. Substitute with any other cucumber.

Cuire au poisson a Tahitian dish of fish wrapped in ti leaves. Cuire means cook; poisson means fish.

Cumin seeds also known as jerra. Available in spice section of supermarkets.

Curry powder commercially prepared mixture of any combination of spices: cardamom, chili, cinnamon, cloves, coriander, cumin, fennel seeds, fenugreek, mace, nutmeg, red and black pepper, sesame seeds, saffron, tamarind, and turmeric. Available in spice sections of most supermarkets.

Daikon a white-fleshed Asian root that can grow to a length of 14 inches and weigh from 4 to 5 pounds. Used in Japan for soups and pickles, or eaten raw. Flavors range from mild to spicy hot. Available fresh, pickled, or preserved, in most Asian markets.

Dalo Fijian word for taro.

Dashi-no-moto instant fish stock available in granules and in tea-bag-like pouches. Substitute with regular-strength chicken stock.

Fa'aipoipoga Samoan name for celebration, specifically for weddings.

Fa'a toa Samoan word for ceremonial monetary donations.

Fafa Tahitian name for taro leaves.

Fa'i Samoan word for cooked green banana.

Faikakai traditional Tongan breadfruit pudding.

Fai lautusi Samoan name for person selected to handle "working money."

Fa paku Samoan phrase describing the bun of hair worn by a traditional dancer.

Fausi traditional Samoan pudding with coconut milk.

Fe'i Tahitian word for "banana."

Fennel seeds greenish, brown seeds of the fennel plant. Available whole or ground, in the spice section of most supermarkets.

Fiddlehead edible, young fern shoots that are tightly coiled and resemble the head of a violin. Available in specialty produce markets.

Fiji Bitter beer premier beer of Fiji. Named for its bitter flavor. Substitute with any dark ale.

Fijian dark rum dark rum sold in Fiji and throughout the South Pacific. Known for its spicy flavor. Substitute with any dark rum.

Fingota Tongan name for raw shellfish.

Fish sauce concentrated salty, brown liquid made from anchovies fermented in brine. Sold in bottles or cans. Available in Asian markets.

Five-spice powder *see* Chinese five-spice powder.

French beans any young green string bean.

Fumet French word for fish stock or broth.

Garlic chives long, thin, flat stems resembling chives. Also called "Chinese chives" or "ku chai." Available in Asian or specialty markets.

Gazpacho cold tomato-based soup, coarsely blended.

Ghee clarified butter.

Green tea made from tea leaves that are steamed and dried, creating a greenish yellow brew. Available in teabags or loose, in most supermarkets and Asian markets.

Grenadine pomegranate juice. Sold in bottles in the liquor section of most supermarkets and liquor stores.

Guava juice juice from the guava fruit that is grown in most tropical climates. Available canned or frozen, in most supermarkets and Asian markets. Substitute with orange juice.

Haere mai Maori phrase for "welcome."

Hangi Maori word for earth oven.

Ha'u 'o kai Tongan phrase meaning "come and eat."

Haupia Hawaiian coconut milk pudding.

Hawaiian red pepper another name for red chili pepper or Hawaiian red chili pepper. Available in most supermarkets and Asian markets. Substitute with any hot red chili pepper.

Hearts of palm edible inner portion of the stem of a cabbage palm tree. Available canned or bottled in most specialty markets.

Himene Marquesan word for song or hymn.

Hoisin sauce a sauce made with fermented soybeans, garlic, rice, salt, and sugar. The flavor is sweet and spicy. Available in bottles, in most supermarkets, or in Asian or specialty markets.

Hot chili paste also called *sambal oelek* or Chinese garlic-chili sauce. Available in the Asian sections of most markets.

I ka ohana Hawaiian phrase used as a toast; means "to the family."

Ika vakalolo Fijian phrase for fish boiled in coconut milk.

Imu Hawaiian word for earth oven.

Jerra also known as cumin seeds. Available in spice sections of supermarkets.

Kabocha Japanese sweet pumpkin. Available in Asian markets.

Kaffir lime leaves glossy, dark green leaves used for cooking. They look like two leaves that are joined end to end. Dried kaffir lime leaves, with a flora-citrus aroma, can be found in Asian markets. Fresh leaves, which have a more intense, fragrant aroma, are sometimes available.

Kahlùa coffee-flavored liqueur made in Mexico. Available in most supermarkets.

Kalofai Samoan slang for "too bad, so sorry."

kalua Hawaiian word for food baked in an earth oven or imu.

Kalua pig Hawaiian word for pork baked in an earth oven.

Kamau Hawaiian word for a toast.

Kana vakavinaka Fijian for "eat heartily."

Kaoha Marquesan for both hello and good-bye.

Karanga Maori word for a chant announcing the arrival of an honored guest.

Kasava Fijian word for tapioca or cassava.

Kauri tree indigenous tree of New Zealand that resembles a California redwood.

Kava powdered kava root that is brewed then squeezed to make a favorite drink in the South Pacific.

Keikei part of traditional Tongan dress for women—a pandanus waistband (with dangling strands of seeds) used to secure the ta'ovala.

Kiawe wood Hawaiian for mesquite wood.

Kina Maori word for sea urchin.

Kiwi fruit a fuzzy, edible fruit with lime-green flesh. Commonly grown in New Zealand. Available in most supermarkets.

Kokoda Fijian word for marinated raw fish.

Kona resort and fishing town on the southeast coast of the Big Island of Hawai'i.

Kumala Tongan word for sweet potato.

Kumara Maori word for sweet potato.

Kupe galuenga Samoan phrase for "working money."

La'ie small town on the north shore of the island of O'ahu in Hawai'i.

Laulau Hawaiian word for a meat dish wrapped in taro leaves, then banana leaves and baked in an imu or underground earth oven.

Lavalava a cloth that is wrapped around the waist, forming a skirt. Worn by both men and women in the South Pacific. Known as a "pareu" in French Polynesia.

Leek a liliaceous plant similar to the onion, having a cylindrical bulb and leaves that are used in cooking.

Lemongrass a citrus-scented grass that adds a distinctive lemon flavor and aroma to the cuisine of Indonesia, Malaysia, Indochina, and Thailand. Its long, woody stalk grows from a base that resembles the white part of a green onion. Available in Asian markets.

Liliko'i concentrate juice from the liliko'i or passion fruit that has been processed and condensed. Available in the frozen food sections of most major supermarkets.

Liliko'i juice juice from the passion fruit, a tangy, plumlike, multiseeded tropical fruit. Available in frozen concentrate, in most supermarkets or Asian markets.

Lime zest the tart, aromatic outermost skin of a lime. Only the colored portion of the skin is considered the zest.

Limu ogo Hawaiian name for brown or dark green Japanese seaweed. Narrow with branch-like sections. Sold fresh in Asian markets. For ogo there are *no substitutes*. Omit from recipe if necessary.

Lolo Fijian word for coconut milk.

Lomi Hawaiian word for massage.

Lomi salmon Hawaiian side dish made by massaging or mixing salted raw salmon, tomatoes, and onions.

Long rice threadlike noodles made from mung bean flour. Soaked in water before cooking. Available in Asian markets, or in the Asian sections of most supermarkets.

Lu'au Hawaiian word for party or celebration, a feast.

Lu'au leaves Hawaiian word for "taro tops" or taro leaves.

Lu ika traditional Tongan dish: sautéed coconut milk and onions wrapped in talo or taro leaves.

Lupulu Tongan dish of taro leaf–wrapped corned beef in coconut milk.

Macadamia nut round, oily nut with creamy, slightly crunchy texture; grows on trees in macadamia orchards on the Big Island of Hawai'i, and in other parts of the world.

Mahimahi Hawaiian word for dolphinfish.

Malae Samoan name for courtyard.

Maloelele Tongan word for welcome.

Malohi Tongan word for strong.

Mango oval tropical fruit with golden-orange flesh and an enticing, aromatic flavor; skin color ranges from yellow-orange to burgundy to green; from a quarter pound in size; available in the produce sections of most markets. Substitute peaches or nectarines.

Mango puree the mashed meat of a mango.

Maohi name of the original Polynesians to settle in French Polynesia.

Maori name of the native people of New Zealand.

Maoritanga Maori word that describes the Maori way of life.

Marae Maori word for house grouping or village.

Marinade sauce used to soak meats and vegetables before cooking.

Masala a basic East Indian spicy mixture used to season meat dishes, curries, and vegetable dishes.

Mea lofa Samoan gifts of thanks.

Mesclun a mix of young salad greens, usually containing dandelion, mixuma, oak leaf, radicchio, and arugula. Available in supermarket produce sections and specialty produce markets.

Mint leaves pungent, aromatic herb available in most supermarket produce sections.

Mirin Japanese rice wine.

Miso fermented soybeans mixed with crushed grain. Available in powder or paste form in most Asian markets. Used in miso soup and other dishes.

Miti Tahitian name for "coconut."

Miti sauce coconut milk–based sauce used to season fish in Fiji.

Moce. Au sa tatau meu sa lako Fijian phrase for good-bye.

Moko Maori chin tattoo.

Moonfish also called opah. A very large, bright silver, bony fish.

Mushroom

Button mushroom small, young cultivated white mushrooms. Available canned or bottled in most supermarkets. Substitute with any mushroom.

Oyster mushroom grayish or tan. Found in Asian markets and some supermarkets. Has very disagreeable taste when eaten raw. When slightly cooked, possesses a mild flavor and succulent texture. Substitute with any mushroom.

Shiitake mushroom from Japan and Korea, these dense, dark mushrooms are usually dried, then soaked to moisten before using. They have a meaty flavor. Shiitake mushrooms are also sold fresh in both Asian markets and supermarkets.

Straw mushroom also known by the Japanese name *enoki*. Creamy colored Japanese mushrooms with tiny round caps atop slender stalks up to 5 inches long. Sold in small plastic bags in Japanese markets, and in some supermarkets.

Mustard

Chinese mustard spicy hot mustard sold in jars and used as a dip for meats, seafood, and savory pastries. Available in Asian markets.

Dry mustard also sold as powdered mustard. Mustard seeds are harvested, dried, and ground to form an aromatic powder used to flavor marinades, curries, dressings, and sauces. Available either sweet or hot.

French mustard generic term for mustards made with coarsely ground brown mustard seeds. Available in the spice or condiment sections of most supermarkets.

Mustard seeds most common are the large white mustard seeds. The main ingredient in American-style mustards. Sold in the spice section of most supermarkets.

New Zealand green mussels bivalve mollusks found off the coast of New Zealand. Sold in supermarkets frozen, previously frozen, or canned. Substitute with any green mussel.

New Zealand oyster a variety of oysters cultivated off the coast of the North Island in New Zealand. Available fresh or frozen, shelled or unshelled. Substitute with any large oysters. (Do not buy fresh, unshelled oysters unless they are alive and full of water.)

New Zealand spinach small, flat, spade-shaped leaves covered with fine fuzz. Available in specialty produce markets. Substitute with any variety of spinach.

Nifo 'oti Samoan shark's tooth necklace.

Nunu Tahitian name for nanny.

Ohana Hawaiian word for family.

Olives

Black olive also called "Mission olive." Ripe green olive that obtains its characteristic dark color and mild flavor from lye curing and oxidation. Available in supermarkets, canned and bottled.

Niçoise olive small, oval olive cured in brine and packed in olive oil. Available in most supermarkets or specialty markets.

Onaga Japanese name for red snapper.

Onion

Maui onion sweet, mild, crispy, and moist onion grown on the slopes of the volcano Haleakala on the island of Maui in Hawai'i. Available in some specialty shops. Substitute with any large, sweet onion.

Pearl onion mild-flavored, about the size of a small marble. Available bottled in supermarkets.

Spanish onion large, spherical, mild-flavored dry onion. Available in most major supermarkets. Substitute with any large, dry onion.

Sweet onion any sweet, mild-flavored onion. Available in supermarket produce sections. (Examples: Maui onion, Vidalia onion, Walla Walla onion, Oso sweet onion, Rio sweet onion.)

Ono also called wahoo. A member of the mackerel family. Often used in sashimi.

Ota wild ferns that grow near streams.

'Ota 'ika traditional Tongan dish; like Hawaiian poke, but with coconut milk.

Ota seisei the young, unfurled fern top. Substitute with fiddlehead ferns.

Oyster sauce thick brown sauce with the subtle flavor of oysters. Made from oysters, brine, and soy sauce. Used in many stir-fry dishes.

Pago Pago capital of American Samoa, pronounced "pahngo-pahngo."

Pahu Polynesian drum, made by pulling animal skin tight over wooden base.

Pala Maori name for abalone shell.

Pale headband worn by a traditional Samoan dancer.

Palusami Samoan dish of baked taro leaves, onions, and coconut milk.

Pamplemousse very large grapefruitlike fruit grown in the South Pacific and in the West Indies, also called pomelo and *jah bongg*.

Pandanus also called screw pine or (in Hawai'i) hala. In the South Pacific, the leaves (*lauhala*) are stripped of their thorns and woven into floor mats, clothing, sleeping platforms, sails, and wall coverings.

Pane po po traditional Tongan cobblerlike dessert made with coconut milk.

Panko packaged Japanese-style fine bread crumbs. Available in Asian markets or in the Asian sections of most supermarkets.

Papaya melonlike fruit with smooth, yellow or orange flesh and a shiny green-to-yellow skin. Each usually weighs about 1 pound. Available in most supermarkets and Asian markets.

Paprika a powder made from sweet red peppers that have been dried and finely ground. Paprika is a Hungarian word meaning sweet pepper.

Pawpaw term used in Tahiti for papaya.

Pea

Split yellow pea yellow-colored pea that has been dried, and split along the natural seam. Available in supermarkets. Substitute with green split pea.

Sugar snap peas also called sugar pea. A cross between English and snow peas. Available seasonally (from spring through fall) in most supermarkets.

Peach mango a variety of mango with bright orange-pink meat. Substitute with the meat of any other large, juicy mango.

Penne pasta large, straight tubes of macaroni pasta cut on the diagonal.

Pesto uncooked basil-garlic sauce used to flavor pasta, fish, or meat dishes.

Pilau traditional spicy Fijian rice dish of East Indian origin.

Pimiento large, red heart-shaped sweet pepper. Sold canned or bottled year-round in supermarkets.

Pineapple, fresh fruit of a tropical spear-leafed American bromeliad; its edible pulp consists of the flowers fused into a compound. The yellowish flesh is fibrous, sweet, and juicy, and near the darker colored base sweeter and more tender than near the top. Available seasonally in the produce sections of most supermarkets.

Pineapple juice juice of the fresh pineapple. Available canned.

Pipi Maori word for small shells.

Plum sauce also called duck sauce. A sweet-sour condiment made with plums, apricots, sugar, and seasonings. Available bottled in Asian markets.

Po'e traditional fruit pudding from French Polynesia. Made with tropical fruit and coconut milk.

Poha Hawaiian name for "gooseberry."

Poi Hawaiian word for mashed taro or breadfruit.

Poi balls Maori dance implements used to simulate the rhythmic sounds of rowing a canoe.

Poisson cru traditional Tahitian ceviche made with lime juice and coconut milk. Poisson means fish; cru means raw.

Polenta cornmeal mush, a staple of northern Italy.

Powhiri Maori word for an official Maori welcome.

Prawn large freshwater shrimp. Sold 10 to 15 pieces per pound.

Pua'a Hawaiian for pig.

Puha Maori name for fiddlehead (early fern shoot).

Pukana Maori tongue tattoo.

Pulehu Hawaiian word for grilled meat or vegetables.

Puletasi traditional Samoan female dress.

Pupu Maori word for traditional reed skirt worn by both men and women.

Red snapper deep-water fish, also known as onaga.

Rice

Basmati rice the name Basmati is literally translated as "queen of fragrance." Grown in the foothills of the Himalayas, this long-grain rice has an aromatic, nutty flavor, and a fine texture. It can be found in Indian and Middle Eastern markets.

Wild rice also called "Indian rice." A long-grain marsh grass native to the Great Lakes area of the United States. Known for its nutty flavor and chewy texture. Available in supermarkets.

Rice noodles made from rice pounded into flour. They look like long white hairs, are thin, brittle, and opaque, about 5 inches long, and have a distinctive flavor. Sold in Asian sections of most supermarkets, or in Asian markets.

River kai Fijian river clam.

Rock lobster also called spiny lobster. All the meat is in the tail. Rock lobsters have no claws. Available at the fishmonger or in supermarkets. Sold fresh or frozen. Substitute for any lobster meat.

Rosemary a member of the mint family. Rosemary is highly aromatic, with a flavor combination of lemon and pine. Available fresh, in the produce sections of supermarkets; and dried, in the spice sections.

Roti unleavened griddle cake much like East Indian chapati. A staple in Fijian cuisine.

Roulottes pasties filled with meat and/or vegetables. Sold by street vendors in Tahiti.

Rourou Fijian word for taro leaves.

Sabayon a foamy, custardlike mixture of egg yolk, sugar, and wine or rum. Also called zabaglione.

Sake yellowish, slightly sweet Japanese rice wine.

Salade d'rous Tahitian version of Russian Salad.

Salt

Hawaiian salt also called 'alaea salt. A red salt made from sun-dried seawater. Available in specialty markets. Substitute for any rock salt.

rock salt white or pink coarse sea salt. Available in supermarkets.

sea salt (*see* rock salt).

Sambal sauce also called "sambal oelek." *See* Chili garlic paste.

Samosa East Indian word for fried, triangular pastries filled with vegetables or meat.

Sapa suey Samoanization of the word chop suey.

Sarso black mustard seeds.

Scallions another name for a variety of onion greens. Most commonly called green onions.

Seaweed used in South Pacific, Japanese, and Chinese cooking. Available fresh in Asian markets.

Sesame seeds, black also known as black goma.

Sesame seeds, roasted native to Indonesia and East Africa. Sold raw or roasted, with or without their hulls. Found in the spice sections of most supermarkets.

Shallots more like a garlic than an onion, with a head composed of one or two cloves. Has a mild garlic flavor. Sold in most gourmet produce sections in supermarkets.

Sherry, dry a fortified Spanish wine, amber in color; sold dry, medium-dry, or sweet. Used for drinking and cooking.

Shinshu miso soybean paste with a golden yellow color and mellow flavor. Shinshu miso paste is available in Asian markets. Substitute with any miso paste.

Shiso an herb, beefsteak begonia leaves; almost round, thick, fleshy leaves that are red on the undersides.

Shrimp

Baby shrimp also called "miniature shrimp" are sold 100 per pound.

Bay shrimp also known as "small shrimp," sold 36 to 45 pieces per pound.

Large shrimp sold 21 to 30 pieces per pound.

Medium shrimp sold 31 to 35 pieces per pound.

Saltwater shrimp usually meaning bay or baby shrimp.

Sole also called *solea Jovi.* Fish of the flounder family, with a flat, elongated-oval shape. Available at your local fishmonger.

Somen noodles delicate Japanese noodles usually produced from hard wheat flour mixed with oil. Most somen are white, but you'll sometimes see a yellow variety that contains egg yolks. Available in the Asian section of supermarkets, or in Asian markets.

Soybeans, whole red, yellow, green, brown, or black in color. Sold dried, and must be soaked before use for cooking. Available in most health food stores, supermarkets, and Asian markets.

Soy sauce dark, savory, and salty, soy sauce is one of the most versatile and frequently used Asian seasonings. Made of soybeans, flour, yeast, salt, and sugar; saltiness varies from brand to brand.

Spearmint of the mint family. This aromatic herb can be found fresh in the produce sections of most supermarkets.

Spinach a power-packed vegetable, spinach provides large amounts of vitamins C and A. Available in supermarket produce sections.

Spring roll wrappers also called egg roll skins or wonton skins. Thin, wheat wrappings, usually sold in square sheets. Can be found in the Asian section of your supermarket. Keep refrigerated.

Star anise reddish brown, woody fruit of the *Illicium verum,* a small evergreen tree native to southeastern China. Also known as *badian.* Introduced to Europe by an English navigator in the late sixteenth century, this irregular, eight-pointed star is one of the spices used to create Chinese five-spice powder. Available in the Asian sections of local supermarkets.

Su'a Samoan word for distribution of gifts after a wedding or large gathering.

Sui fa'i Samoan name for cooked green bananas.

Sweet and sour a flavoring widely used in cocktail drinks. Can be found in most grocery store liquor departments.

Sweet basil aromatic herb native to India. Available fresh in the produce sections of most supermarkets.

Sweet potato the orange-colored edible root of a tropical American vine, often confused with the yam, which is starchier and less flavorful than the sweet potato. Available in the produce sections of most supermarkets. Substitute with fresh yams.

Szechuan peppercorns wild berries from the prickly ash tree. Substitute with black peppers.

Tahitian crayfish Tahitian name for lobster. Usually referring to rock lobster. Substitute any lobster.

Tahitian vanilla bean vanilla bean grown and processed in Tahiti. Known to be one of the most flavorful vanillas in the world. Available in specialty markets. Substitute with any vanilla bean.

Taiaha long Maori ceremonial spear.

Talking chief Samoan chief whose primary duty is to negotiate family business.

Talo Tongan word for taro.

Tamarind also known as Indian date, the fruit of a tall shade tree of Asia and northern Africa. The 5-inch-long pods contain a pulp that when dried becomes sour. Pulp concentrates flavors of chutneys, curry, and other dishes. Substitute with lemon juice.

Tamarind pulp the sour-sweet insides of the tamarind fruit, used in East India to flavor curries and other dishes. Available in East Indian and Asian markets.

Tamure name of fast Tahitian dance.

Ta'ovala traditional Tongan dress; a finely plaited pandanus-leaf mat worn around the waist.

Tapioca bread unleavened bread whose main ingredient is tapioca flour.

Taro nutritious, starchy tuber used for making poi, a staple starch in the South Pacific. Available in Asian markets, some supermarkets, specialty markets, and health food stores. Substitute with potatoes.

Taro leaves the large, elephant ear–shaped leaves of the taro plant; used throughout Polynesia as a deep green vegetable, and to season meat and fish dishes.

Tarragon an herb, can be purchased either dried or fresh. (Always use fresh herbs if you have the choice.)

Taualuga traditional Samoan bride's dance.

Teletautala Samoan for "talk too much."

Thai fish sauce a thin, salty, brownish gray sauce. Known as *nam pla* in Thailand, this particular type of fish sauce is much milder than the Japanese, Chinese, Burmese, or Vietnamese versions. Available in Asian markets, or in the Asian section of supermarkets.

Thyme leaves from the aromatic plant native to the Mediterranean region. French thyme is the most common. Usually sold in the produce sections of supermarkets with the fresh herbs. Ground and crushed thyme is also available in the spice section.

Ti leaves leaves of a Polynesian and Australian woody plant of the agave family. Available in florist shops. (Substitute banana leaves, corn husks, or aluminum foil.)

To'ere Tahitian/Marquesan wooden drum used for the fast-moving Tahitian dance.

Tofu fresh soybean curd; bland and therefore versatile. Readily absorbs food flavors. Available in Asian markets, health food stores, and in the produce sections of most supermarkets.

Toko Maori ceremonial genealogy stick.

Tovioka Fijian word for cassava.

Triple Sec strong, clear, orange-flavored liqueur used to make cocktails. Available in liquor stores, or in the liquor section of your supermarket.

Trout a large group of freshwater fish grown commercially throughout the United States.

Turmeric powder made from the dried root of a tropical plant related to ginger, with a bitter, pungent flavor and an intense yellow-orange color. Available in the spice section of your supermarket.

Umala Samoan word for sweet potato.

'Umara Tahitian word for sweet potato.

'Uru Tahitian word for breadfruit.

Vinegar

Balsamic vinegar a vinegar made from a white grape juice and aged in wooden barrels for a year. It has a very dark color and a mellow flavor that is picked up from the wood of the barrels.

Blackberry vinegar a vinegar made from aged, distilled blackberry juice. Available in the supermarket condiment section or in specialty markets.

Red wine vinegar French-style vinegar made from red wine. Available in the condiment section of supermarkets.

Rice wine vinegar Japan's relatively mild rice vinegar, the type most often found in Asian sections of the supermarket. Chinese rice vinegar—white, red, or black—has a stronger flavor.

Tarragon vinegar white vinegar infused with tarragon flavor. Available in the condiment section of supermarkets, or in specialty markets.

White malt vinegar made from malt barley. Available in the condiment section of supermarkets.

Vuaka vavi Fijian word for roasted pork.

Wahoo also known as ono or mackerel.

Wakame Japanese seaweed.

Wana Hawaiian word for sea urchin.

Wasabi paste paste made from the hot, green root called Japanese horseradish. Available in the Asian section of supermarkets.

Wasabi powder powder made from the hot, green root called Japanese horseradish. Pungent root with an extremely strong, sharp flavor. Popular condiment for foods in Japan. Available in powder or paste in Asian markets.

Water chestnuts tubers of a marsh plant with a crisp texture and sweet flavor. Available canned, or sold fresh in Chinese markets. Canned water chestnuts are offered whole or sliced. After opening can, rinse well, and peel before serving. To store, cover with cold water, and refrigerate for up to 2 weeks (changing water daily).

Watercress a member of the mustard family, with crisp dark green leaves that have a slightly bitter and peppery taste.

Wero Maori chant of welcome to test the bravery of a guest.

Wharerunganga Maori learning house.

Whikorero Maori speech of welcome.

Index